Comp████ey

Making Serious Dollars ($60,000+) In High-Tech Consulting

By
Alan N. Canton

Adams - Blake Publishing
Fair Oaks, CA

ComputerMoney

Making Serious Dollars ($80,000+) In High-Tech Consulting

By
Alan N. Canton

Published By:

Adams - Blake Publishing
8041 Sierra Street
Fair Oaks, CA 95628   U.S.A.

Copyright © 1993 by Alan N. Canton

First Printing 1993
Printed in the United States of America

ISBN 1-883422-01-9

Library of Congress Catalog Number: 93-071430

Table
Of
Contents

CHAPTER 3

CHAPTER 4

CHAPTER 5

CHAPTER 6

ACKNOWLEDGMENT

This book is dedicated to Jane Schweitzer and Helen Sperling for their faith, love, advice, and guidance. Without them, this work would not have been possible.

I also want to acknowledge three long time friends, Richard Kent, Ira Einhorn, and Bob Kern.

Finally, I salute all of you who have the courage, ambition, and motivation to pitch the corporate world and take your roll of the dice in your own consulting business.

ABOUT THE AUTHOR

Al Canton has been an independent consultant for fifteen years. Born in 1947, he grew up in Great Neck, New York. Mr. Canton holds a BA degree from the University of Virginia, and an MA from the College of William And Mary. He started out as a school teacher and taught the entire 8th grade in an 8 room school house in Webster Springs, West Virginia. After graduate school, where he was introduced to computer technology, Mr. Canton worked for EDS in San Francisco and Dallas. Tired of making Ross Perot richer, Mr. Canton, on a whim, started his own consulting company in 1978. Over the years he has taught technology courses at National University and has given seminars on computer consulting throughout the country. Mr. Canton is married with four cats.

NOTES FROM THE AUTHOR

What Is "High-Tech"?

I chose the term "high-tech" because it is the most encompassing one I could come up with to describe the genre of skills that are transferable to the consulting business. To me, high-tech means computer literacy. I don't mean just programming, but any activity that involves knowing how to use, manage, create, extract, synthesize, or extrapolate information via "the machine".

I believe that anyone who can "operate" a computer for the benefit of another, has high-tech skills that can be sold on an independent basis. I use "computer skills" as the common denominator for defining high-tech because I can't think of any technology position today that does not require the knowledge of computer hardware and/or software.

Because my high-tech skills are in the software development arena, and because the majority of high-tech consultants are involved with software, this book emphasizes the programming and analysis areas of consulting. However, if you are involved in engineering, design, systems integration, CAD, CASE, training/education, technical writing, repair/maintenance, project management, site design, security, data center operations, etc., there is a world of opportunity open to you and this book should be able to help you realize it.

On Style

I have tried my best to make this book gender neutral as much as possible. When I use only "his" or "her" it is out of stylistic consideration and should not be considered a "political" statement.

Please Write!

Let me know what you think of this book, how it helped you, how it can be improved and anything else I should cover in future editions. Contact me via the publisher's address on the back of the title page. I will reply to all letters.

1

WHAT THE CONSULTING BUSINESS IS ALL ABOUT

What is Going On Here?

It has often been said that either you *work* for a living or you are a *consultant*. It is an almost magic word conveying a sense of eclectic omnipotence, a mastery of discipline or perhaps even a mystical clairvoyance. When you are a consultant you do not have to explain anything to anybody; after all *you are a consultant*. Now, this covers a multitude of sins. How many people who, having been out of work during the recent recession, when asked what they had been doing during their employment hiatus have said, "well, I've been doing some consulting." In fact, to many seasoned personnel people, the word "consultant" is synonymous with "out of a job".

The vast majority of men and women who run American industry view this occupation with an almost superstitious awe. They may have little idea what a consultant does or what consulting is all about, yet they hire hordes of these mysterious people to solve their problems.

Management believes in the existence of the magic-bullet, thus an increasing number of consulting miracle-workers can be seen skulking the corridors of every American business enterprise.

Consulting: Call It What You Will

One definition that has made the rounds is that the consulting industry is made up of a group of people, who know nothing about your business, but whom you hire to solve all of its problems.

Another one that has been heard is that consultants are a group of people who know more and more about less and less until they ultimately know everything about nothing!

And finally, there is the maxim that a consulting firm is made up of people who have a Phi Beta Kappa key at one end of their watch chain... and no watch at the other!

Depending upon your experience with consultants or your experience in the consulting field, you may or may not agree with the above characterizations. The point to be made, however, is that a clear-cut, concrete definition of the business is just about impossible. Indeed, consulting tends to be all things to all people.

The definition that I put forth is very simple. *A consultant is a person in business for him/herself, representing no other entity, who provides an intangible service for a customer.*

> *COMMENT: I will fudge on the "in business" clause so as to include the large group of people that work on a W-2 basis for what are called "body shops" (I shall call them agents or brokers). These W-2 people would probably rather work as an independent (1099) but for reasons we will get into later, don't. However, they are at risk in that they are on short term projects with the understanding that when the work is finished, they are also.*

What about the so called "consulting houses"? This will put me at odds with all those fine people who have the word "consultant" on their business card *but* who work for a company; be it a Big 6 accounting firm, EDS, Computer Associates, etc. As much as I like you folks, you are not consultants... you are employees. That means that the check is never in the mail, and you don't have to worry about being "respected" in the morning! You may walk and talk like consultants, but since you are not accountable to your own bottom line, you are wage slaves... not consultants. You are *not* at risk.

> **TIP**: By reading and applying the information in this book, you can change all of this.

It's Business As "Unusual"

Let's take a brief look at what the business is all about. A key point here is the word "business" because, in every sense, consulting is a business. I'm not talking about those rare dollar-a-year people, perhaps retired and living off of a good pension who enter consulting just to keep busy. I'm talking about people concerned with the bottom-line.

Having asked a number of consultants at a recent convention whether they considered themselves first as an independent business person *or* as a member of a "profession", each responded that they were business people first and foremost. While many hedged and called themselves "professional business people", when pushed further on the subject, most had a higher awareness of being in a business for a profit as opposed to being a member of a profession (with whatever connotation the term brings to their mind).

But I Want To Be a Professional

It seems that if everybody does not want to be a consultant, they at least want to be a "professional". Perhaps it is because "professionals" do not seem to work for a fee, but instead are engaged in the pursuit of furthering the knowledge of the "profession".

> **COMMENT**: If you really believe this, you truly need this book! It's reality check time!

There are damn few "professional" doctors or lawyers who work for less than the going rate in their fields, and even fewer high-tech consultants. If you are thinking of joining the ranks of consultants, or are in the business already, do not delude yourself into thinking that you hold (or will hold) some lofty title as a member of a profession. You had better consider yourself first and foremost a business person or you will never make it in the industry. If you do not have to put bread on your table as a consultant, then by all means consider yourself a "high brow" professional. However, if your car payment is dependent upon receiving a fee for service, you better get the mind-set of a business person.

In my seminars, I have been accused a splitting hairs over this business vs. professional issue. Not so. In the real world you will discover that business people attend night class and seminars to *hear* from the "professionals". But *business people* sign *real contracts* with other *business people* ... not "professionals".

So why are consultants often termed as "professionals"? Probably because so many people outside (as well as inside) the consulting industry have at one time or another referred to consultants as members of a profession.... the oldest profession! More on that later.

The Doer, nor Originator

Our business is rarely the originator of a client's policy. True, we may break our collective arms patting ourselves on the back about the wonderful ideas we come up with, but most often these ideas are the means to an end, an end set and determined by those who are running the business. We may design the slickest claim processing network or write the most terrific optimized SQL code that has ever been done. To us these are instances of original thinking. The reality of the situation is that *someone else* determined that there should be a claim processing network in the first place. Someone other than us decided that SQL should be used to solve the problem.

While many management consultants have been signed to sit in a quite room and come up with ideas about what *should* be done; to come up with a new product, process, or organizational scheme. However, this "think tanking" tends to be the exception in the high-tech consulting industry.

Whether we be programmers, managers, consultants or whatever, we seem to have a rather high opinion of ourselves. I remember one banking programming manager telling me that his DP group really ran the entire bank. When I asked what new banking policy the group had come up with, he just could not admit to any. He finally came up with the notion that ATM had been the idea of the MIS department. He was quite sad to learn that the "idea" of ATM had been proposed by a senior teller, who never seemed to have money in her own checking account and thought it would be neat if her account could be debited automatically by her grocery store before she had a chance to spend her bucks on non-essentials.

But I will humor you. Let us suppose that the MIS department (Management Information Systems) does come up with a great idea for the business entity. In how many companies can the MIS management approve on the idea and make it policy? It was not so long ago (during the user-be-damned era) that people really thought that the MIS department actually ran the company. This was an illusion. The reality is that the MIS department is merely the tail at the end of the dog. I am not saying that MIS people don't have powerful positions in their company. However, their power stems from being the only people that can effect of implement policy. The policy (many times poor policy) is set by executive management. Someone made a decision and the computer department was *told* to do it.

edit

Well, for the most part, we consultants are even *further removed* from the decision making process. Management decided what was to be done and by the time most consultants reach the scene (sometimes of the crime) the MIS department staff has decided how to do it. The specs were written and the consultants were told to follow them.

So, we go in and design the file structure, the job flow, and then code the programs. Maybe no one actually looked over our shoulders and inspected our code or design. But direction is usually applied. Consultants complain bitterly about the number of times they have suggested better ways of doing things only to be told "how" the staff wants it done. Again, for the most part we *implement*, we don't *originate*.

To Be Objectively Objective

In discussing what this business is all about, I must spend some time talking about the concept of objectivity. Did you ever read the sci-fi classic *Stranger in A Strange Land* by Robert Heinlein? The author had a group of characters who were termed "fair-witnesses" - people who were trained in the art of objectivity. They were to be used as both observers of an incident and as potential jurors. They were trained to see and tell the truth.

This is a basic tenant of computer consulting. We are supposed to be objective. This is what makes our proposals valued to senior management. Nothing will ruin a consultant's credibility quicker than to be seen as being in the hip-pocket of a major manufacturer of either hardware or software.

We consultants deal in the hard facts and cost figures and *not* in the arena of corporate politics. Now, whether this objectivity can always be maintained, is open to question.

Here is a short incident I remember from a few years ago. A consultant, when asked to give a recommendation as to whether an installation should go the central data base route or the networked distributed path, found himself in a quandary. Knowing quite a lot about programming in data base languages from shared logic machines, he knew that should the company go the mainframe route there would be quite a lot of work for him and his associates. On the other hand, the distributed processing route would freeze him out, since he had little background in microcomputer programming. The question arises: could this person be objective?

Before we answer, a more important question should be asked. *Could MIS management, with their political wars waging at full blast be any more (or even equally) objective?* After all, this involved over a quarter of a million dollars.

In this case, the consultant went with the networked approach. Although he was "on the bricks" a few months later, the strong recommendation he received from the client helped him get another project within two weeks of leaving (they don't always work out this well!). The essence here is that when we speak of consulting, we are talking about people who can (or should) be able to put themselves above the battle; who can measure the facts with regard to the overall result for the client. Management knows that it cannot expect the above of its own staff, so they call in the consultants. While objectivity is not achieved 100% or even 90% of the time, so long as management cannot reach even a 50% rate of objectivity (usually due to their own internal politics) we consultants will continue to act as "fair witnesses".

Give Me Independence Or ...

Another important factor that earmarks the consulting business is independence. Consultants feel very strongly about their ability to pick and choose the type of assignments that they take on. And, in many cases this might be a bit overstated. There is nothing like being between contracts for three or four weeks to help persuade you to take on an assignment to write and design an access-method in RPG somewhere in East Tennis Shoe, Nebraska!

Research over and over cites the "freedom of movement" issue as being one of the more favorable factors of consulting. There are many in the business that will refuse to sign long term contracts, even if the money is above average, so that they can preserve their freedom of access and their level of visibility to the high-tech community.

Consultants acutely feel that is it necessary for them to float from assignment to assignment, if not only to maintain their so callod visibility, but also to help them from going stale. While this "movement" motivation is strong, it is changing, as many companies are using what might be called "resident" consultants. But the romance is still there. We see ourselves as riding into town as a hired gun (For a Fistful of Dollars) to "right" all the wrongs and get things back together again. Everyone sings our praises as we ride into the sunset(to the tune of the William Tell Overture) in search of other dragons to slay. (Who was that masked person?)

We are all really *independent entrepreneurs*. Just about all who enter the field have had an apprenticeship as an employee of several firms. After may years of working for a wage, the entrepreneurial bug bites and the wonderful thought of working for oneself becomes the motivating force for a programmer, designer, engineer, analyst, or manager to take the plunge; often giving up a high paying and secure position to do so.

It is rare to find a person who has been successful and happy in a high-tech consulting role to later go back to the world of full-time employment... and be happy. Even during the latest recession, most consultants resisted the urge to find a safe haven until business picked up. (There were not many media stories of consultants finding full time jobs... but we saw many clips and articles of previous full-timers becoming consultants).

See Me, Touch Me...

The consulting game is not played in the back room, but right out there - up front and in center court. Visibility is a constant. From the moment the ink sets on the contract, to the moment you get your final payment, you are in a highly visible position in the highly visible computer or engineering department. This visibility comes as a shock to many who first enter the practice, as they figure that they would be treated as an ordinary employee with no more or less visibility than any other programmer/analyst. Wrong.

The employees know you are there. You may not think they know, but they know. This is not to say that you are going to get the royal coach service from management (in fact, it will probably be just the opposite when it comes to creature comforts). You are costing the company a lot of money. Often times you will be making, on an hourly basis, more than the person you are assigned to, and sometimes more than even his/her boss. Believe it - they know who you are!

While visibility is a given, it is not nearly the factor that "accountability" is. If, in the sporting world, you are only as good as your last game, those men and women in the consulting game know that you are only as employable as the reputation you create on your last contract. It doesn't matter that you have pulled four MIS departments out of the techno-graveyard in the past 16 months. Nobody cares that you once fixed that accounting problem and saved the company from an embarrassing audit. If, on the last contract, the project gets screwed up (or you screw it up) guess where the buck is going to stop?

If there is one item that is absent in American business, it is accountability. It seems that nobody wants to take responsibility for anything anymore.

The consulting industry, on the other hand, strives for accountability. It is not only a major factor why people enter the business, but also a major reason why so many technology shops rely so heavily on consultant personnel. The average programmer or analyst or engineer knows he only has to do a passing job and perhaps live a year longer to receive a raise (and in some job markets, he doesn't even have to do a passing job). The independent consultant, however, knows that this job could be either the last or the springboard for the next. The consultant knows that, as an independent business person, he or she *must* perform.

There is something about being "on the edge", of knowing that you have to "make it happen". So often, people say that they enter the consulting business because they were just plain bored from their day to day jobs. They were looking for the "great and terrible". They wanted the accountability factor. So many of us need to "know" that what we do really makes a difference. Unlike any experience you might have as an employee, if you do "good" in consulting you be will richly rewarded. If you do badly, you won't just miss out on a raise or get a simple reprimand. You will be history.

Getting It Done Right, The First Time

Beyond accountability in dollars and cents, the consulting industry actually feels that it has a moral responsibility to its clients. Consultants may not admit it but pride often runs a close second to the dollar.

Why pride of workmanship has disappeared from the American way of industry is a great mystery, one that industrial psychologists will ponder for a long time to come. But consulting, almost by its nature, attracts people who either have, or want to have, pride in their work. The industry appeals to creative individuals who want to stand up and be counted.

We are not usually aggressive types. We are not the type of people to be on some kind of a power trip. None of us expects *Pomp and Circumstance*" to be played when we walk down the hall!

But this pride factor is so present in the personality of consultants, that industrial psychologists have repeatedly tried to find out what motivates people to leave full-time employment for the uncertain future of consulting.

While there has probably been ten zillion words written on the search for motivation, the answer is easy. Consultants are in business *for* and *by* themselves. It is pass or fail every day. They must do a better job than the average employee. They feel totally accountable for their performance. They have no illusions about the cold facts of the business world. Those who satisfy the needs of their clients will live to work another day. Those who don't won't. It is called accountability, pride... survival.

Now, follow this line of thinking. Every high-tech installation makes great claims about how goal-oriented they are. They send their managers to all sorts of conventions and seminars, usually held at a post resort. These off-site meetings (the legal jargon in order to take the tax deduction) almost invariably center around the setting of priorities for the coming quarter or fiscal year. However, more often than not, they end up as low key buck passing affairs, each manager trying to blame the other for the fact that more projects were screwed up than were completed. It is almost a maxim that all projects start smoothly, roll right along, and then seem to stop dead at the ninety percent stage of completion. Why? Is it management? No! It is the nature of the people doing the work.... the programmers, engineers, analysts, and designers.

It is sad, but true, that most programmers and analysts make lousy business people. For the most part, they fail to see the big picture, their role in it, and more importantly, they don't care to. Programming and analysis is almost an art form. To most practitioners of the art, doing it is more important than finishing it (and selling it). In high-tech, to think is to create. The usual pressures of deadlines or cost effectiveness are just not concerns to most high-tech workers. The method actually becomes the madness. So what if management wants it by next week and only wants to pay so much for the system? Well, most programmers and analysts feel that if the company wants it done, it will have to be done the way the technology people want to do it!

But this arrogance is not their fault. They were not trained in business, and if ever the difference between a business mind and a technical mind was to be measured, it would be in the approach each takes to the completion of a project.

In every computer department there are a few programmers and analysts who have a good business background and who understand the roles of production, profit, and loss. These are the people who become consultants.

I am leading you to the conclusion that since almost every high-tech consultant has at one time worked as a programmer, than as an analyst, and then a manager, the above observations have not been lost on us. We have all seen projects stall and die.

Thus, the consulting game has for a long time centered around this flaw in so many computer departments: Project completion - getting it done right the first time! It is no secret that many managers have brought in a consultant or two, not for their technical expertise, but to stimulate staff productivity. One manager of a large computer manufacturing company when interviewed for this book said:

> Whenever I bring in an outside consultant, the in-house staff grumbles. But all of a sudden, more and more user complaints get solved in less and less time. It is like having an invisible butt-kicker around to keep my guys from drinking coffee behind the printer instead of being on the terminals where they belong.

Another manager remarked that by having a consultant in the group, the staff was able to pull together and work as a team against what they saw as an outside threat to their job-security. And a third project manager said:

> By having a consultant around, I became a better manager. I was paying all that money out of my entertainment budget. I was going to make damn sure the guy had plenty of work to do. It improved my planning skills and got the system running in much less time. I wish we could have afforded to have our whole staff as independent consultants.

Maybe the reason we are able "to get it done" is because we all have a strong sense of guilt. While some consultants have boasted at conventions and get-togethers that they have the easiest job going, the vast majority actually feel guilty when there just isn't enough to keep them busy. When the machine goes down or turn-around is slow, most consultants have conceded that they feel guilty about charging for hours not actually engaged in the "technology arts". So they check out and go home.

While this says one thing about honesty and ethics in favor of consultants, there is also a lesson to be learned. The average computer person believes it is the responsibility of the company to pay him or her for the privilege of breathing the corporate air. This is not to say that most employees are lazy and not productive. But, how many have ever written a check back to their company for time that they were not actually doing what they were being paid to do?

So, perhaps it is guilt that keeps the mind of the consultant focused on project completion. This could be the reason why many consultants become the real movers and shakers in the course of a major project. They only *want* to *get it done*! To the consultant, getting it done and getting a good "rep" is just as important as *doing* it.

The consultant is able to bridge the technician/businessman gap. Consultants want to keep busy. They want to stick to the game plan. They want to get it over with. It seems that many corporate employees simply want to find the slickest way to shift bits on a terminal. Consultants on the other hand are motivated to sift sand on the beach in Mazatlan. And the airport is only as close as the end of the project.

What is consulting all about? It is a business that is made up of independent, objective, visible, and goal oriented people. It is about doing a good job, working hard, getting paid well, taking a risk, being your own boss, and rising above the crowd. You will see all of this in the following pages.

THE ROLE OF CONSULTING IN THE COMPUTER INDUSTRY

People Who Need People...

There is absolutely no way to describe the high-tech information systems industry, much less define it. We had enough trouble trying to pin down a definition of consulting. Anyway, this is not a book on the data processing industry directly, so there is no reason to walk you through a zillion words on the what the industry is or is not. If you are *not* already connected with the computer industry, any definition will do. If you *are* in the industry, then you have your own preconceived notions about with it is all about, and don't need any other ideas to confuse (or enlighten) you.

Since the vast majority of the readers of this book are people who either want to get into the consulting game or are in it already, it is necessary to spend some time in discussing what your role to the computer industry will be, or already is.

If you put two high-tech types in the same room, what you will not get is a discussion on the relative merits of OS/2 versus Windows. The first topic of conversation will be somewhere along the lines of what company (or group) is doing what exciting project and "are they looking". High-tech people are notorious for exercising what personnel managers call "job mobility". It is no secret that a manpower crunch in on and will probably continue will into the 1990's. If there are no hard statistics to back that up, at least evidence can be found by reading the Sunday classifieds or by looking at the job orders at your nearest friendly headhunter's office. The info-systems market is booming, even during the recession. One MIS manager, when interviewed said, "A good technical person can get a job nowadays by just driving into the wrong company's parking lot.".

> **COMMENT**: Not too long ago, a large electronics firm in the San Francisco area held an open house in their parking lot. That's right - drive-in interviews. It may not be long until the only people making house calls will be data processing recruiters!

Obviously, the consulting field is affected by this people shortage. Many people in the industry have cited the shortage of qualified technicians as the cause for the rapid rise in the use of consultants. Said one respondent, "if I could hire good, hell even average, technical people, I wouldn't use nearly all the consultants we have working here."

Now this suggests that there is some evidence to prove that the growth in consulting is due to the "people" gap. But, upon deeper inspection of the industry, we see that the talent shortage is *not* the *main* reason for the increased use of contractors.

In the first place, there are always programmers and analysts looking for work and MIS departments that seriously want to hire (lure away) people, can do so. It may cost, but it probably would not cost as much as most consultants. If a company is serious and knows how to recruit, then the people can be "gotten" (maybe "had" is a better term).

In addition, more and more firms are going with entry-level people and putting them through an in-house training program. There is no shortage of young men and women (as well as older people changing careers) who thirst for computer training. The community colleges are full of people seeking a certificate in information systems. A company like EDS, that offers entry-level people very thorough training, has no trouble attracting candidates.

Now Playing Second Base...

It is not the so called "people shortage" that has directly contributed to the increase in the number of consultants. The real growth can be attributed more directly to the need for workers on a temporary basis.

The computer department in any company is more project-oriented over the long term than any of its sister departments. While the sales department might need more people during the holiday season, or finance might need to gear up during a year-end audit, the computer department constantly has short-term projects which can't be assumed as spillover work for the current staff.

For example, when the technical staff in the manufacturing group have finally gotten on board with the "new" system and are fighting the daily fires of maintaining the product, there is always some vice-president who wants a new reject analysis system. The MIS department could hire more staff, but what is to be done with them three months down the road? Fire them? What kind of reputation would the company receive by so many short term hirings and firings? There are very few companies who want the reputation of being body-shops.

> *COMMENT: There is a large defense company that for years would hire a boatload of technical staff in anticipation of getting a big government contract. They would then have these newly hired, high salaried people sit around and write documentation until the contract was received. If the company got the government work, all was well and good until the systems were in place and the programmers were, as they called it, "de-activated". But if the contract did not materialize, these unfortunate souls found themselves back in the headhunter's office sadder but wiser. After about two years of this the company could not hire a technical person for love or money (neither of which they had much of).*

You Want It When?

Here we see the major role of the consulting business to the data processing industry. MIS shops need great flexibility in order to handle its manpower assignments. The timing of user requests is unpredictable. An MIS department might go for six or eight months without the need of a major staff increase to handle the workload. Then business conditions change and the "request for system services" forms come out of the woodwork. Everyone in every department wants something done with their system.

The MIS department usually cues up all these requests and handles them on a "crash" basis with the existing staff. However, here is what happens.

The staff complains (justifiably) about never seeing their wives or husbands or kids. They quit in droves and the projects get backlogged even further.

The managers find pink slips in their pay envelopes. New management is hired, a re-organization takes place (it seems that no department enjoys re-organizations more than the MIS department), and someone gets the bright idea of calling in some contractors to get the work done.

Everyone yells about the price until the cost of not getting the work done is weighted against the ability of the business to *stay* in business. The consultants come, the work is finished and everyone is happy.

> *COMMENT: Unfortunately, nobody seems to remember the lessons learned in the process, so that the whole thing repeats itself eight months later.*

This need for flexibility is also seen when the work gets highly technical. When a company goes through a conversion or an upgrade, the need arises for a hoard of highly trained specialists to get the company over the hump in the beginning stages. The consulting industry provides a mechanism which management can utilize in bringing people with specific (although somewhat narrow) skills to the project.

The Best and Brightest

Management has to also face the question as to just what level of skills they want to pay for in their full-time employees. Without getting into the argument as to what technical people should be paid compared to the rest of the organization, I believe that most of the work done in most computer installations is not so difficult that it requires a software wizard. Most business programming today is maintenance work done in

COBOL or some 4GL. Do most companies need a complete staff of $50,000 a year programmers to do this work? Hardly.

Many companies realize this and are relying on consultants to provide a higher level of technical skill when the need arises. It may sound boastful, but the fact remains that the consulting industry provides the MIS department with more competent staff than a company could hire on its own. If you ask if consultants are "better" than the full-time people, the answer nine times out of ten is *yes*. (In research for this book, I have asked!). Maybe not every one, but by and large, managers believe that consultants are more capable.

> **COMMENT**: *Why are they better? They have to be. A consultant who does not out-produce and isn't technically superior to the majority of the client's programming staff will not last long in the business. Management may be slow, but it is not stupid (in the long run). A company will not pay $50 an hour for someone equal only to their $20 an hour staff member. No rocket-science logic needed here!*

Leveling The Playing Field

The amount of talent available in any field is always limited and in the computer industry it often gets stretched rather thin. Programmers and analysts are pretty much like any other business people... they all want to work in the limelight, they all want to be in the center of power (or the storm). They all want the best in the way of office conditions, access to technical mobility and a parking space close to the door! And there are many companies that can offer all of the above, including a better than average salary schedule.

Do these firms have the "best" staff? Well, that of course depends on what you consider as "best." There is no way any of us can agree upon what criteria one has to measure up to in order to be considered "best" in the business of working with computers. However, doesn't common sense tell us that a "more competent" staff would be found in a company that is financially stable, growing technologically, and people-oriented, than in a company that is non of these? Again, there is no definitive answer, but common sense does suggest that these would be the companies having the "best and brightest". And research suggests that most often, companies with the above attributes and which are on the leading edge of computer application technology usually have a more technically experienced staff than firms utilizing older and less complex technology.

This is not to suggest in the least that less technically advanced firms are not pleasing places to work. I am only saying often there is no need for their staff to be up on the latest in application techniques, database concepts, or perhaps client-server methodology. And we are not looking at a big vs. small competition. There are many small organizations utilizing up to the minute technology and involved in every way with the latest high-tech "buzz word of the year" concepts.

> **COMMENT**: I want to coin a new buzz-word: techno-gap (made it up myself... not bad).

What I see happening in almost every city is a techno-gap between companies that have the latest and greatest and those who don't. And with this gap comes the so called "brain drain" (no, I didn't invent this one... it's a British term) in which the bigger more technically complex firms are able to attract and retain the better employees. Thus, the available "best" talent in the computer industry is not evenly stratified, but is concentrated in those firms where the people perceive that the best opportunities for growth and mobility will occur.

What does this have to do with consulting? Simple. Unlike employees, consultants are motivated first by money and second by technical challenge. The small company that would like to hire a full time person to help out with a new project can't attract the candidate(s) they want for the reasons outlined above. So, they enter into the consultant market and contract with a top technician to get the job done. It may cost more in the short term, but the small firm is able to remain competitive with their larger brothers by being able to hire talent by the pound.

It has been noted by observers of the employment scene that the availability of a large free-lance consultant force in any market will tend to narrow the technical gap between the "space age" installations and those still in the (often comfortable profitable) "technical stone-age". This highly skilled computer talent available to these firms helps to even out the technical manpower pool.

This often overlooked role of the consulting industry can prove vital to the small company just starting to compete in the big time. The thousands of high-tech consultants that will forsake the plush offices and the latest technology to work in the basement of a young, but up and coming company provide a stabilization mechanism on the data processing industry as a whole. By spreading the available talent, consulting makes it possible for *all* companies to continually grow technically and thus remain competitive.

Make It Happen... Now!

Along this line, consulting also plays a role in the development of advanced technology. There have been many software houses that have come up with a better idea (often in response to a customer need) in a particular application area. It is not unusual for management to "put out the word" and pull in the top people in the field for what often becomes a bone-crunching, break-neck assignment.

When the "best" work with the "best", lightning often strikes. Would this lightning occur if management had to hire employees with the constraint of having to find something for these people to do after the project was complete? The hassle of hiring this way would give many people in management a desire to overdose on Maalox!

The consultant army provides a mechanism for a company to achieve high productivity, fast results and a high degree of accountability when business cycles dictate or when specific technical needs arise. We have played the role of catalyst in high-tech by not only stabilizing the available pool of talent among many types of installations, but also of allowing a company to take a chance on a new technology product or technique. Many new applications or software products have gotten off the ground through a pilot program staffed by consultants.

The Black Hats

Now all of this looks pretty good for the consulting industry. Perhaps you may think that consulting is the best thing to happen to information systems since recycled paper. Well, there is no doubt that consultants play many beneficial roles to the computer industry as a whole. But there are some *negative* points that should be mentioned here, just to keep things in proper perspective.

Consultants in the traditional fields of management and finance have often been criticized for coming into a company, asking a lot of questions, collecting their high per-diems, and leaving without accomplishing a damn thing. And there is not much a company can do, beyond giving the consultant a bad reference.

Fortunately, this has not been too prevalent in the information technology industry, perhaps because the results of a consultant are more readily measurable. However, it does happen. There are cases on record where consultants have come in and made things much worse than before they started. There are instances of systems which continually blew up. There is the case of the ton of undocumented code.

Fortunately these incidents don't occur often because, while there are incompetent consultants in this field (as in every other field), most get weeded out after a very short period of time.

Many of the problems with consultants are due to bad management of the consultant's tasks. But this must be understood in the light of the fact that most managers have never managed consultants before. Many managers assume that consultants don't need management and that magic things will occur all by themselves!

Kickin' Butt

A main complaint about consultants has been "attitude". Many people new to the consulting business have little idea about consultant-client relations. They think they are supposed to be the office "butt kicker".

> **COMMENT**: Hopefully, this book will help them get their act together.

Some of these young consultants have been known to come on like they were the greatest thing since high-density disks. They feel, in their need to make a good impression, that they have to ride roughshod over everyone, kick some butt, and in effect, they make real asses of themselves. They attempt to circumvent the client's channel of decision making by going over the project manager's head, or worse, they make important decisions themselves without consulting anyone. One MIS department secretary remarked:

Some of these consultants come in here and act as if,
whey they say jump, because they are highly paid, the
rest of the staff should ask how high!. Some of these
people should take all of their money and buy
themselves a set of manners!.

I Wanna Be Like You, Dad

Another problem has been with the type of consultant who tells the
regular staff only about the good points of the consulting business and
leaves out all the difficulties involved in starting and running a practice.
This leads to a good deal of staff envy. Envy is particularly increased
when management goes out of its way to give the consultant special
system privileges, such as access to the printer room or access to the
password files. Staff conflict can cause a project to go south in a hurry.

Finally, we see the case of what happens when staff members work
for the first time around consultants and the idea pops into their heads
that they want some of the action too. More than one top-notch
company programmer has been launched into this business by the
dreams of glory and riches. Client companies are not happy to lose their
top people, whether it be to another company or to the consulting
industry.

All That Glitters...

So we see that consulting plays many important roles in the data
processing industry and serves, in the most part, as a very positive force.
However, one role it does not play is that of a panacea.

If anything, we consultants usually play the role of the scapegoat.
When a project is well thought out *and* the consultants are brought in to
help get it done, *and* they are well-managed, *and* everything goes
smoothly from the first line of code to the installation of the system... it
is the management and company staff that receive the bulk of the credit.
This is the way it should be. After all, consulting is, as we have seen,
merely a tool to be used by MIS management to accomplish their tasks.
When the tool is used wisely in the hands of a skilled staff manager,
there is no reason why things should not go well and why he or she
should not get the credit.

However, when the computer takes a machine check, *or* a key employee quits, *or* the user changes the specs during coding, *or* those new terminals don't arrive when the salesman said they would, *or* when they do they are not really compatible with the mainframe, *or* when the manager doesn't really give a damn about the project in the first place, *or* the project fails for any reason and every reason beyond the human imagination (whew!)... who is around to pass the buck to? Take a guess.

Many years ago a friend of mine was a consultant at a company called Four Phase (no longer in business). These folks made minicomputers as well as the software to run them. He was blamed because he wrote some very efficient code which showed up a bug in the compiler. Because of the compiler bug the entire project had to delayed. Instead of blaming the compiler writers, my pal got the boot. They said he should have written the programs in "such a way" as not to bomb the compiler! Nothing like clear headed management.

> *COMMENT: I'll bet you can buy a Four Phase machine real cheap nowadays!*

The point to be learned here, especially for those thinking about going into the consulting field, is that when a project fails, someone is going to get the blame. And it is always easier (and more believable) to blame an outsider.

> *COMMENT: One manager had this to say about consultants: "To me, having some contractors around makes good sense, insurance-wise. They tend to spur productivity and they usually know what they are doing. When things go right, I look good. But when they don't, I make a claim against my insurance and just get rid of the consultants. They take the heat while I put on my dancing shoes to get things back on the road again. I usually do this by hiring different consultants. All in all, it's not a bad deal."*

SO YOU WANT TO BE A CONSULTANT
(Are You Sure?)

Is This You?

U p to this point we have talked quite a bit about consulting in very general terms. By now, you are probably asking yourself when will you learn just how to do it. Well, that time is at hand. You have read what consulting is all about and all the wonderful things the industry does for the high-tech world. You just can't wait to get into it, can you? Most likely you are a better than average technical person working for a good company, earning, say, around $35,000 a year. You have a good boss, interesting projects, and growth opportunity. But, you want to get into consulting.

Let's ask one important question. Why? Well, that is an easy one, you say. You've heard about those big bucks out there, those high hourly fees or fat per diems. You've seen consultants come and go as they please, and you want the chance to be your own boss, to work for yourself, to be the captain of your own ship. Oh, the thought of working for three months and then going off into the wilds of Acapulco, armed only with a sombrero and a glass of brandy! What a life it must be, you say. And where else will you get the opportunity to branch out, expose yourself to new systems and hardware, to attain a degree of technical sophistication which you can use to write your own ticket? Finally, how else can you become a power, a person of wide influence in the business community; one whose opinions are solicited to help shape the mission-critical systems of the future? The answer, you say, is *consulting*. By now you have it all planned out. You know all there is to know. Consulting is where you are going to *make it*.

Relax. After reading the long-winded paragraph above you are probably thinking that you are going to be shot out of the sky to crash and burn among the wreckage of all your dreams of glory and riches. Not so, as this is not one of those books that glorifies an occupation by saying how tough and rotten it is to get in and how meager are the rewards for all except the cream of the crop.

Instead, we are merely going to deal in the facts of the matter (with maybe a few of the author's opinions thrown in for your consideration and/or rejection). First of all, everything you think you know about consulting, *except the money*, is a myth. Does that mean your ideas are untrue? Well myths do not become myths unless there is some basis in fact to make them repeated so often that they become believed. Yes, you have heard a lot of myths about consulting, and like most myths, they tend to accentuate the positive and ignore the negative. So if you want to get into consulting, you might as well get your head on straight from the beginning. It is your future, so you might as well know both sides of the business before you take the leap.

If I seem to be dwelling on this at too great a length, it is only because most people who have jumped into consulting and have washed out, did not have the opportunity to have all the facts laid out in front of them. With dollar signs gleaming in their eyes, they leaped into a contract, found themselves to be very unhappy in the role of consultant, and were not prepared for some of the pitfalls that would traverse their path. They bottomed out, not because they were incompetent or lacked the proper technical skills, but because they did not know what the business was really all about, what would be expected of them, and what types of problems they would have to cope with after they left the corporate womb.

So let us look at the myths that have grown up around consulting and try to separate fact from fiction. There will be no scare tactics and no gloss over; just a simple word of caution. If people seem to only *hear* what they want to hear, then it is doubly true that when they *read*, they believe only what they *want* to believe. Don't let this happen to you. Don't take on the casual "well, this won't be the case with me" syndrome. Maybe it won't. Just maybe.

Give Me Money or Give Me ...

As we mentioned in the first chapter, people don't go into consulting for sport or passion. They go into it for *money*. That's right, money. People may be embarrassed to admit it, but it's the honest truth. All the high minded phrases that you hear about dedication to "profession" and fascination of the "art" is, for the most part, a lot of hot air. No matter how many times a consultant emphasizes that it is the idea of working for himself that keeps him going, don't you believe it for a second. *The first and number one thing which attracts people to the business, and keeps them in it, is the high monetary satisfaction one can gain.* This is not a myth, this is reality.

Let's take a look. First you have to figure out what you now get paid. To keep things simple take your gross yearly salary and divide it by 2000 (50 wks. x 40 hrs.). This will give you your hourly rate.

> *COMMENT: What about benefits? Unless you are getting some pension or profit sharing, or you are receiving some added spending money through your benefits then you can forget them. You can't take the company retirement plan that vests you in ten years to the Safeway to exchange for a rib steak. We are talking cash only.*

Using the above formula, if you earn $35,000 a year, you are making $17.50 an hour. This is not bad. But you have heard that as a consultant you can make between $25 and $45 an hour. While rates vary according to geographical location, market conditions, and the overall economic picture of the region, the above figures are pretty representative.

Let's take the amount of $35 per hour. This translates out to $70,000 a year.

> **COMMENT:** *If you get $40 an hour you make a cool $80,000 per year. There are many consultants who receive $50 and more for their services. Multiply that by 2000 hrs. and see why people talk about big bucks.*

There is no doubt that the money is out there. Is it any wonder that programmers and analysts crank up their ten megabyte monster machines, do some simple arithmetic, and rush out into the consulting world like a chicken with the colonel behind them? And if you are already in the consulting business, do you remember back when you were a employee and some agency called you and told you about all this wonderful money that was out there? There are a lot of myths in this business, but the money is not one of them.

Now numbers don't lie. But you should pay close attention to what follows because there are a few facts about the money that you should be aware of. Again, no scare tactics. And, yes, you will make more as a consultant. But how much, and is it *worth* it, should be your main concerns.

Time Is Money

Most consultants are paid a flat hourly rate for the hours that they actually perform services. Every person contemplating an entry into the consulting business figures the projected income from the business based upon full-time work; that is, forty hours a week for fifty weeks a year (2000 hrs.). *In no way is this going to be the case.* In the first place, your clients will most likely be closed on the major holidays, as well as many of the minor ones. However, these are of little concern as they are anticipated and most consultants would not want to work during these breaks anyway. But you must understand, that at $280 a day ($35 x 8 hours) these holidays can add up to quite a bit of lost income; income that a full-time employed person receives.

There are also a number of non-billable days other than holidays which are sometimes beyond the control of the consultant. For example, if the network goes down for any considerable length of time, your client is (if they are wise) going to call you off until the problems are fixed. There are also times, usually during month-end processing, that you will get no test time at all and the project leader may suspend work for several days until the production crunch is over. Should the project manager have to be away on business, he/she may request that you not report until their return. This may also happen when a key user checks out for a short time. There is also the possibility of your need to travel to a remote site. Now, in some instances, you may be able to bill you time and travel expenses. But most clients, while happy to reimburse you for actual out-of-pocket expenses for travel days, will be very reluctant to pay you your normal hourly rate while you are spending six or seven hours sitting on a plane to Paducah. And of course, there will be those days that you will not want to work for personal reasons. Perhaps there is a seminar you want to take. Or perhaps you want to attend a convention or computer exposition. There are those half-days you will spend prospecting new clients. And finally, there are those days which we term "mental health periods", when you just say to hell with it all and take a day on the beach, on the slopes, or in another time warp.

While all of the above examples do represent a loss of income to the consultant, in many ways they can be controlled. However, the final case, the one most consultants (and those thinking about being consultants) fear the most is the lay-off, or being "on the beach" as it is so commonly called.

There are some very privileged consultants who never miss a day between contracts, either because they know the techniques of marketing or they are so well known that they actually have a backlog of clients waiting for their services. This, will not happen to you for the first two or three years that you are in the business. Resolve yourself to the fact that you will definitely spend several weeks in the marketing process, looking for that next contract.

There is absolutely no way to predict just how many weeks a year you will be without a contract. The word-of-mouth figure that is passed around is four to eight weeks a year without income. And this can rise considerably during a recession period.

Taking the figure of six weeks, for a consultant who receives $35 an hour, this represents $8000 of lost income.

> **COMMENT:** *I believe this is a fair figure, although my research shows that most consultants do not want to admit just how much "down" time they actually have in a given year.*

Make no mistake, it is this "on the beach time" that will *make or break* a consultant's income picture. Signing a two-month contract for $40 an hour will not compensate if it takes another six weeks to land the next contract.

You see, unlike soap manufacturers, we cannot "create" a need for our service. The need must be present. All the slick brochures will not be worth their printing and postage in a locality where the economy is in the dumps. And when the whole country goes down the tubes for a year, as happened in 1991, well the consequences are obvious.

> *TIP: While you should be concerned with the above, it should not overly scare you. If you know how to market, make a name for yourself, and are willing to travel, there is always work somewhere for computer consultants who know what they are doing.*

So let's add up the damage. If we figure that you will have 30 working days of down time , that you will have 5 days of "Oh hell, I don't want to work" days (including sickness, seminars, etc.),an 10 days of holidays, we have a total of 9 weeks of possible lost income.

Let's figure that you get $35 an hour or $1,400 per week. On a fifty-week year, that is a gross of $70,000. However, our 9 weeks of non-billable time comes to $12,600 so that we gross $57,400.

> *COMMENT: The figure of $35 dollars an hour is pretty average for a consultant, based upon my survey in early 1993. While some consultants in particularly hard hit areas of the country, recession wise, have to work in the $25 an hour range, the overwhelming majority of experienced consultants surveyed say that they bill between $30 and $50 per hour. The higher figure is on the coasts, with the lower figures in the south and heartland areas.*

You should take a long hard look at the figures that you come up with based upon your part of the country. (Later on I teach you how to come up with the prevailing rates in your locality). While you may be lucky and be able to undercut the amount of "down" time, there is the possibility that you might become victim of a local recession. The point that should be getting through by now is that the gross figures that you have heard in the hallways and near the coffee machine are merely "best case" dollar amounts, and do not necessarily reflect the actualities of the business.

> COMMENT: Still, $57,400 is not a bad dollar figure to be earning; and we are talking "average" billing rate.

Risk, Reward, and Taxes

If you are like most people contemplating the leap into consulting, you are probably making in the area of $35,000 (1993 figures). Many ask if it is worth the risks in leaving a nice, safe, secure (right!) company for the perils of consulting.

From a financial viewpoint, resolving this risk/reward issue centers around the fact that since a consultant is in business for themselves, he/she enjoys the last really good tax shelter available. As a $35,000 a year worker, unless you have a large family or a lot of interest or medical deductions, you will be lucky to take home two thirds of what you make.

The reason people do will in consulting is because they are "paid" to take a "risk" by being able to deduct anything that is business related (a fine line at best). It is important to note that while the gross amount a consultant can make is not as high as it first looks, the dollar amount is still higher than working full-time. Some people would say that based on our preceding example, a $22,400 ($57,400 - $35,000) increase in gross earnings is a *good* justification for all the risks one finds in the consulting field. The *great* justification is in the relative tax advantages of being self-employed which can yield a significant increase in "bankable" dollars over being an employee.

It is not the intent of this book to serve as a tax manual for the consultant or those considering entry into the field. But a few observations are in order. You need to be less concerned with the amount of gross earnings, and more concerned with the amount of money that you need to cover your expenses.

A simple example will do, but this is only a generalization. If an employee makes $35,000 a year and has 15% of his gross ($5,250) as itemized deductions, he pays tax on $29,750. At a 33% tax rate (combined state, local, federal, etc.) his taxes are $9,817, leaving him with a $25,183 (gross income - taxes) profit.

Now perhaps he/she was able to get some of these "living" expenses calculated so that the tax bill is lower. But with the new tax laws it is damned hard for the wage-slave to deduct real living costs (beyond the mortgage) from their taxes. For example, if the employee's answering machine goes on the "fritz" and a new one costs $100, the employee might be able to make a claim that the machine is needed for their work. But it is doubtful that too many people would want to be in that employee's shoes trying to legitimize such a deduction during an audit.

However, if a consultant has to buy a new answering machine, it is a business expense and can be deducted as a cost of doing business (on Schedule C).

Using the same simple example, our $57,400 consultant can lower his taxable income by *business expenses* of 40% of his income, or $22,960. He also can lower his taxable income by 10% for itemized deductions, or $5,740. This lowers his taxable income to $28,700. He still has to pay state, local, and federal taxes (assumed at a 36% rate to account for the 'effect' of self-employment tax - which is calculated and deducted from gross), so his tax is $10,332 leaving him a gross profit of $47,068

What happened here? The wage earner has a gross profit of $25,183 the consultant had a gross profit of $47,068.

Our wage-slave friend has $25,183 left to live on. From this figure he has to buy his new answer machine, pay his rent and utilities, pay for auto expenses, his vacation, his cellular phone, etc. Let' assume that his "living costs" are $1,500 a month. This leaves him with $7,000 ($25,183 - $18,000) as a "profit" to put in his saving account. This is 20% of gross earnings ($7,000 / $35,000).

Our consultant was able to "include" many of his living expenses into "business expenses" of $22,960 and thus was able to lower his/her taxable income figure. Let's say that there are still $500 a month of expenses that the consultant can't write off. This leaves him/her with $18,108 ($47,068 gross - ($22,960 of business expenses + $6000 of personal expenses)) "profit" to put in the bank. This is 32% of gross ($18,108 / $57,400).

The wage earner showed a "profit" of $10,783. The consultant had a profit of $18,108 or a difference of $11,108. *That is not bad considering the risk is manageable and you will be doing basically the same type of work.*

> **TIP**: A quick and dirty way to "ball park" how much more you will put in the bank (i.e. net profit) by consulting, multiply your expected gross in consulting on a yearly basis (figure in down time) by 32%. Take 20% of your current gross. Subtract the second from the first. For example if you make $40,000 a year now and you expect to charge $45 an hour for 1640 hours, then you will gross $73,800. 32% of that is $23,616. 20% of your $40,000 salary is $8,000. Subtract ($23,616 - $8,000) and you can expect to bank $15,616 more than you do now. This is just an estimate.

What this boils down to is that a consultant may pay more in actual dollars to the tax man, but as a percentage of his take-home pay needed for goods and services, his tax can often be far lower than that of the salaried employee.

If all these tax matters tend to confuse you, have little fear. They confuse everybody. That is why there are people who earn a good living in deciphering these matters for everyday people (and perhaps due to accountant's pressure for complexity, we may never get a simple tax code). If you do nothing else before you decide to enter consulting at least consider going to a tax advisor. They may be expensive, but they have the answers to the questions that you are probably asking and which this book does not address.

> **TIP**: Try to remember this fact: people and companies do not become rich by making a lot of money... they become rich by keeping most of what they make from the government.

Bottom line, the bucks are there. If you are smart and get good advice on tax matters, as well as accounting procedures, you stand a good change of coming away with a nice piece of change. But first, you have to get paid, and that can become hassle number one.

Fast Pay, Slow Pay, No Pay

Do you pay your bills a day or two after you receive them? After opening your dentist's bill, do you immediately write a check for his services? Probably not. If you are like the majority of us, you will first pay those bills on which the collector can and will take action. (We have all received that cheery little note from the phone company). Your average, plain vanilla, client will be no exception. The amount of revenue and size of accounting bureaucracy will determine (almost in direct proportion) how long the wait at the mailbox will be.

In the first place, to most companies you are not a person, but a vendor. You are not looked upon as an employee who will raise hell if you are not paid on time. You are also not considered as a supplier of their raw materials which, should you decide to withhold, would threaten the existence of the firm. Unfortunately, you will be put into the vendor class, along with their plumber, electrician, and coffee-person.

While your services may be deemed as highly important at the time you render them, by the time your client is ready to pay, your invoice has ceased to be a top priority item. This is not to say that you will never get paid. There are no multi-million dollar companies who wish to jeopardize their reputation, credit rating and perhaps a law suit by ripping you off for a few thousand dollars. To them, it is just chicken feed. It is money that, if they did not pay to you, would end up going to the government anyway.

The problem here is priority. Those services that the client relies upon to stay in business and which at the same time have some "leverage", will rise to the top of the collating sequence when pay codes are assigned. Those other vendors (like us) get the "slow" pay codes. But don't regard this as selfishness. It is just good business. In the same way that you do not feel highly motivated to pay the plumber for last month's visit, most large clients feel that the world will not cave in on them if they do not bust their buns in getting a check to you. After all, they have received your services already. The programs are running or being designed, and there is little leverage that you can really exert. You can terminate your contract, but they know that you won't. And *you* know that you won't, because there is always another consultant out there waiting to take over.

The logic behind not paying you is called the "float" You may not be aware of it, but many large firms loan their reserve funds to financial institutions on an overnight basis in return for the interest that can be received. It is not a high rate, but if a one hundred and fifty million dollar company can float two million dollars a night, at a rate of 1.75% over a year, that comes out to $35,000; enough to pay at least one programmer's salary.

> *COMMENT: Some companies have arrangements to leave certain amounts in float each night. If it comes down to paying you or having this fund drop below the arranged level... well, you know the answer. True, if the company needed the money, they would use it in a minute. But your invoice does not, and never will, constitute a critical need.*

Even if you are with a company that would like to pay you within ten days of receiving your invoice, the sheer weight of the accounting bureaucracy would prohibit this. First of all, just because you sign a contract does not get you onto their vendor file by the next cycle. The scenario usually works this way. The project leader and you arrange for a rate and sign a contract. A purchase order requisition is sent to the department secretary. When she gets around to entering it (usually when enough of them pile up to call in a temporary data-entry clerk) it will then go back for review and signature. When enough of these are collected by the secretary, they are sent over to the division comptroller for approval. From there it will be routed to the accounts payable section, where you will be formally accorded vendor status during the weekly or monthly batch cycle. They will assign a purchase order number, without which no invoice will be accepted. All of this paper must be copied for both your file and theirs.

If all of this seems tedious, remember that you have already started work weeks ago (perhaps months ago) and your invoices are piling up because the department is waiting for a purchase order number. When your first invoice reaches accounts payable, a pay code will be established, probably one which puts you on a 45, 60, or 90 day pay cycle. It is quite possible that, by the time your first check arrives, your contract is either up and you are with another client, or the amount of the purchase order has already been exceeded and you have to go through the whole process all over again. This is not to suggest that you will not eventually get paid. However,, the trick is to receive your funds before you are eligible for Social Security... or food stamps.

A small company presents a whole host of different problems. In companies where money is very tight, the possibility exists that there will not be funds in the till to pay you until some of the company's customers pay their bills. And when they do pay you, there is no guarantee that the check won't bounce all the way back. The small firm may routinely process all their vendor transactions quarterly. Or they may sit on all your invoices until the project is complete. Or the company may be dissolved by a partner's illness, death, or dissatisfaction. Or a government contract may not come in. Or the company may get swallowed up by some giant conglomerate. Or ...... (fill in your own horror story)

> *TIP: While I will deal with brokers later, working through a broker as an independent still leaves you victim to the vicissitudes of client payment procedures. Don't let them tell you otherwise.*

Watch The Cash Flow

So, whether you contract with a small or large firm, you can count on having a cash flow problem. This is compounded by the fact that more and more companies are using out of state (even out of region) banks for their accounts payable. If your Florida company banks with the Ride 'em Cowboy Bank of Boffo, Montana, your client can count on a extra six to ten days of float before the check clears. Not only do they know this, but your bank also is aware of the fact. After all, don't you think that your Florida bank has an account for the Atomic Can Opener Company in Platypus Falls, Idaho? To protect themselves, the bank may put a ten-day hold on these funds, thus keeping you from enjoying the (very ripe) fruits of your labor.

And there is the U.S. Postal Service. I need say no more.

> *COMMENT: In my locality, the Postal Service has improved quite a bit from ten years ago. They are still not Fed-Ex, but they are better then before.*

Because of the imbalance in cash flow, you will have to plan your purchases and expenses accordingly. But then again, you are a business person (remember) and this is just exactly what business management is all about.

> COMMENT: If you can't manage your own business, who in the hell is going to be stupid enough to bring you in to help determine the course of theirs?

If you can work with little down-time, you will make good bucks. But your checks will come to you in drips and drabs. In the long run, you will do well, but as John Keynes said, "in the long run we are all dead." In the short run, especially if you are just getting started, you will know what it is to wait for the mail person and then go back upstairs to a meal of either tea and toast, or steak and Lowenbrau. Unless you become expert at managing your finds, your love/hate relationship with the mail will not continue for long. You will be out of business and back in the headhunter's office looking for the steady income of full-time employment.

Bills, Bills, Bills

Let me say a few words about expenses. First and foremost will be the expense of getting a contract. This will entail travel, postage, printing, phone bills and perhaps a suit and haircut. Once you are established, you will have need for an answering service or machine, regular office supplies, educational materials (such as books and periodicals) and perhaps even a small office.

> TIP: Remember when you were an employee and you could raid the company supply cabinet? No way, friend. You may get away with it a hundred times, but let one envious employee make an issue of it, and you will be out on your butt faster than a keystroke. And if the word gets around, you are history in this business.

The above expenses will be minor compared with the amounts of money you will have to fork over for whatever benefits you desire to have. If you think non-group medical coverage is cheap, wait until you see just where the "good hands insurance people" have you by! You will also have to buy your own life insurance and disability insurance. Your auto insurance might also take a leap upward, since you will be, as they see it, a greater risk; using your car for business purposes.

Of course there are taxes and license fees. Since no income tax will be withheld, you will have to pay your taxes quarterly, based upon an estimate. Thus, another dent in your cash flow. And, in order to render unto Caesar, you will need your own army of consultants... lawyer, accountant and tax advisor. (Here is the "pay them now or pay them later" thing... either you need them to *keep* you out of a jam... or to *get* you out of a jam.) Have we mentioned Social (in)Security taxes at 7.5 percent?

What's In a Name?

There is another "expense" associated with being a computer consultant, but this one is not so easily measured in monetary terms. For lack of a better phrase, I call it the "good name" cost.

When you are (were) a salaried employee of some organized business enterprise, you have a degree of "merit" in the financial, as well as social community. When it comes to applying for a loan or credit card, or receiving a membership at a golf club, or renting an apartment, the fact that you regularly "work" somewhere carries with it an aura of maturity, stability, credit worthiness, and reliability. The simple fact that others with whom you do business on a day-to-day basis know where you are going to be from 9 to 5 each day, gives you a certain degree of social and economic respectability.

After all, you are a working person, not a lone-ranger or gypsy-type, moving from one garden patch to another. Because you earn a "regular" salary, you have an economic "good name". People are not afraid to offer you credit terms because they "know" that you have some money coming in on a regular basis. On a social level, others can identify with you easier, since, like them, you have to be in at 9, you work for a boss, and inflation is always greater than your last raise. In other words, you conform to the normal standards that members of our industrial society have determined to be acceptable.

Now the truth may be that you outspend your income by a hundred dollars every month and are mortgaged to the hilt. But you have a *steady job*! You are a stable breadwinner.

As soon as you junk all of this stability and go out on your own, you lose your "good name" and become what might be considered a "risk". Other business people such as your dry cleaner or florist may identify with your struggles, goals, and ambitions. Your banker may congratulate you and pat you on the back, praising you as an inspiration to all who desire to get ahead. The hidden fact of the matter is that many business people do not want as their credit-customers people who have taken the risks they have taken. They want regular working stiffs with steady incomes that can be *attached* if necessary.

Your "good name" is gone. You no longer enjoy a steady income but depend upon (as they see it) the whims of luck and circumstance for your bread and butter. The sad fact is that the financial community would rather you earn a steady $30,000 as an employee than a hefty $65,000 as an consultant.

> *TIP*: If you don't believe this go to your nearest car dealer and make an application to lease a car. Give them the name of where you were previously employed (or are employed) and see how they smile at you while the salesman fills in the form. Then go to another dealer and tell them right up front that you are a consultant and see how fast the salesman leads you towards a cash deal. Or go to any real-estate office and tell them that you are self-employed as a consultant and you will hear a lot of bull about money being tight and lenders being loaned up to the limit.

The money people do not trust you. You are placed in the same class as writers, minor league ball players, college students and palm readers. Even if you are experienced and can show a healthy bank book, you will still be looked upon with skepticism and asked the eternal questions about your ability to make a forty dollar a month payment.

Whatever credit you have going into consulting you will be able to keep. However, getting extensions of all accounts or opening new ones will be difficult until you have been a cash customer for a while. So, if you want to buy that first house or get a loan for a new car, do it now before you enter the consulting business. You may not be able to do it for some time afterward.

> *COMMENT*: Even after 15 very profitable years in this business and a strong balance sheet, I still get turned down for those "pre-approved" credit card applications I get in the mail. Being self-employed can be a credit death wish.

Tennis Anyone?

The social scene is something else again. As a salaried employee, more than likely most of your friends were close to the same salary bracket as you. You probably did not go out drinking with a $90,000 a year vice president, or play golf with a $15,000 typist. It seems to be a curious fact of the industrialized society that people seem to be most comfortable around those who earn approximately the same as themselves.

As soon as you leave the ranks of the $25,000 to $40,000 programmer/analyst class to go into consulting, you are the one who becomes an outsider. Your friends, both in and out of the information systems industry may not know beans about consulting, but they know that you are not stupid. You did not leave a sure fire $35,000 a year position in order to make any less or even just a little more money. They will have no real idea what you will actually be earning, but they know (or at least suspect) that it will be a bundle.

You will find that they will treat you with respect (maybe jealousy), but you will notice that you no longer will be one of the "group" anymore. You have (in their opinion) stepped up. Your old friends won't desert you. But you may find that invitations to dinner or cocktails will not arrive as frequently as before. It is not that they feel that you are too good for them... it is that they feel they are not good enough for you. It sounds stupid... because it is stupid. But it is a fact of life. It is just another of the costs you will have to pay for going into the "big time".

Did I Get Your Attention?

If I have painted a rather sullen picture about the rewards of consulting, it has been only to dim the blinding gleam of dollar signs glowing in your eyes. Too many good computer people have been led astray by those who did not paint the whole picture for them.

There are tangible rewards to being a consultant, but there are also risks and opportunity costs that have to be considered. Perhaps not everything I have talked about in this chapter will become part of your experience. Perhaps none of it. As long as you are aware of the risks, then you are much better prepared than thousands who have come before you. One ex-consultant who was not prepared told me:

When I first started as a consultant, I thought I had found the key to the vault. But when I did not get my first check until two months after the project was over, I realized that, for me, the rewards were not really worth the problems.

Well if they *are* worth it to you, and you can put off for the short run what will be yours in the long run, then you *can* achieve success as a high-tech consultant.

> *Perhaps it is this specter that most haunts working men and women: the planned obsolescence of people that is of a piece with the planned obsolescence of the things they make. Or sell.*
>
> *Studs Terkel*
>
> *Working (1972)*

WORKING FOR YOURSELF

A Little History, A Little Advice

Some years back there was a radio and then television show about a man who went into business for himself. He had previously worked for a large, well respected organization, and he served in a professional capacity with the outfit. Although the firm was well-managed as a whole, his division ran into some unexpected competitive situations and suffered quite badly; such that the entire division was literally desecrated by the cut-throat competition. Although this man suffered much pain and anxiety at the dissolution, he still felt that the company's service was viable and he, with the help of a friend, became a *consultant* to the industry that his one-time parent company still functioned in. He felt that by working for himself, he could maximize both his efforts and his profits, more than by joining another division of the company. He set out to develop his own working philosophy and style of operation. It was not too long until his reputation had traveled throughout his geographical area. Because of this, he was continually called upon to solve the most challenging problems of his industry.

In case you don't recognize the show or the man, we are speaking about the "*LONE RANGER*".

> *TIP*: Re-read the opening paragraph again slowly and then think *about it!*

There are probably a hundred or so books that have been published on the joys and rewards of working for yourself. Obviously, you are aware of these rewards or you would not be interested in being a consultant. The drive to be one's own boss cannot be developed through words on paper. Either you have the motivation or you don't. And if you don't, then stay the hell out of consulting, as you will become very unhappy.

The literature about working for yourself abounds with discussions on taking direction, being responsible, making it happen, doing your own thing, having "it" your way, pleasing yourself, etc. And there are as many good reasons to work for yourself as there are good reasons to work for somebody else. But most people who work for themselves, when asked why, would probably not cite any specific reason. They will tell you that they do it *because they like it.*

You have to intrinsically believe that working for yourself is going to be "good". That is all I am going to say about it. Either you believe it or you don't. It you need it proven to you, then find a good book on the subject (there are many), as I am going to confine the discussion to the specific facts about being your own boss as a high-tech consultant in the data processing industry.

The One Man Band

Consultants in all industries are to some respects "lone rangers"; yet this is even more evident in the high-tech services. Management consultants for a long time have found the team approach more beneficial to their clients. Companies today don't hire one consultant to solve a distribution problem. They call in a whole team of consultants and direct them to come up with the answer.

But in most MIS departments, the problems and desired results are usually not beyond he grasp of one person. And unlike their management consultant counterpart, in software systems the consultant is usually brought in, not to find the problem or even to find the answer, but rather *to do the work* of solving the problem. Management knows that they are at point "A" and want to get to point "B". They bring in consultants to get them there in a hurry and often the work can be handled by one or two persons working alone.

This is not to say that there aren't teams of consultants working together on projects. At least they are called "teams". But in reality each consultant pursues a mostly solitary path in programming, design, analysis, etc.

It would not be unusual to find yourself as the only consultant on a project working with three or four employees. Or you might "be" the project, working completely independent of others. You will literally be a "lone-ranger" out there, facing attacks from hostile quarters without anyone to help you out or back you up.

The Working Guest

You will be a guest in the house. You will not be "taken in" as one of the family members. You are going to be treated just as you would treat the man or women who comes to paint your living room. You may offer them a cup of coffee and be friendly, but you hardly expect to be friends. If you are working on an independent project, you are going to bear the entire responsibility for its success or failure. If it goes well, you may not get any of the actual credit. But, if it gets screwed up, you will take all of the heat. In many cases, being a consultant can become very lonely work. You may have very little intercourse with the other staff members, and after some preliminary meetings, you may have no contact with the users. And in some cases you may be given a book of specs, and told to work on the problem (either design or programming) off-site.

> *COMMENT: This can be great. Almost every consultant surveyed said that working part of the year at home was one of the real pluses of being self-employed. With today's technology; a modem, a fax machine, a PC, and a scanner, even large projects can be done from a consultants home office. You can't beat the commute! However, may contractors remarked that extra discipline is needed to meet deadlines (it is easy to procrastinate or find other distractions).*

One programmer/consultant reported the following about working alone:

> I walked in at 8:00 A.M. and at 8:05 I was handed a
> three ring binder of about forty pages. This contained
> all the specifications of the proposed system, the file
> layouts and the reports that the company requested.
> They had all the labor and yield calculations figured
> out, and even contained instructions on how they
> wanted the programs structured. For two months, I
> became a programming machine. The project was
> easy but, as I worked all day in a quiet room writing
> code, I grew increasingly tense, due to the lack of
> human contact.

The relative isolation that you will feel is very real in the consulting world. This is not because you are working for yourself, but because you are working alone. It is very possible that you will find yourself in a position where nobody knows what you are really doing and nobody cares how you are doing it. All they will care about is that on a certain date, they can shovel in the data and send the reports to the users. They brought you in because you are better than their staff. With as little direction as possible, they want their system up and running.

If you get to work with other consultants on the project, you will escape many of the lonely aspects of this business, but if you are the sole contractor on the project, it might be you against the world.

"You Go The Ten Rounds By Yourself"

This quote is from an article I saw about a third rate "Rocky" type ex-boxer. When you are in the ring, there is no one who can help you. The responsibility factor that we alluded to in an earlier chapter deserves just a bit more attention. When you are an employee, you may have responsibility on paper for the success or failure of a project. But in reality, it is your boss who will get the heat if things go bad. After all, programmers and analysts are a valuable commodity today, and even incompetent ones are not fired.

> **COMMENT:** *In fact, even incompetent managers are not fired... merely assigned somewhere else where then can do little damage. And you wonder why the rest of the world is beating the hell out of us?*

In short, there is really little accountability put on the staff programmer/analyst. If a project is two months late, or user requests don't get taken care of on time, most computer people have little to fear. If their company doesn't want them around anymore, there is always another company that will employ them and perhaps at a better salary. Most technical management types know this and do not exert a lot of time or effort into motivating people to get the projects done on time and in budget.

As a consultant, you are going to have to face accountability measurements like you have never seen before. Your name is going to be on the system and your reputation is going to be at stake.

> **TIP:** *Try this experiment. Find two programs, one written by a company programmer and one written by a contractor. Ask the project manager about each program. Odds are that he will tell you <u>when</u> the company employee's program was written. But he will <u>absolutely</u> tell you that other program was written by a <u>contractor</u>, and will probably know the consultant's name. This is* accountability!

If a staff programmer screws up a system... big deal. But, if you do a less than adequate job...it might be your last as a consultant. A good number of consultants entered the business thinking the good thoughts about being able to come into the office at 10 and leaving at 3. They did not stop to realize that every job could turn out to be their last. There is nobody to pass the buck to.

But don't toss and turn all night worrying about your new found accountability. As long as you are aware of it, it probably will never be a problem. On the other hand, don't become the consultant who thinks he/she is so good that no matter what happens on a project, they will come out of it smelling like a rose. Not true. It new was... and never will be.

Will You Still Need Me, Will You Still Feed Me...

When you work for yourself in your client's shop, you will face two very distinct extremes: the love/hate relationship that the staff will have for you. In most cases, the management will treat you very well. They have a problem, they hired you, and they really want you to succeed; if not only for the good of the company, but also to justify the decision they made in bringing in a consultant and paying the rate.

Management knows right to the penny what you are costing per hour, and thus, you are likely to have easy access to them and the user community. No cost effective manager wants to keep a $35 an hour contractor cooling their heels in the outer office.

Whether it be true or not, management will often consider your work more important than what the rest of the staff is doing. You may receive those little system privileges that you never had as an employee. Your batch jobs will be given a higher priority. The operations staff will answer the phone when you call. You may have access to the printer room and have priority delivery of your reports. The data entry section will get your stuff out the door overnight. And most importantly, those big decisions that must be made by the manager will be taken care of and not left in an unread stack of memos on his/her desk.

All of this can be very satisfying and may be one of the reasons that consultants can accomplish as much as they do in such a short period of time.

> **COMMENT**: It would be interesting to see how much an average technical person could accomplish if given free and easy access to the tools of the trade. How productive would an employee staff be if they were all treated like high priced contractors?

Don't let this go to your head. In the first place, you are not getting all of this special treatment because they "like" you. In the second place, you would not be there if they didn't desperately need you. It is purely an economic consideration. You are a squeaky wheel... so you get the grease from management.

But, you are likely to get something a lot heavier than grease from the staff. They could probably cite a hundred specific reasons why they don't want you around, but all of these reasons can be grouped under two labels: fear and envy.

We Have No Fear But Fear Itself

For some reason, computer people are a paranoid lot. When you come into the shop they are going to feel that you are there to show them up and give management a reason to replace them. There is never any justification for this fear, but it persists in almost every shop. Technical people are never afraid of screwing up when there is no one around that could replace them, but let a consultant come in who, in ten days, finds out all anyone needs to understand or maintain the system, and the staff people become just a bit irritable

As a result, they will break their necks to see that their production keeps pace with your own. As I said before, there is nothing like an outside consultant to spur the technical staff into action. All of a sudden those user requests seem to get quickly resolved.

> **COMMENT:** *Management knows this and it could be one of the chief reasons for your presence.*

The fears of the staff can take many forms but the result of these fears is the same. The staff members do everything in their power to keep vital information from reaching you. Technically, you are probably more experienced than they are so they can't beat you there. But they know the system and they may use this knowledge as a weapon against you.

You have several things going for *you*. First, you have worked on systems like the one you have contracted with. Two, the program code is available and the code does not lie (usually!). And three, you have easy access to management and even easier access to the user staff. The user staff is probably ticked off at the staff people anyway and will bend over backwards to give you any and all information about what happens when the system is run.

If their fear is not justifiable at least it understandable. You probably remember how you felt the first time a hot-shot consultant came in to bail out a project you were involved in. The contractor was an outsider, not one of the gang, and you were not overjoyed in having this person around... especially if you were the shop "heavy".

I have found that the more technically capable the staff is, the more they will resent your presence on the project. Said one contractor:

> I was convinced that one guy stayed up very late every night, searching the CICS manual for some obscure term that nobody ever heard of, just so he could spring it at me in the morning; trying to make me look like a rookie... and I was programming CICS when he was in junior high!

Fortunately, you will find that the resentment of the staff programmer is short-lived. As soon as they understand (or are made to understand) that you are simply a hired gun and not there to replace them (at any price!), the quicker will their defensive wall lower. Sooner or later, they will know that you do not know everything about info-systems, and their confidence in themselves will rise enough so that they will not have to take out their insecurities on you. As soon as they realize that once the project is complete you will be on your way, their hostility will begin to diminish and you will have a more cooperative associate to work with.

If you have some common sense and follow the advice in the later chapters of this book, you will have no trouble in handling the fearful staff member. Their feelings are understandable and predictable. It is not your success that they fear. It is the possibility of their own failure.

Basic Instincts?

The staff members who are jealous of you is another matter. In every shop you are going to run into some people who just don't like consultants. My research shows that with these people you are dealing with a whole range of psychological problems commonly know as envy.

Whether it is because you make more money than they do, or because you can come in at 11 and leave at 3, or one of the dozen other reasons that these staff people find to envy consultants, you are going find people who really hate your guts. As a colleague of mine reports:

> It seems that on every project there is always one programmer or analyst who is always downright nasty to me. And always, he or she is someone who is not in my group or even on the project.

This kind of problem is much harder to deal with because you never really know the basic psychological problems that this person has. In many cases you will be dealing with a person who not only has nothing to lose if you fail, but he/she might have something to gain. And many times their tactics are really noxious.

This is the person that will claim you are cheating on your hours. If something goes wrong with any system in the shop, it is this person who will try to pin some blame on you. It is this person who will crack those nasty little jokes about how all consultants cheat their clients and actually screw things up worse than before their arrival.

This jealousy sometimes takes the form of the silent treatment, where you might share an office with a person who never even says "good morning". But as soon as he hears you talking to your spouse on the phone, he/she will hit the manager's office at a dead run to complain what a disturbing factor you are in the office.

When you worked full-time you could deal with these people because you had a power base and could handle the office politics. But you are out of that loop. So what do you do? I'll talk about some solutions later, but don't expect miracles. Professional envy exists in all occupations. But, because you are a consultant, you become like the substitute teacher you used to haze in grade school. When you were an employee you could deal with these guys. Now you are working for yourself. You have a reputation to maintain. Think about it.

I Am... Somebody

The traditional reason for working for oneself has been stated as the desire to be one's own boss. Many people who feel alienated from the goals and objectives of the organization that they work for leave their jobs in droves each year to enter into business for themselves... to be their own boss. It is a normal desire for people to feel that what they do for a living is important to the whole scheme of things. Technical people are no different.

How many times have you busted your buns in fixing or designing a system, only to feel that, everything considered, it really wasn't that important one way or another? How many times have you felt that what you do is not important to the real success of the business? Well, you are not alone. More and more technical people are beginning to feel like very small spokes in a huge wheel. For many computer people, once they have mastered the technology, the satisfaction they used to receive from technical work seems to diminish. One very successful consultant told me:

> When I was working full-time, I had done it all.. from writing compilers to on-line network design. I was bored. I was bored because I could not get connected with what I was really doing. It was just another system. Somehow I wanted my work to mean more to me.

If this is one of the problems that you are facing, then you should take a good look at being a consultant. While the business may not solve the problem completely, it will go a long way towards giving you that sense of job satisfaction that you enjoyed earlier in the career.

If you have done your homework (like reading this book) before starting out on the consulting road, the day you clean out your desk, hand in your ID badge, and leave the warm corporate environment to walk out into the chilled night air... that day you shall remember always as the one where you took a step in controlling your own destiny. On that day, you stop being an employee and you become an enterprise. The decisions you make about what contracts to accept, about how you will market yourself, about how you will manage your time and money, are some of the most important you will make.

In many cases, you will be making decisions, that, as an employee, were made for you (usually by committee!). Whether you strike it rich or you go bust will be largely on your own efforts, your own good (or bad) judgment. For the first time, you will really feel that you are in control of your own life. At the highest level, you are going to be your own boss. You will decide where you will work, what kinds of projects you will work on, what you will get paid, when you will work, etc. Nobody is going to pressure you into anything. You are the boss.

Notice, I used the term "highest level of decision making". I don't want you to get carried away on a power trip. Yes, you will have power over your own life. But remember this. Many of the decisions or choices you will make will not contain viable alternatives. For example, let us say that you are asked to sign a contract for three months with a company which would help give you some visibility in the industry; and the project will be an interesting one. But what if you know that the project leader is going to be a pain in the butt?

On the "highest level" of decision making, the choice is yours. However, what is the alternative. Either you take the contract and earn the bread, or you don't. You might say that this would be the same choice if you were an employee and were transferred or got a new boss. But there is a big difference. As an employee, you have a position in the organization; you are part of things. Within limits you have some direction over your own affairs. True, you can't dictate policy, but you can play politics. As a consultant you are your own boss but you only have the option of taking it or leaving it. As an employee, you would have the opportunity to engage in some tough office politics and perhaps wangle what you want. You could devise a strategy (and there have been a million books written on corporate politics) to get off of one project and on to another, especially if you saw the change before it occurred. As a consultant, however, this opportunity does not really exist.

You have to ask yourself just what level of decision making do you want to be on. Do you want the freedom and independence of consulting, or do you want the power and authority of being a corporate person.

What's Your Game, Can Anybody Play?

The desire to plot a course of action, plan it out, market it, administer its completion and then take the credit is a very powerful motivation. These are the factors why good people remain in the corporate environment. Say what you want about corporate life, if you come up with a good idea that can save or make money *and* if you have anything at all on the ball, in most corporations you will eventually get a shot at making it happen. It may not be overnight, but sooner or later, your turn will come.

Living in the corporate world can be looked on as a game, and there are a great many people who enjoy the competition. They find it fun to play. Have you ever felt the satisfaction of coming up with a good idea for a system and getting it completed, especially if it was over the objections (and forecasting of doom) from your office competitors. Many observers speak in pejorative terms when mention is made of office politics. But for many players, it is the only game in town.

> *COMMENT: To many, being in the thick of a department fight, in determining whether to firm goes proprietary or open system for example, can be very stimulating. They love the politics. And by politics, I am not talking about endless (and mindless) memo writing. I mean power... the making of decisions which will effect the course of events for the organization for the foreseeable future.*

When you first started out in technical world you joined a company and they put you on a system that you were to learn and maintain. As time passed, you got to know all there was to know about that system. When someone wanted the system to do something different, they had to come to you. You might have only written three lines of code a week, but you had power, you had authority. Your files were not used and your data was not extracted until they came to you for advice. You had an important place in the shop (although at the time you probably didn't realize it, because you had access to information no one else had.

Then came a point where the system had to be enhanced and you were the one to design, chart, code, test and install the programs. You were a decision maker. They might not have been life-or-death decisions, but you did make decisions. Understand this. You couldn't set your own pay or choose your own boss, but you were able to act in a decision making capacity. You had a power base from which you could enlarge your visibility throughout the organization. You could use this position and through some politics, you could become a very important person in the company.

> *COMMENT: One of the great features about consulting to me is the lack of politics. I hate playing politics. I just like doing the work (programming). I guess I am just a nerd at heart.*

You may say that politics is of no interest you. But, before you commit yourself, at least understand the ramifications of what consulting will be. Understand that you can't play in the corporate game as a consultant; you are merely a spectator.

Happy Hooking?

Earlier I talked about the "oldest profession". You will become subject to what may consultants refer to as the "whore principle". I know this is not the most appealing description of consulting, but it is a fact that you had better be aware of before joining the "profession". The lady of the evening has the opportunity to work where she wants, when she wants and with whom she wants. The terms and conditions of sale are the same as the consultant. She must always please her client before herself.

> **COMMENT**: *There is broad academic debate in business schools about whether the consultant works for himself or his client? Is he* really *self employed? This is one of those circle-type "chicken versus egg" questions that professors love to spring on their students. Some take the view that anyone who sets his own rates and hours is in business for himself. But the opposition says that there is no such thing as a self employed person because everyone always works for a boss or a customer. Go enroll in an MBA program and contribute your opinion!*

The "whore principle" simply describes consulting as a mix between business and pleasure. The pleasure comes from the fact of your being able to act as an independent, to not get involved in the day-to-day hassles of your client. Ultimately you can determine where, when, for whom, and for how much you will provide services. These are decisions you get to make. You are independent... at least up to the time you sign the contract.

You can shop to your heart's content, but once you check into the "client hotel" everything else is up to the management. This is when you cease to be an independent business person and start becoming the whore. At a recent meeting of a California consultants association, one person had this to say.

> Before I started out, I really believed that I would be
> my own boss. But it wasn't so. True, I could make
> the up-front decisions, but I found that once I got in
> bed with the client, it was their needs not mine, that
> had to come first. It was really shattering.

You may steer the boat, but your client will determine its direction. When your client says jump, it will be you and not the full-time employee, who will say "how high?". When it comes to technical questions, such as whether to use a random or sequential update technique in a program, you will have pretty much carte blanche (mainly because nobody really gives a damn). But, when the question arises about whether the system should be procedural or object-oriented, in most cases you will not be consulted for your opinion.

You were not signed to find the problem or to find the answer. These were done before your arrival. You were brought on to implement an already established solution. Thus, you must see yourself not as a mover and shaker of policy, but as an implementor of their policy.

Like a whore you are there to perform a trick and to get out. You will have no effect on the firm's data processing goals and objectives. More than any employee, you will have to do exactly what management wants. You will not have any power base and you cannot politic for what you think should be the goals of the organization.

I can't stress this too strongly. To the client you are a high priced piece of meat. If you fail to give satisfaction, it is not likely that your phone will ring soon afterwards. It is true that you may get some privileges of the house, but you will not be a player of the game. You will be more like one of the pieces on the board.

It's Fee For Service

If you don't understand the whore principle you will not be successful in consulting. It's that plain and simple. But if you are not able to adapt yourself to this role, all is still not lost.

There have been many consultants who, in the course of doing a project for a company, demonstrated the exact talents that the company was looking for in management. There are lots of examples of people who have dropped out of the consulting business to take a job with their client doing what they loved best... the game of corporate business.

In the next chapter we will talk about what the work will probably be like. Lots of the time it will not be all that interesting. You will end up doing many of the same types of contracts. You won't be able to take part in politics either. Thus, you better (like the whore) be in this business for the money.

I will say it again and again. It's the money, stupid! No matter what you have heard or read (including this book), it is all about money. Consulting will often be like any other occupation. Many plateaus, some valleys, few highs. It better be the money, or you will probably be very unhappy working for yourself.

Where is Your Head, Now?

The concept of working for themselves is a very powerful motivation for most people. But so many have started a business without knowing all the ins and outs of what they were getting into or their own needs and desires.

You have to ask yourself some basic questions about what you ultimately want. I think I have given you some objective glimpses into what working for yourself will be like... the good parts and the bad.

To thine own self be true.

Knowledge - Zzzzp! Money - Zzzzp! - Power! That's the cycle democracy is built on!

Tennessee Williams

The Glass Menagerie (1945)

THE WORK

Hi Ho, Hi Ho, Off To Work We Go

This is a story about work and play. It happened recently. A consultant new to the business went to a computer exposition and happened to run into a friend of hers from the company where they had both been employees. Since the consultant had not seen this friend for quite some time, the friend was naturally curious about what our hero had been doing. The consultant went on an on, telling her friend abut how she was able to leave at noon and play golf, about how she could vacation when she wanted and about how she could pick and choose her projects. The friend finally interrupted her and asked when was the last time she had "done" any of these "consulting perks". The consultant replied, "I didn't say I did. I just said I could." The two parted. The friend left to play volleyball at his company sponsored tournament. The consultant, though tired from a long day, trudged off to the booth of a large hardware firm in order to sell her services and make a possible contact.

You have heard the phrase that there is a time for work and a time for play. The corollary to this is the concept that if you want to stay *busy*, become employed. But, if you want to *work*, then become a consultant. Because, the simple truth of the matter is that you are going to work hard.

Please don't let this confuse you with the idea of being *challenged*. Working hard and being challenged are not synonymous terms. You may be challenged some of the time. But most of the time you definitely are going to work.. and work... and work.

Borrrrring!

Many people go into computer consulting thinking that they will get to work on those projects that either weren't available at their old company. Or they hope to work on a level of technology much higher than available at their old firm. The choices were supposed to be endless!

I've seen this over and over. There is nothing so forlorn as a sharp programmer, hot in CICS and relational database methodology, who finds himself with the choice of either going hungry for another three weeks, or signing on to a PDP-11 batch shop and sitting at a keypunch machine (they're still out there).

Remember when I said that by being a consultant you could choose your assignments. I never said that any of the choices would be terrific! It is a cruel fact that many programmers and analysts think that being a consultant, by definition, means constantly working on interesting projects. They all think about those exciting contracts where they can utilize new hardware and the latest in software techniques.

If you are a technical person thinking about the business, don't believe this. And if you are already in the business, you know it is just not true. The fact of the matter is that often you will be called in, not to do work that is so difficult that the staff can't do it, but because *the work is was needed yesterday and there is nobody in the shop free to do it.* You will be brought in not so much because have space-age technical skills, but because you know the basics of your craft so well that you can do twice the work in half the time. It is the old "we don't want it good... we want it Tuesday! " paradigm.

Many times you will be called upon to do the work that nobody else in the office *wants* to do. Remember when you were a programmer or analyst and the management gave you an assignment that you just didn't want to do? If you were smart, you suggested that they bring in an outsider to design and program it. You had some power. You were just not going to let them assign some dull, back breaking project to you.

While we all want a contract to work with the latest object-oriented techniques, or whiz-bang hardware, it seems that we often wind up re-working some system that is currently a "non-performing corporate asset". If we don't re-invent the wheel, we often build one that probably rolls along a little bit smoother, but is still a wheel. There are times when we all felt that if we had to write that same inquiry and display CICS code one more time we would throw in the towel and sell encyclopedias! I am telling you the truth. It is not always fun and games.

Yet there will be good times. If half your projects are dull, the other half will be beyond excitement. There will be projects you hope will never end. There will be assignments where you learn more in three weeks than you could in three years full-time. There will be contracts were you work with the most wonderful people you could imagine. There will be experiences that you will remember all your life. While 50% of your work will be routine, you can count on the other 50% being simply terrific.

> **COMMENT:** *Several years ago I worked on a health care project for the State of California. Not only was the work terrific, so were the people. They even gave me a wall plaque that reads : Al Canton, Often Wrong, But Never In Doubt. It is one of my most valued possessions.*

You Load 16 Tons ...

Then there is the matter of hours. How many *real hours* of work does the employed computer person really put in? Whatever the figure is, you as a consultant will definitely put in much longer hours. The days of long morning meetings, bull sessions with your friends, or chit-chat with the users are going to be over for you. In some shops they will try to turn you into a robot-like programming/design machine. I've been on projects were the deadlines were so tight that people have actually worked 48 hours straight, designing while they were coding.

> **COMMENT**: *Some shops will literally lock you in a room. There is a state office in California that has the notoriety of making their consultants fill out a form before they are allowed out of the "secure area" to go to the bathroom.*

As a consultant, you will be expected to keep all of your "non-productive" activity to a minimum. When that big user meeting comes up, you will often be excused right after you present your material. In the first place, they don't want you privy to all the gossip that goes on in those meetings. In the second place, they are paying you a small fortune (by their standards) to *work*. That is what they want you to do. *Work*. If you are not coding, or designing, or testing, then you have no business being there that day.

It is not just the hours. I find that I don't usually work much past 8 or 9 hours a day, but they are a solid 8 hours. Writing six or seven hundred lines of code before noon can leave you pretty washed-out and sometimes the only thing to do is to go home and re-charge.

The company wants twice the amount of work done is half the time. This is the way that they cost justify you. While they don't want you to drop dead at the terminal, do understand that you will often be working against critical deadlines. The pace can get hectic.

There is no way to easily generalize about what your day will be like, you can be assured that it will pass quickly. Most shops will have plenty for you to do. A friend of mine reports:

> As soon as I got in I would find a stack of listings from last night's cycle. I would not stop for coffee. I would not reach for a doughnut. I would go directly to the terminal! As soon as I had debugged last night's test runs and fixed some compile errors, I would start or continue working on another module. I had to have the skill to juggle three modules at once. I would be designing one, programming another, and testing a third. This balancing act was not hard to accomplish once I learned time management. By the time my contract was up and I had finished three back-breaking jobs, I knew more about how the company was run than the president."

The lesson to be learned here is that as a consultant, you may not always find more challenging work than what is available at your current company, but you will be able to dabble in many areas of high-tech. And, as you get more and more experience in different applications, every project you take on will get just that much easier. You can get an awful lot of application experience in a very short time. Plus in most shops you can work your own hours, and many times you can work off-site.

Learn and Earn

The question is always asked about the possibilities of receiving technical growth through consulting. I believe it was easier about five years ago. However, the possibility exists if you are continually called on by those companies in your area that utilize the latest hardware and software. But many consultants find that they get technically out of touch a few years after entering the consulting business and find it necessary to actively engage in a continuing education process.

The reasons for this technical obsolescence is two fold. First, many of those choice jobs, such a database, object-oriented techniques, networking etc., are often reserved for the client's own top people. More and more companies are getting actively involved in the technical development of their people and are becoming more reluctant to call in consultants to do the "exciting" work. Thus, many of your assignments are going to be on projects that their employees could (perhaps should) do, but, because the staff members are being pulled for bigger and better projects, the firm decides to bring you in to do this grunt work. In many cases, you will be working on the projects the users have been screaming for, but haven't received because the regular staff are off in a corner doing new enterprise-wide design work.

The second reason you will become insulated from new technology is that few firms will pay you to "attempt" something that you have never done. When a company interviews for a consultant, they want someone who has done in the past just exactly what the firm wants done now. Nobody cares that you have a strong interest in network design, have read every book out there on it, and would work your buns off for half the price for the opportunity. They want someone who can cobble together a quick and dirty network scheme. No company wants to invest $40 to $50 an hour so that you can improve your skills.

You must understand one thing. For the most part, your work will consist of tasks that you probably have had the most experience in. If this is in CICS programming then this is what most of work will be in, at least when you start out. Even if you are a seasoned bit twiddler, a lot of the assignments that you will be offered will be at a lower technical level than you might be used to. If you have done it before, your client will have faith that you can do it again, especially if the "it" is a lower technical life form than what you "actually" know and are truly capable of.

> *TIP: There are ways to get around this and market yourself to a broader segment of the data processing community. Unfortunately, in order to overcome the narrow minded attitude of many firms, you have to create a subterfuge. Sometimes you have to lie! I'll talk about this later.*

What's Your Application?

While it may be harder to obtain technical growth (hardware and software) you will be able to gain broad application experience. It is becoming more and more important in our business not only to be good technically, but also to have a firm knowledge about the application you will be working on.

I believe that programming today is becoming easier and easier. Only a few years ago, most applications were written in an assembler language that really required the programmer to know not only the language itself but about the hardware also . There was a real skill in just knowing what 287 different assembler instructions would do. As one instructor of data processing pus it:

> The 4GL's are idiot languages. They are not hard to understand, they are easy to develop expertise in, and they are just about self-documenting. Nowadays, it is not the language that is important, but how to use it in the context of a specific application. A fifth grader can learn a 4GL. But can he understand the intricacies of a manufacturing system, even if the entire system is coded using only combinations of 15 or 20 simple functions?

While you may not become a technical guru through a career in consulting, you will have a great opportunity to become something more important. You can become an "expert" in many different applications in just a couple of years. While full-time programmers may spend years working on only one system, you will have the chance to gain expertise in many different applications. And the time has come when clients do not just want technical people who can design or code. They want application experience in addition to data processing knowledge.

It is fine to sell yourself as a hot-shot coder or designer who knows how to use ten different languages or design methodologies. But when you can sell yourself as not only a competent technician, but also as a master of several applications, in the days to come the demand for your services will far exceed that of the traditional "heavy".

> *COMMENT: As I said before, much of your work may not be that technically stimulating. The real contribution that you will receive will be experience in a wide variety of applications. Some of them you will like... some you won't. But all of them will make up a set of skills immediately transferable to a large number of clients. If you want to work, this is important! Just coding won't cut it anymore. Now they want "industry experience".*

I have not mentioned this before, but it must be obvious to you that *flexibility* and *marketability* are synonymous. Knowing a lot about "one thing" is great, as long as work in that "one thing" is available. And if you are interested in only one type of applications, you would be better off taking a full-time position. It is true that many consultants specialize in only one area, say marketing or inventory applications. But over the past number of years I have found that these people have found it harder and harder to market themselves *vis a vis* the full-time technical representatives of the software firms that sell vertical market software packages. These firms will sell a client not only the software package (say a hospital system) and also market their own in-house consulting force. Clients tend to opt for these people before they call on an independent, even if the independent may be cheaper and better.

> *TIP: Some consultants align themselves with vertical market developers and get referrals from them for either overflow work or for work in geographical areas the seller can't adequately provide services for. This might work for you.*

"I Am The Greatest"

The mere fact that you are in business for yourself, doing what others who are employed full-time do, will lead to feelings of envy and admiration on the part of your client's staff. I already covered the negative side of this. I saved the better side of this picture for now.

Whether you are really good at your craft or not, when you first come to the client's office, they will at least *think* you are good. The logic is simple. You are a computer person, able to make a living by working for a variety of companies. You are hired solely on your technical and application expertise. The regular staff is going to conclude that you must be better than the average person in order to continue getting contracts. They may not say it in so many words, but they will think it... just the way you once felt about outside consultants when you were a full-timer. You might not have liked them, and you might have been fearful of their presence, but you had to admire the ability of a person who could make a living doing what you were doing and be self-employed.

The regular staff is going to think that you are good, and they will waste little time in finding out just how good you are. Here is where the ego trip comes in.

When you first arrive the staff will be testing you. If you are working with rookies, then this will be no big deal. Most of the time, however, you will be working with top staff members and you are going to be asked a lot of questions. Only some of these are going to be for their edification purposes. In other words, they are going to want to know just how well trained you are.

After you survive the first inquisition of your first contract, your ego will be boosted with the knowledge that *you really do* have a thorough command of your craft. There is no better feeling in the business world than to work around top people and know that you are just a little bit more knowledgeable then they are. If you are not better, at least you are equal. There is an old saying that first-rate people surround themselves with first-rate people. Second-rate people surround themselves with third-rate people.

One of the real joys of consulting is to be accepted and respected as equals with the sharpest people in the shop. Why will your ego be boosted? Listen to John Bolton, a consultant from New Jersey:

> When I was employed as a senior software engineer for a large insurance company, neither the management nor the other staff members seemed to care that I was really good at data processing. My pay was locked into the company salary schedule and nobody went out of their way to single out, develop, or recognize exceptional talent. As soon as I went into consulting, this all changed, because both the client and I knew that I was there because I was good. They wanted the best to work with the best. It was really a good feeling."

Once you survive the first assault, and assuming you are accepted, your reputation will make its way around the shop to the point where the more junior staff members will be constantly bombarding you with their particular programming problems. You are the outside expert in their craft, and they are hoping to make use of your skills for their own improvement. In some cases, you will take the role of mentor and it will give you great satisfaction in helping a junior person to understand new and complex concepts. If you think accomplishing a difficult task is rewarding, wait until you find out how much satisfaction there is to be gained by teaching another person a new technique and seeing them bring their skill levels up.

In some shops you will become sort of a trouble-shooter for the junior members on the project (and even for some who are not so junior). This will be especially true when it comes to debugging. There are many consultants who spend a considerable part of their day (by direction of management) in helping the staff members solve their problems.

While some shops will expect you to be merely a coding or design machine, there are some enlightened firms that believe that they are also paying for the extraction and use of some of your experience. They are hoping that you will leave them not only with a well written, efficient new system, but also with some of your skills and expertise transferred to some of their staff members. To insure the validity of their investment, smart clients will pay you the highest compliment and ask you to teach a course on some area that they would like their people to know.

Let me point up a negative item I sometimes hear about teaching. Some consultants feel that they could be cutting their own throats by helping client staff. They say that if the staff get better skills then the market for top notch consultants will become limited. Please, don't buy into this. There will always be a market for good people in high-tech, because it is a knowledge profession. Do your best to help anybody in your client's shop who desires it. If asked to hold a series of seminars, do it. If you are the only person who knows how to turn on the Magic Micro, and they ask you to train one of their people, do your best.

True, there may be less work at that shop in the future once their people can operate the Magic Micro. But, when your next client calls this client for a reference and is told that you not only got the new system going, but also trained the staff in how to solve the Magic Micro mystery, you will be able to write your own ticket.

> **COMMENT**: *You have never really been on an ego trip until you get a call form a new client who wants you to come in solely on the reference his friend gave him last weekend while playing golf. It's a rush.*

Facing The Draft

Any strokes your ego receives from being really good at your craft will be tempered by the fact that consultants are usually considered hired-guns and, as such, nobody is going to pay much attention to your personal needs, especially when it comes to working conditions. You can expect to sit at the oldest beat-up desk in either the draftiest or hottest location in the building. Any phone messages you get will be late in getting to you, and nobody is going to take much time in making you feel "at home".

On short contracts, you probably will not even be spoken to about any subject other than your work. You will not be included in all the good gossip, and people are not going to relate to you much beyond a simple "good morning".

If you have a problem, no one will be too interested in discussing it with you, unless it relates to the project. Said one consultant who wants to remain anonymous:

> Whenever I have the need to talk with somebody, I mean just to b.s. with them, I know it will be impossible at the office. I know they don't hate me or anything. It is just that since I am an outsider, they don't seem to care that I am a human being also. It can be awfully hard being an iconoclast, especially if you are an outgoing extroverted person like I am."

Indeed, this is one of the reasons that many people give up consulting work in a year or two. In some cases, it is due to outright hostility on the part of the client's staff. But in most cases, it is just the plain lack of human involvement that working consultants miss in everyday office life. It is like moving to a new city every three months. You are never there long enough to really feel a part of things; and you never get to make long lasting acquaintances. Many consultants have told me that once they fall out of love with their craft or the money they can earn, there is little motivation for them to get up on the morning and go to the client's office. Those who have lost the urge to create good software usually leave the business to take a job as a project manager for one of their old clients.

> **COMMENT:** *My advice holds. You have to be in it for the money. If you are not, you wont' be in it for long.*

> *Leadership and learning are indispensable to each other.*
>
> *John F. Kennedy*
>
> *Remarks prepared for delivery at the Trade Mart In Dallas (November 22, 1963)*

ARE YOU QUALIFIED ?

Overqualified... A Personnel Invention

Personnel people in American industry have developed a curious new phrase which they apply to people who are looking for employment but to whom personnel don't wish to hire - "overqualified". Now seriously, how can you be overqualified for a job. Either you are qualified and can do the work, or you are not qualified and can't. Nevertheless, many world-be employees seeking an entry-level position or a career change have been condemned as overqualified and, thus denied the chance to get their foot in the door.

Remember the days when the bright young college graduate got his or her first job by starting in the mail room? Today, if you have a degree in anything, you can have a rough time getting in on the ground floor. The argument is that a highly motivated person would not be "happy" working in a menial job, such as sorting mail.

This is stupid. It seems to this writer that while people should not settle for employment below their capabilities, it makes sense for companies to employ aggressive and motivated people at the ground floor level, so as to give them the work experience, personality development, and corporate cultural "training" that they will need to rise to their capabilities.

Where does this fit into consulting? Simple: You cannot be overqualified.

However, you can be under-qualified. So what we shall do here is take a brief look at the types of traits and knowledge one would need in order to be a success in the computer consulting business. One word of caution. Each of the items I shall discuss is exclusive of the other. If you lack one or two, we are not drawing the curtain on you. This is a general discussion because there is no "carved in stone" personality type or experience background that will insure success in this (or any) field. You may possess all of the qualities I talk about and be a flop, or have none of them and be a success.

What I will discuss are the skills and traits which my research shows are the ones a consultant should have to attain success and happiness. I am going to describe the kind of person who should and should not be a computer consultant. All I ask is that you take this as a rough guide which you can use to measure yourself. You may fit the pattern, or you may be the exception that proves the rule.

From Flakes to Gurus

Let us first look a the commonly held (and misunderstood) concepts that many people have about consultants . It is not too flattering.

The first of these myths is that all of us are "flakes". If the word "flake" brings no connotations to your mind, then you will have difficulty in understanding what I am talking about. There is no way I can describe the type of person that has the "flake" label. One manager described a flake as a person who was totally unreliable, someone who could not be depended upon to be in any one place at any given time. Another friend described many consultants as "flaky non-conformists" or prima donnas.

Many technical employees feel that consultants are just plain "weirdoes". Where this notion came from is a mystery, but perhaps it evolved from the opinion held by the general public about computer people being "nerds". You know, the idea where we are a strange lot, walking around with our heads in a cloud, using strange words and thinking in on/off absolutes. And then there is that damn pen and pencil pocket protector! So, if high-tech people are strange, then consultants must be even stranger, right? The old image of the IBM'er with his white shirt, dark suit and military crewcut is still prevalent in many parts of American industry.

The second myth about us is that we are outcasts and misfits. Consultants (of all kinds) are often labeled as people who can't make it in the traditional business role of employee or manager. Either we cannot conform to the rules, or we cannot handle the pressure. Many managers think of consultants as people who are losers in the corporate game; people who are routinely passed over time and time again for management positions, so that the only way that they can attain some self worth is to quit the game and "do their own thing".

Here is the image of the long haired, bearded guy with beads and rhinestones, who sits all day in a dark room drawing funny pictures on yellow legal pads.

OK, the stereotype of the corporate dropout does have some merit, as there are many consultants who entered the business because they really did grow tired of the corporate game. They knew that they had an employable skill and adopted the attitude that if corporate America wanted them, it would have to be on consulting terms... hair, beard, and all. One middle level MIS manager I spoke with said:

> To me, all consultants really do resemble the hired-gun of the old west. They do the job, but they have an 'I don't care and to hell with you' attitude. They are a bad influence on my people. But we need them. I try to live and let live.

Finally, we have the stereotype myth of the consultant as some kind of guru. He or she is a person who talks way above your head and is almost unapproachable. Consultants are supposed to be extremely smart, but like all geniuses, we lack common sense. We are people who cannot see the forest for the trees, people who can't possibly use any word less than four syllables. Said one user:

> The consultant that we had in here the last time was probably the smartest woman I have ever met. However, she could not see that our difficult problem

really had a simple solution. She just wanted to make things more difficult than they had to be. Her motto seemed to be that if the solution was easy, then it wasn't really a problem and thus, it won't be worth solving!

You have probably heard other characterizations of us. You may even believe them. Or, you may be a consultant helping to establish the validity of these stereotypes! The real truth (as you might have suspected), is that we consultants are not much brighter, enlightened, or non-conforming than the rest of the computer services industry taken as a whole.

If anything, most of us are probably a little more introverted and more confident than our full-time counterpart. Yet, I doubt that most people listening to a casual conversion between an employee and a consultant, who was who.

The traits that I shall discuss are present in all good business people. However, if you interview several consultants before you enter the business, or if you work around many of your consultant colleagues, you will probably find as I have that the items that follow (which I shall arbitrarily call 'qualifications') are highly visible.

The Eagle

There is a very well known software service company whose symbol is the eagle. They have a motto: "Eagles don't flock, you have to find them one at a time."

> **COMMENT**: *The corollary to this (when I worked there) was that: "Eagles don't flock around!"*

Whether or not this is true in the zoological sense is debatable, but there is no question when it comes to consultants. You have to be an eagle, you cannot be one the a flock (or a turkey).

You are a loner. This should not be confused with being some kind of far out neo crazy. What I am talking about is the "corporate" loner. The type of person who enjoys the participation in a team sport above that of individual competition, is not going to be happy in his own consulting business. The corporate loners are people who physically and mentally separate themselves from the rest of their colleagues. It is not that they do not like their fellow workers, they just see their work in narrower limits.

Most people think of themselves as part of some amorphous "we", fighting against an equally amorphous "they". The loners, however, see their work as a test between themselves and "it". If the team succeeds and the loner does a less than adequate job, he/she will take little comfort in the success. They will have failed, if not the team, at least themselves.

This is an attitude thing. Some have characterized it as an egotistic quest for personal glory. I don't think this is accurate. I believe the loner simply cannot equate his/her own efforts with that of the business entity as a whole. They work not only to achieve the company goal, such as a new program or making the big sale, but they also work to achieve some personal goal. This personal satisfaction remains separate of the outcome from the whole.

Consulting is a personal service and the person who enjoys the individual challenge of doing "it" alone is the one who will succeed and be happy. The man or woman who enjoys (in fact needs) the support of a peer group will find that consulting is a very lonely occupation. This is because consultants are not usually part of a group that can give counsel and support. If you are a consultant you are hired to work on a problem. You alone. You have to be the kind of person who likes to work independently... not as a hermit, but as someone whose ultimate satisfaction will rest upon his or her own decision and actions.

Happiness does not come from merely solving the problem. It is the fact that *you* solved it. It is important to understand this because many of the tasks faced by consultants are not of the highest magnitude of difficulty. If just getting *it* done is the main thing in your life, then you will probably not be happy in the field. Pride in accomplishment is an important trait.

Many people pride themselves on the ability of solving problems in a short time. This is fine. The same goes about solving a really big problem. A consultant will take pride, not in getting it solved, but rather form the fact that he did it mostly on his/her own. .. whether it was a simple program bug, or a complicated network design problem.

> *COMMENT: The eagle flies high and proud. It is immaterial what he does today; whether it is as simple as catching a mouse, or complex as building a nest. It does not matter. He is an eagle. He and the other animals know that. It is enough. (The poet in me speaks).*

What Moves You, Better Groove You!

A loner is, by definition, self-motivated. Whether it is money, success, independence, or just a desire to work as little as possible, in this business you must be motivated by factors outside the corporate environment.

We all like to be "stroked", to be told that we are good, needed, and an asset to the company. There has been much written on management motivation theory in the last several years. There is the theory X and theory Y type of environments. There is management by objectives. There is that famous pyramid of ten or twelve needs . There are Atila the Hun methods. There are 10 minute management paradigms. There is tough minded management, touch and feel management, consensus management, and zero sum management.

All of these are fine if they have meaning to you. If you need someone to offer you a carrot and a stick, then stay where you are or go back to full-time employment. The truth is that your client is not going to spend one second trying to motivate you to do the job. Hell, one of the reasons you are there is so he or she doesn't have to spend time on the management function.

I said earlier, nobody in the shop is going to give a damn about you or your needs for motivation. As far as they are concerned, your prime motivation is the money they are paying you. And if this is not your prime motivation, then you better find one close to it. You better be motivated by the freedom, independence or any of the things I talked about earlier. Because if you are thirsting for that word of praise from the project leader, or a standing ovation from the users, then you better think again... you would do far better to drink from the well of the corporate environment where such occurrences are much more frequent.

Many consultants think that it will be the work that will keep them going. But as I said before, many of your assignments are going to be well below your talents. They will not be the most interesting exciting projects each time. You will have to be turned on by something else, and that something else will have to come from within.

Do not rely on anyone else to give you the motivating factor that gets you up in the morning. As was told to me at a database consultants' convention:

> After I had started consulting, I realized that a great deal of motivation I had for working full-time was due to the people around me and my boss. It was just a terrific place to work. It wasn't until I had left that I found that I really missed the old place. Fortunately, I am one of those people that can be bought, and the extra money easily compensated for what I had left behind.

> *TIP*: The best advice I can give you is that you should find out what turns you on about consulting and "go" with that from day to day. If you find it difficult to be motivated from within, be assured that you will find it impossible to attain any motivation from without.

Bright and Perky

There are many other personality traits that one could or should have to be successful in the field of consulting, but I shall discuss only one more before turning to those qualifications which are more business-oriented.

This personality trait is probably the most important and most difficult to explain in words. Simply put, you must have an "up" attitude about *you*. You should feel good about yourself.

This probably sounds like a crock to you. It seems that every other article in today's literature is about feeling good about something or other and/or how to develop some sense of personal happiness or tranquillity. If you are not a happy person in your life in general, it is doubtful that simply having some business cards and letterhead printed proclaiming yourself as a consultant is going to give you what you are looking for. And the money you earn will not be worth a bit bucket if you can't enjoy it.

If this sounds like a detailed explanation of the obvious, just stop and think about all the people you know who are really upset with their lives. Whether it is social or business, you know these sullen and "always down" people I am talking about. They may be able to get by in the shadow (or anonymity) of the corporate environment; but they will wash out in consulting.

This is because you simply cannot take problems to your client's office. Nobody is going to be interested in them. I am not saying that you have to be brightness and light *every day*. Obviously, you are going to have your bad days. That is when you stay home.

You are asking for consulting suicide if you go to your client's office without a clear head ready to do their bidding. And on the same level, if you think that becoming an independent business person is going to solve whatever personal or personality problems you have, then you have not read the previous chapters too carefully. Being a consultant is tough enough. But trying to do it with some other thing hanging you up will find you headed ultimately to a long session with another member of the consulting industry... your psychologist.

TIP: A happy consultant is a productive consultant, and a productive consultant is a successful consultant, and a successful consultant is a happy consultant!

Wanted: Self Confident, Sales Oriented Person...

The concept of having an attitude of success if often referred to as the "sales" personality. This is an important asset to have or develop. You've heard it said a million times... you sell yourself. It is true. You are the product. While not everyone is going to buy you, if you have an attitude of success, an innate optimism and an outgoing articulate nature, it will not bother you to be rejected. We all hate rejection. However, if you have good self-esteem, you will have a good weapon to fight the depression that repeated rejection brings.

I have no lessons on how to achieve this attitude of success. There are many books on the subject, all of which will probably seem overly simplistic (at least they do to me). My observation is simple. If *you* don't think you are worth hiring, then *neither* will your potential client. I am not saying you should keep pounding away forever or that eventually success will ultimately come your way. For all I know you might pound away and be a total flop. Who knows? There are no simplistic guarantees that if you make so many sales calls, one has to click. This may be that stuff that million copy best seller books are made of, but it is certainly not true in consulting.

> *TIP: As I see it, there is a simple rule that I have followed for fifteen years. If you feel good about yourself and have a good sales approach, you might fail. If you have problems, low self esteem, and can't sell yourself... you will fail.*

It's Only a Game!...

What I have discussed up to now are personality traits found in people of all walks of life. They are not necessarily developed traits from one's experience in the business world (although they might be). Feeling separate from the pack, being self motivated, having an attitude of success will probably make you successful in any business or social endeavor. And, of course these traits are equally important in consulting.

But what I want to talk about next are some items that you should have acquired directly from your experience in the work-a-day world. You are probably not born with them, and they probably were not acquired at an early age. The qualities (qualifications) I will discuss are learned attributes, and you will possess them if you have had a wide background in the business world, especially if you have been in data processing or engineering for any length of time.

Business is a game. Some rules are written, some are assumed and some are made up along the way. Most are occasionally broken. I have already spoken about the rewards for winning; and the penalties of losing are obvious. While entry to the game is initially open to any player, the chances of just breaking even, much less winning, are very low for the marginally qualified. Just wanting to play the game sets you apart from the spectators who are content to remain on the sidelines. They may have all the qualities to be a participant or even a victor, but they don't choose to be a player. Why? The main reason is their fear of risks.

Whether it be the loss of money, time or prestige, most people feel secure in the role of coach or fan, rather than player. This is understandable because, in the end, we are not really just talking about a game, but survival. Out of work... out of food! I have talked about what motivates a technical person to leave a nice secure position and go it alone. These motivating factors are very important. But there is another characteristic that successful consultants have attained. This is the entrepreneurial spirit. They want to play the game, not watch it.

The Key Is Risk Management

There are hundreds of reasons why some people are happy to work for others, and some people are only content if they are their own boss. Probably the overriding difference between these two groups is their understanding of what business is all about and their acceptance of risk.

I purposely said that business is a game because if you are going to go into business you must treat it as such. People who feel that work is their whole life and the most important thing in it make the best employees. Every company wants the man or woman who works-to-live and lives-to-work. You've seen them at the office. Their only interest is in the profit or loss of the company, their only goal is to get finished with one project so that they can start on another. These are the people who will most likely end up in the executive suite and perhaps will be contracting for your skills. But they do not, or cannot, accept risk.

The entrepreneurial spirit has, from time to time, been defined as the desire to be the boss. Well, these people would qualify. But they don't play our game... mainly because they do not see business *as a game*. Instead they see it as life itself. The person with real (for lack of a better term) venture initiative is one who does not see business as the end-all and be-all of life. It is merely a game.

I find that those who are not so deadly serious about the final score are the people best able to manage the risk. The key word here is *manage*. What is the risk? Failure. Managing failure is what it is all about.

Whether you measure failure in terms of money or time, in reality it is failure that is the big risk. As long as you are an employee, you have little fear of failing. There is little that you could do to get yourself fired. Even in severe recessions when management wants to cut their labor force, the one classification of employee this is not going to end up on the cut list is the engineer, computer programmer, or analyst.

This is not quite so in the consulting business. The risk of failure is always present. Any day could be your last. And it could be some time before another contract comes your way. There is no unemployment benefits for consultants. Only unemployment. There is no safety net. Coping with risk is what you ante up in order to play the game of computer consultant.

What Kind of Risk Manager Will You Be?

In our business there are two kinds of players. First there are those that accept the risk but are so completely horrified about being between contracts for even a day, that they suffer anxiety attacks two weeks before the end of any contract, and will accept any contract at any rate in order to keep working. After a couple of years of this, the pressure causes them physical and mental illness. Programming, analysis, and design under tight deadlines is stressful enough. Add to this the fear of being out on the streets, and you have the making of a cardiac patient or a substance abuser. Fortunately, most of these consultants are smart enough to realize the symptoms and they go back to full-time employment. The point is that they should never have gone into consulting in the first place.

> **COMMENT**: When I wrote the first and even second editions there was no expression as "substance abuser". I used the word "alcoholic". I've known several candy nose consultants as well as several heavy dopers. Heavy alcohol consumption has always been a factor in data processing; consultant or employee. I've never known why. Let me know if you have a any hard research on the subject.

The second type of consultant simply takes a "what the hell" attitude toward the whole thing. They feel that if they are out of work... they are out of work. So what? It won't be forever. Basically, they see this as just one of the plays in the game. And it is, to them, all a game. If they win (by working a lot and making good money, then great. If they loose (by being on the bricks for several months), well... you can't win them all!

Either way, the person with real venture initiative simply recognizes the risk, but does not dwell on it. Working is not *the* most important thing in life. Important yes, but not at the expense of health or happiness. This, in essence, is what risk management is all about. You must be willing to take the risk of failure, accept it, and not give a damn one way or another. It almost comes down to what your parents told you when you joined the little league (hockey team, basketball team, or whatever),... just playing is ultimately more important than winning or losing.

The consultant who is going to be successful, and by this I mean financially, physically and mentally, is one whose life is not completely involved in the ups and downs of business. When we all started out on our first few jobs as a wage-slave, we dreaded the idea of failing, of not pleasing the boss, and especially of being fired. But I believe it is the person who has failed, who has incurred the wrath of management, who has been canned, and who has survived, is much more likely to enjoy and be successful in his own consulting business.

They have been up... they have been down. They know they will be up again. Most importantly, they don't give a damn. The current phrase for this is "chilled out". Whatever term you apply, however, it is an attribute that the entrepreneur must possess. If you have been fortunate, you have developed this attribute through having had ups and downs in your business career. You have coped.

> *COMMENT: The person who, when "up", only fears being "down", and when "down" fears never getting "up" again is not cut out for the pressures that consulting. Period.*

How Deep Are Your Pockets?

Many ventures are started by people who, by appearances, don't seem to need more money. They are already well off. When was the last time your heard of a poor person starting a business? The reason for this is that it takes money to make money. It is expensive for most firms to get off the ground.

Fortunately, this is not true of the consulting business. Being a consultant is a low-overhead proposition. You need not invest in costly equipment or hire expensive labor. You can run the whole thing out of your living room, or the back seat if you are on the road.

While there is a low entry-cost to the business, there is one cost you should not overlook. You still have to eat, pay the rent, and gas up the car while you are waiting for that first contract, are between contracts, or waiting for the check to arrive. So while you will not need vast amounts of money to get into the business, you still need ample funds to carry you over until your boat comes in.

TIP: When your boat comes in, try not to be at the airport!

You must be a good money manager. There is no way anyone (or any book) can instruct you on how to be a good money manager. By this time in your career, either you have the skill or you don't. There are many technical consultants who make over $150,000 a year, but because of bad management, are continually broke. This is because they have no discipline. When they see that long awaited check for $10,000, they rush right out and spend it as though in a vindication of self-denial.

Good money management is simply the timing of your expenditures so that you don't have to hock the family dog to pay your bills. When I asked several computer consultants about how much money they would recommend always having on hand before entering the business, they stated an amount equal to eight months of their basic expenses. Thus, if it takes you $2,000 a month to live rock bottom, then perhaps $16,000 in the bank at all times would be a conservative figure. In these inflationary and uncertain times, many consultants I surveyed try to keep at least one year's basic living expenses in reserve. Of course, if you have a working spouse or domestic partner, then perhaps this reserve fund is not totally necessary. Whatever the case, a good sense of money management is a very desirable qualification whether you are in business for yourself or not.

COMMENT: It is not money that is the root of all evil.. but the lack of it!.

Are You A Quick-Study?

Every time you switched jobs, you had to go through the oft-quoted "learning curve". In some applications, it took weeks before you really knew what was going on. You won't have that luxury in consulting. You must have the innate ability to learn quickly.

When you sign the contract, you will be expected to hit the ground running. You will have to read vast amounts of code or documentation, and obtain much information from both the staff and users in order for you to do what the job calls for. Many people in the business feel that having the ability to grasp new ideas and concepts quickly is not only an ability grounded in experience and intelligence, but also in attitude. I have found from speaking with consultants that those who are afraid to "do it" (learn new stuff), just can't, no matter how hard they try. I honestly believe that this quick study-ability depends on whether or not you *think* you can learn new things.

Okay. This sounds overly simplistic, but many consultants who have been contracted to solve a range of problems on applications they knew nothing about, say it is true. If in your past experience you have had a success pattern of learning quickly and getting things done quickly, then you have this important qualification. If you haven't had the experience, but *think* you can do it, my research shows that you probably can. It's an *attitude*. A young programmer consultant from Denver reports:

> For a while, when I first started out, I always seemed to get contracts on systems I knew. Then I signed on to put up a payroll deduction system using CICS. What I didn't know about CICS would fill volumes. But hell, to me, programming was programming! I took the manuals home and over a long weekend gave myself a cram course in on-line techniques. I might not have written the best code, but it got the job done... on time and within budget!"

But It Is 'Quality' B.S.

You must have a quick mind and a quicker tongue. Some call it the power of persuasion, and some call it being a bull-artist. Whatever you call it, make sure you have developed it.

You may be the sharpest software designer in the world, but if you can't convince someone of it, big deal! You have to know what to say and when to say it, especially when you are asked some stupid question by the user. We all know that there are three entities: the truth, the whole truth, and nothing but the truth. You will need the good business sense to know which one of these to tell the client.

There is an old story about the senior analyst/project leader who designed a master file update system. He then gave the specs to a junior staff member who did the coding. All did not go according to the specs, however. It turned out that if the last transaction was an "add", the transaction record was eaten (went into never-never land... disappeared). The deadline arrived and the system *had* to be installed or all hell was going to break loose from the vice-president of finance. The junior programmer bashfully told the designer about the flaw and apologized for not being able to fix it in time. He was terrified that the project leader was going to make him tell the user. The project leader, being a woman of some experience said not to worry. She went downstairs to the user and explained how the programming staff had built this wonderful *feature* into the new system. "Add" transactions would have to be input first by the clerks because, after all, they were the most important part of the application. You could always change or delete on the next cycle, but "adds" had to be done right away because the vice-president said ... bla, bla, bla. And on and on she went until the user believed that he had the greatest file update system ever invented... that his department was on the leading edge of technology!

> *TIP: Pure bull. Sometimes it can be worth pure gold. And as the song goes... you have to know when to hold them, and know when to fold them. Sometimes consulting is like a poker game.*

Skills, Skills, Skills

Finally, I want to discuss the most often-asked questions about qualifications. What skills do you have to have to be a consultant? How good in the craft do you have to be?

You will often hear the war stories that some consultants tell about how they took a few semesters at night on data processing in the local community college, while they were driving a cab during the day. They then opened their door, walked out, and proclaimed that they were consultants. Next, they offer full orchestration and four-part harmony about how they learned on the job. Twenty years ago when nobody knew anything about data processing this might was very possible. It still is now, but it will take more than one or two courses on hardware or software.

It may be a seller's market on the full-time employment scene for anyone who even whispers that they have some computer knowledge, but it is not that way in the consulting world. Companies may hire just anyone on a full-time basis, but when they choose consultants, they demand that they get their money's worth. They call in a consultant because they need the best talent they can get. Money is not the sole object. Performance (or at least the promise of it) is. If you lack all of the other qualifications I have outlined above, you may get by; may even succeed. But if you are not damn good at what you do, and if you do not like what you do, you haven't got a chance of succeeding.

How good is good you ask? It is a question of degree. You must be as good or better than the full-time programmer's skills at the going salary. I cannot overemphasize this. You must know all aspects of your craft. Some aspects you will know better than others. Some you can pick up quickly. You must "appear" as an expert or, at least, *capable* of getting the job done.

There are a million things you could know and make a living as a consultant. I can't possibly cover them all. In some markets certain skills are more valuable than others. So I shall divide this discussion along three major division points: Mainframes, Micros, and Others.

COMMENT: I deal mainly with software skills. While this is not only my specialty, research shows that these are the areas in which most high-tech consultants work and where most of the opportunities for both entry and growth seem to be.

A Song Sung Blue

Since Big Blue's mainframes are still the dominant force in the Fortune 5000 world, let me talk in terms of consulting using IBM technology. In the first place you absolutely must know JCL. You must know it cold. That includes the use of Procs and JES commands. You absolutely must know how to override DD statements, as well as EXEC parms. Condition code logic is important. You must be familiar with symbolics and how to override them in both catalogued and in-stream procs.

Unless you can maneuver in ISPF, don't even think about doing any consulting in a blue shop. You will also be expected to know how to use PROFS so you can get E-Mail from the project manager.

The various TSO commands are also important, especially with respect to getting stuff to the printer.

Knowing REXX or the other script type languages won't hurt but you can usually pick this up through study and on the job trial and error. It is not hard.

As for analysis, blue shops love so called recognized methodologies such Yourdon, Orr, etc. These shops also seem to enjoy fooling with CASE tools.

You will have to know VSAM concepts and commands but in most shops virtually all the VSAM stuff will be done for you by the systems people.

CICS (if you don't know what it is, don't worry about it) is a world of its own, and an awful lot of consulting is done on this platform. The same goes with the various "big-time" database products... ORACLE, DB2, IDMS (yes, it is still around), and IMS.

> *TIP:* If you are a CICS person, don't drop these skills just because IBM seems on the wane. CICS is being ported to UNIX and will have an important role as an OLTP monitor for smaller platforms. Companies will be able to convert all their massive CICS COBOL programs to cheap hardware

Down To The Micro Level

Obviously you must know MS-DOS, and an knowledge of OS/2 would not hurt either. On the micro side, so much of it revolves around the ability to cobble together various pieces of hardware and get them all to work. Knowing how to use had tools is a must... you will be taking lots of boards out, jumping them, and replacing them.

COMMENT: *There is a risk to this. With software there is not that much damage you can do to the hardware. But you can break the users machines quite easily when you start pulling them apart. Many years ago I blew up a client's PC when I pulled a board from a slot and had forgotten to turn of the power. The repairs cost $900 out of my pocket. Be careful out there!*

A great deal of micro consulting also revolves around putting in networks, tuning them, and debugging them. Thus, you should have a good knowledge of Novell because many of clients will have this installed. At least know the various Novell commands and utilities.

The whole world is talking about client-server. You will be expected to understand these concepts (you will probably be the only one!).

TIP: *I carry with me a few disks with an editor, communications program, debugging tools, and a few other utility programs that I find useful when I go to a client (usually a small business) with a micro problem to solve.*

I'll talk more about languages later but I want to mention both C and xbase. The xbase variants (dBASE, FOXPRO, Clipper etc., are especially popular and getting more so each year. While C is used for the underlying system work, the xbase languages are becoming the application of choice for so many businesses.

The Other Side Of The Moon

There are a zillion other platforms out there on which you could stake a consulting practice upon. There are still lots of DEC, Data General, Unisys, etc. clients out there. Obviously you have to know these platforms in order to consult on them.

But the platform that everyone thinks about when they think "other" is UNIX.

> *COMMENT: Why the world wants to migrate to UNIX is a mystery to me as well as others. It is 20 years old, clunky, temperamental, and enigmatic. It doesn't do anything "better" than a proprietary OS. You get more hardware for your buck, but after hitching together desperate pieces of silicon and software you also get more ulcers!*

I think UNIX holds a terrific opportunity for consulting. It is not hard to learn and there is plenty of available information at your local book store. Anyone can become a UNIX consultant with a few months of study. You must know the 'C' language but it is fairly easy to pick up.

Assuming you also know C, you have to learn the shell script language (either Bourne, or C Shell) and master the arcane UNIX commands, if you are not using a graphical front end.

You will also have to understand UUCP as well as the MAIL system. UNIX communications is a pain, but it is learnable. The same goes for terminal setup.

X-Windows and Motif are also becoming standards so you should have some understanding of how they work (or don't work).

Finally, you will have to know the vi editor. If you are coming from a micro world and have never used a line editor, welcome to the stone-age!

> *COMMENT: vi is a full screen editor but it's a dog! Many UNIX shops are installing ports of MS-DOS editors and word processors, so if you know Word Perfect you may be spared the pain and suffering of the vi editor. Did I say it loud enough...it's a dog!*

Are We Speaking The Same Language?

Because so much high-tech consulting is revolves around programming, let me spend some time on languages. If you are not going to earn your living as a programmer consultant, it still would not be a bad idea to have some knowledge or background in a programming language.

There is the sad story of the programmer who had spent over ten years working in assembler language. Realizing that his market was limited, he went out to the local community college and took courses in five higher level languages. He really thought that by taking a few courses, he could approximate the knowledge and experience he had in assembler. His first contract was in PL/1. It took him twice as long to finish it than the client had allocated. He was let go.

The point to take from this is that it is not necessary to be a walking encyclopedia of computer languages. You only have to know two: C and COBOL.

First let me say a few words about COBOL. We all know that COBOL is a pain in the butt. However, you will find that many of your clients are committed to it, so you might as well get used to it. And knowing COBOL is not just limited to a MOVE or a nested IF. You must know how to do double subscripted tables. When I first wrote *Computermoney* I really thought that COBOL would fade gently into the night. Ten years later I am still waiting. I find that it not only won't go away, it seems to get more robust. And as downsizeing picks up speed, many COBOL application are going to be ported to smaller machines with graphical front ends. There are tools available to make this all possible and to enable COBOL to survive. I don't know if this is a good thing, but it will be a fact, so you might as well keep your COBOL skills up to par.

Everyone thinks that C is new. It is a twenty five year old language developed in the UNIX labs. Even though it is old, it is stronger than ever. If you want to consultant as a programmer in the 90's you better learn it. It is the language of choice for many software developers and it is quickly becoming the de facto standard in object-oriented programming.

> **COMMENT**: *As for C, it is a language I know well, make a lot of money with, and truly hate. I find it to be cryptic, it allows the programmer to write programs that are impossible to understand, and it has too much punctuation. But I don't make the rules... I just play by them. If they want to use C, it is fine with me!*

It is also helpful to have another language on your shelf as inventory. It is probably not as important to be expert in the second language unless you expect to do a lot of work in it. Having a good language manual around and reviewing it once a month will keep you current enough so that if you get a call for a very lucrative assignment for a three week bout with dBASE you can at least make it through the early rounds.

> **COMMENT**: As I'm sure you have guessed, I am very partial to the xbase variants as a means to making a consulting dollar. I think every computer consultant should be able to get round in one of the flavors of xbase as a "fall back". There is almost always xbase work to be found, and the rates are relatively high.

While I am on the subject of languages, there is another point I want to make. Programming is programming. Except for form and syntax, there is not a whole hell of a lot of difference in programming in COBOL, C, Foxpro (an xbase variant), etc. The words and symbols are different, but the overall logic will not vary much. Just because you can recite all the COBOL verbs or C string-functions does not a programmer make. Anybody can code. You know it and so does your client. What the client is ultimately paying for is both the solution-logic as well as your programming methodology.

Give a sixth-grader a good course in C and then give him a data processing problem, say a file update via SQL. Sooner or later he will come up with an answer and the program to accomplish it. The design and logic might resemble spaghetti. Clients don't want complex and convoluted systems. There are hiring you to bring them a logical mind and an orderly organized approach to programming and system or network design .

> **COMMENT**: Before I went into programming I read those little government pamphlets about "your career in data processing." I remember all those nice phrases about having the abilities to systematically sort through problems, using inductive or deductive reasoning and being able to "think logically". These were all things I never saw on any job when I was an employee. Yet these are the qualities your client is buying.

Is What's Inside Important?

When it comes to computer internals and architecture, most people think that you have to be a whiz in order to succeed in consulting. You do, if you are going to market yourself as a systems integrator. Otherwise knowing the logical I/O design of the back plane of some hot UNIX box will not get be necessary. The system internals of most computers are interesting but I don't think you are going to find that much consulting work in, for example, re-configuring a UNIX kernel. (These are usually employee oriented tasks).

Database and file structure internals are important, however. If all you feel comfortable with is flat files, than stay away from the business. It is imperative that you be able to put up and utilize some of the various database products on the market. You must understand relational file concepts and be able to do normalization. I don't believe you have to be a full bore DBA, but you should be able to speak with him/her and not sound like an idiot. In line with the above, each database product has a whole host of utility programs which you will need to understand.

The demise of the plain vanilla programming consultant is rapidly drawing near. The days of the consultant who was only hot in COBOL batch applications are indeed numbered. The big demand now is for consultants who can talk database concepts and who are knowledgeable about windowing, event-oriented methodology, and object-oriented techniques. In some markets if you are skilled in these areas, you are virtually guaranteed a plentiful amount of work.

> *TIP: Take my word for this. Don't jump on every "new tech" bandwagon that comes along, especially if you live and work in a smaller city. Knowing object- oriented programming is great in San Jose, but you would starve to death in Sacramento. Trust me, I live there.*

If your skills are not up to what your market is looking for (you can read the want-ads to find out) then take some seminars and get some books. In the future (which will arrive sometime next week!) it will be the knowledge of these advanced topics that will separate the "wanna be's" from the *consultants*.

I must say a few words on Computer Aided Software Engineering and structured techniques. Some in our industry feel that CASE limits their so called "creative potential". Some fee that all the ballyhoo about CASE has been a false Messiah. Others think that CASE is the greatest thing since sliced bread.

My attitude is that you better know CASE concepts and use structured techniques, whether you like them or not. From the first day that you entered the data processing industry, the idea of "maintainability" has been preached to you. How many computer marvels have you known in your career whose programs and design resembled thirty miles of bad road? As a consultant, you may get away with systems designed and coded an a random sloppy manner... but only once. The day you turn over one of these dogs to the full-time staff and they run to the boss yelling about how your network design resembles a Jackson Pollock abstract, you can consider yourself unemployed as a consultant. Permanently.

If You Don't Know It, Can You Find It?

When I first got into the software engineering business it was in vogue to administer ability tests to determine whether or not a person was qualified to be a programmer or analyst. Today there is talk about a national certification examination for all programmers. There is also mention made about licensing of consultants (see Appendix).

Whether this is right or wrong is not the issue. The point is, you simply must be in the top thirty percent of your peer group in order to succeed at consulting. It would help for you to "know it all". But if you don't, then it is imperative that you know where to find it". A manager friend of mine was interviewed for this book and talked about this important skill: .

> My experience has shown that consultants are generally more able than our staff, but not by an excessive degree. Their real skill lies in the fact that they have had a variety of experiences, and if they can't remember how to do it, they know where in the manual, in fact, even which manual, to look to find the answer.

No client is going to expect you to know the displacement into the a file control block in order to find the state of the attribute flags. But you will be expected to know what these are and where to find information on them.

So, Are You Qualified?

Only you can answer this, but I have tried to give you some objective (as well as some of my own) thoughts on the subject. If I have overwhelmed you, it was not my intention. But you will have to step back and take a good long look at yourself, your technical skills, business acumen, as well as personality traits.

If you don't see a consultant staring back at you, try to figure out what qualities you think you are lacking. I believe that *anyone* can be a consultant. However, I don't believe that *everyone* should be one!

As I said earlier, the question of what qualifies someone to go into the business has some rather subjective answers. So give yourself credit. I believe anybody can do it, or grow into it; so long as you have a will, you will find the way.

> *TIP:* Some people need to take on a "mind set" about something. Try this. Next time you go on vacation, make believe you are a consultant. Tell those you meet that you are a consultant. Get their reaction. Get a consulting "mind set". When you get home, I bet you will find it hard to go back to work and take on a "wage-slave" mind set. If you believe it, you can do it. It is true. If it wasn't I would never have been able to write a book.

MARKETING

Buyer: Where Are You?

The thing about marketing is that everyone hates to do it. Wouldn't it be nice if we could simply print up some business cards, make a few calls, send a few letters, and then just sit by the phone waiting for those frantic calls from clients begging us to come do a trick for them? It sure would! However, it is not going to work like that. You are going to work your buns off in the marketing department.

It doesn't matter if you are the worlds greatest programmer, analyst, engineer, system integrator, network specialist or whatever. If you can't market, you won't work. This is not to say that you have to like the task of selling yourself. Most of us hate it. But it can be made tolerable and, for some, even enjoyable. There is the success story of one San Francisco consultant, who found that the challenge of "getting" the client to be much more enjoyable than doing the work for the client. He now makes a six-figure income by buying rights to software and selling the product while his employees (and some consultants) do the installation.

> *COMMENT: You don't have to market yourself if you don't want. You can use a broker. But even if you plan to use a broker, read this chapter anyway. The chapter on brokers assumes that you have some knowledge of marketing.*

When I talk to consultants, the successful ones all understand one important distinction. This is between sales and marketing. These are *not* the same, but they are often used interchangeably.

Marketing is the process of determining *who* your prospective clients are, finding out *where* they are, designing a *strategy* for approaching them, and finally, implementing a plan for making *contact* with them. Simply put, marketing is done so that you have a *chance* to sell..

Sales (which I cover in depth later on) is the actual process of turning a prospect into a paying client. I consider sales to be the human dynamic that follows marketing. Some people call it the *pitch*, some call it the *interview*, some call it the *presentation*, and some just call it hell.

Both sales and marketing are symbiotic in that it is hard to succeed unless you are good at both. If you are lousy at marketing you are not going to have many opportunities to make your pitch. If you are terrible at sales, you may make lots of presentations, but sign few clients. You have to be reasonably effective at both.

If you have ever done work for a sales or marketing department of a large company, you have come across terms like positioning, penetration, market share, and others which are even greater obfuscation's of the obvious. Throughout history, marketing has remained rather constant. You have something to *sell*. You must find the buyer and convince them to *buy* it. Sounds simple. But most consultants don't wash out because they are unqualified at their craft. They wash out because they are unqualified at marketing. It is definitely a craft of its own, and it is one you will have to learn in order to succeed.

> *TIP: If you don't want to do marketing of yourself, don't expect to eat very regularly. This is not a scare tactic. Just a simple truth. I'm serious.*

But I Hate Marketing!

Before I get into the "don'ts" of marketing, I want to take a candid look at why so many of us dislike the task, and what can be done to overcome the obstacles.

Number one on the hit parade of objections is the fear factor. Simply put, nobody want to be told that they are not wanted. We don't want to be rejected. This is an *attitude* problem. It is one we all face, and there is no easy way to overcome it.

There is a an entire publishing sector built up around overcoming the fear of sales and marketing. I 'have read most of their books and some are pretty good. What most of them boil down do is the idea of having a positive mental attitude... you *can* do it, others *have* done it, so go out there and *do* it!

My purpose in this chapter is not to be a confidence builder. If you are *absolutely sure* that you *cannot* market yourself, there is probably nothing in these pages that will convince you otherwise. If you have deep-rooted fears about putting yourself out there in the cold, and waiting for the world to take you in, then being an independent business person is not for you. Return this book and get your money back. Everything from here on is directed to the person who is merely *apprehensive* about the possibility of being rejected.

This apprehension is normal. We all have it. If you finally land an interview with a potential client, and he says that he wants to think it over and you don't hear from him, you are going to take it very personally. After all, you put yourself on the line. You are standing up there and daring the world to reject you. And you got rejected. And you feel bad. This is normal. The point here is that you just can't take it so personally. The catch is that there is no set gimmick that I can tell you so that you *won't* take it personally. You have to find your own method. If you like, rationalize it any way you feel comfortable.

> **COMMENT**: I was told that sales and marketing people are the biggest buyers of horoscope books. "It's not my fault... it's in the starts!"

I have found that in most cases, the best rationalization is the truth. The truth, here, is that with marketing (as the song goes), "you know it don't come easy. " If it were easy, everyone would be doing it. It is tough to market yourself, so go about it in a businesslike manner. Don't expect the best case scenario and don't expect the worst. Take a nice conservative "Main Street" banker's approach... things have been better, and things have been worse. If you go into a marketing situation with a "forewarned is forearmed" attitude you have a much better chance of keeping you head together after you have had four interviews and the phone is still deadly silent.

> *TIP: The 'Positive Mental Attitude" people stress that you can be your "own best friend" by keeping up a bright sunny disposition which will affect all who come into contact with you. This may or may not be true. It may work. But you are better off with a real strategy. After you have been kicked in the teeth a few times you could become your own worst enemy !*

The second objection to marketing is also based upon fear - the fear of total failure. By this, I mean going hungry. A manager of a large computer installation told me:

> I would go into consulting if I thought I could get a client. I wouldn't mind getting rejected by a hundred companies, if I could convince myself that I would eventually make a sale. I just don't think I could take the pressure of knowing I had to make a sale in order to eat well!

It is tough to take a risk. You have heard all the stories about the great tycoons who risked it all in order to make a killing. You also probably have friends who once risked it all and went bust. What can I say? The rewards go with the risk.

But risk can be managed and minimized. I tell people not to market in a "must sell" atmosphere. Every book you ever read about getting a job stated that you should never quit your current position until you have found another one. This holds for consulting as well.

I tell people over and over to start looking for the next client a month before the current contract is up. Nobody ever listens to me. (And sometimes I don't listen to myself!) True, there is no guarantee that you will be able to land another contract before your present one expires. But you might.

The Big Crap Shoot!

I talked earlier about all the high-concept terms marketing people use to describe what they do. I will talk later about strategies that you might follow to get a contract. However, what nobody will tell you is that the little voice deep down inside you is correct. It is saying that "the whole thing is a crap shoot!"

Call it fate, luck, being in the right place at the right time, or whatever. A good part of marketing success is derived from "everything just working out." Really. There are no other words to describe it. One consultant termed his experience in marketing as a series of mutually exclusive events, some of which worked out and some of which didn't.

What I will talk about are some things which have worked for others in the business. Doing them all, either well or poorly may or may not have a direct bearing upon your success as a consultant. Knowing the right person at the right time is always better than knowing how to write a great resume. Getting on a plane and by chance siting next to the president of Microsoft or IBM could be best break of your career.

In marketing, you could be lucky. You could randomly pick out five large computer users in your community, write five quick letters, and land a contract inside of 72 hours. On the other hand, you could randomly pick a hundred companies, send a hundred letters, and end up only helping the post office overcome their deficit.

> **COMMENT:** I thought this business was a piece of cake when I got started. I sent off three letters to "test" if I could get a call-back from a company. Two days later National Semiconductor called and hired me. I quit my full time job and never looked back. But it hasn't always been that easy, believe me. Because I got lucky the first time, it made my first dry spell that much harder to take.

What separates the successful consultant from his or her unsuccessful counterpart is their knowledge of the market. This knowledge is gained through diligent market research. You must find out who the buyers of your craft are, and who to contact. Doing all of this at the right time and having a little "luck" does not hurt.

They Must Be Hidden Under A Rock!

Consultants must wallow around in what is called the "hidden job market." When a company is in the market for a computer consultant, they rarely advertise the fact. They do just what you have to do in order to find out what is available out there. They get on the phone and call around. As a manager from the banking industry told me in an interview:

> I may hire some twenty-five contractors a year, but we never advertise. We call our friends at other firms, we ask our vendors, we get referrals from other consultants. Hell, one time I mentioned to my dry cleaning guy that I was seeking a consultant. Believe it or not, he had a customer who was just what we needed and we hired the lady.

If you have ever read any of the many books on the market on how to get a job, you should be familiar with the scenario of the hidden job market. These positions are kept from view, and only those in the know realize that they exist. In order to crack the code of this hidden market, you have to do a PR job on yourself. You have to let everyone, from the Tupperware lady to the president of your bank know that you are available for a contract.

The best way to do this is to call all of your friends, be they in high-tech or not, and simply ask for help. You may think it is demeaning. After all, with a zillion computer related jobs going begging, you may not feel comfortable skulking around saying to the world that you are unemployed or are about to be. Well, relax. It is no big deal. People will be glad to help. After all, they are your friends, aren't they. And to some of them, you might be a customer. Don't underestimate the "you scratch my back" routine in American business. Don't be uncomfortable. Simply pick up the phone and call a friend. Even it is not a close friend, just introduce yourself and state that you are seeking their help in getting a contract, or breaking into the consulting business.

The very worst they can say is "no" and hang up. This will probably never happen. and if it does, well at least you know who your friends are! It is amazing how many people we all actually know well enough to at least give a call. Sit down and make a list, and you will be surprised at how many contacts you really have. Don't limit this list to just computer people. Remember, you are selling you! Seek out people who come into contact with people like yourself. Don't forget your banker, your lawyer, your broker, your hairdresser, your kids' teacher. They are all out there. And one of them is going to know someone who knows someone who needs your craft. Some bright person once reasoned that we are all only seven phone calls separated from anyone in the world! The right seven calls will have you working in the White House.

> *COMMENT: How many people are on your list? The estimate is 250. It is interesting where this statistic came from. Years ago, funeral parlor owners determined that they would have to put out 250 chairs for the average person's funeral. Make your list. I bet it comes close! Don't die just to find out!*

There are three simple "don'ts" and one very important "do" when you are calling people.

First, never beg. You know how you hate being asked for spare change? Well, your friends don't want to hear you pleading for assistance. Even if you haven't eaten for a week, you don't want to sound overly hungry. Simply state your request and go on to some other topic of conversation. The message will get through.

Second, don't bargain. Sure, your friends might like the keys to your ski lodge for a weekend, but they don't want it in exchange for helping you find a client. So, don't promise a reward, a finders fee, or even a free lunch. Nobody wants to feel as if they are being bought.

Third, don't bother them. Never, never, call back with the same request. Have you ever been hounded by a salesperson? Well, your friends don't want to be dogged by you. Call them once, be effective, and hope for the best.

Finally, if someone is instrumental in finding you a contract, don't fail to thank them, not only personally, but by a small token gift - perhaps a bottle of wine or a gift package of fruit. What I am talking about here is elementary psychology. If you keep in mind the three "B's":

- Don't Beg
- Don't Bribe
- Don't Bother

you will be able to cultivate some really good contacts that will pay off for you in the years to come.

One final note to all of this. Call, don't write. It is the personal touch that will get your friends interested in keeping their eye out for your interests. Nothing sounds worse than the form letter sent to a hundred or so of your contacts, that sounds like it has been sent to a hundred or so of your contacts! I know word processors can make magic. But so do your friends. Do it right. Call.

Meet Marian (The Librarian)

So much for the phone trip. Next comes the hard copy research. Make friends with your local library and especially with the reference librarian. What you will be looking for is any information on companies that have computer installations in general, and those that use consultants specifically. There are many business directories out there, and some regions have what are called data processing directories. These are usually put out by a local publisher and contain the name of the MIS director and the type of equipment that is on-site.

Before you go digging around the library, take note. It doesn't matter what you can come up with in an hour or so. The reference librarian can do it in half the time. You are a specialist in your field. They are specialists in their field. Tell the reference person that you are a consultant and you want marketing information. Be honest with them and don't be arrogant. These are highly trained people who are vastly underpaid for their contribution to the community. Wait if you have to. Do not make an enemy of this person, whatever you do. If they are too busy to help, find out when their slack time is.

What you are looking for is not only the firms in your area you should approach, but also the name of the person to direct your marketing to. There are no real guidelines that I can give you here, as each area of the country has their own informational resources. Best case, your librarian will have in a file the name and address of every company within a 40 mile radius that has ever used a computer consultant. Worst case, you will only come up with a list of a hundred or so companies who use computers, must of whom you have no idea as to whether or not they use or have used consultants.

No matter what you come up with, do heed this word of caution. The information you get is more than likely to be quite out-of-date. People come and go in management. Firms change equipment. Some companies are growing, some stable, and some are history. So, don't put a lot of stock in what you find. Also, don't carry this research to an extreme.

Many consultants and aspiring consultants brush off their library skills from their college days and spend week upon week in the large metropolitan library, coming up with reams of three-by-five cards with information on every company in the area. This would be all well and good if you are going to compile a new Chamber of Commerce directory. All you should be looking for is a list of who buys your service and a few pertinent facts about the firm... the CEO, gross sales, and their main markets (i.e. what do they do for a living). This list becomes merely a starting point or staging area from which you will be able to take direct action.

It may not seem worthwhile now but this work will not be in vain. One day your phone will ring from a friend who has a hot tip on a company who might be looking for a consultant. You can go to your database and find the type of equipment they are computing on and other information about the firm. When you call or see your prospect it makes you sound very knowledgeable when you ask if they are still using their Pondasorius 250/4 or have they the downsized to a Lilliput 486? This may not be a big time door opener, but in a competitive world, every little bit can help.

The Subject is Classified

I said earlier that the vast majority of consulting positions are suspended in the muddy waters of the hidden job market and rarely see the light of newsprint. But you should not overlook the classified advertisements. Because of the universal shortage of good computer talent, companies are spending large sums of money for slick display ads seeking full-time employees. Every company knows that damn few computer employees get hired because of a classified ad. But, because their competition is advertising heavily, so too does your prospect.

Anyway, the personnel department needs something to spend its money on so they throw it at the newspapers.

You can glean quite a bit of information from these ads. So clip them, paste them to a three-by-five card and put them in your reference shoe box (or scan them into your database). The company may be looking for a full-time employee, but who is to say that they won't take a contractor?

> *TIP:* If the ad gives a name to contact, and it is not followed by some sort of title that resembles a manager, you can be assured that the name belongs to a person in the personnel department. Personnel people are to consultants that magnets are to floppy disks.

Guilt By Association

There must be an association for every group, cause, idea, disease, or occupation now in existence, that has ever been in existence, or that will be in existence. They all have membership lists and they all publish newsletters. Finding out the type of associations that the firms in your area belong to can be a step nearer to finding who the movers and shakers are in your collection of prospects.

Often companies will disclose important information about themselves in these newsletters, such as some type of expansion or the creation of a new division possibly acquired from another company. I am not suggesting that you go out and join every organization around. In fact, the association approach might be a long shot in many geographical areas. However, you never know what you will come up with. A few well-placed phone calls to the secretary of an association, stating that you are interested in doing consulting work, might just get you a name or two.

Also, don't overlook the possibility that there may be an association in your area for computer consultants. There might be a chapter of the Independent Computer Consultants Association (see Appendix). If there is a chapter, attend some of their meetings and consider joining (however the dues at some chapters are quite steep). The contacts you make with other consultants will be the most valuable you will ever have in your career as a consultant.

You might think that consultants would be very tight-lipped about sharing information of where the work is. Not true. Those in the business for any length of time know that eventually they will have to shake some bushes for leads. The concept is that if I am working and I hear of a project, why not help you out? It probably won't be long before I will want the favor returned.

Just as it was when you were employed full-time, the grapevine is usually the most accurate source of information in any business community. There are always people who have access to information or contacts that you might what to share. Do whatever you can to tap into this rich source of business related scuttlebutt.

I have busted my buns for weeks in the library, on the phone, and with the want-ads. Then magic happens. Some other consultant calls and says, "I know that Boffo, Inc. is looking for two consultants, are you available....?" If you can tie yourself into the information pipeline you can kiss most of your marketing worries good-bye.

TIP: You've played the party game where information is whispered to each player around the table? Well, don't always believe everything you hear; a lot of stuff will be bunk. However, don't be remiss about passing along information yourself. Even if you are not sure of the authenticity, bad information, in our game, is better than no information at all.

Some Conventional Wisdom

If you think that conventions are held in order to make decisions or get some kind of work done, then think again. Conventions are held and are attended in order to share or extract information. You can make more good contacts at a convention in an hour, than by two weeks of cold-calling. Just about every city has a convention bureau, as convention business can represent a sizable share of the city's revenue. Find out who is holding what and where.

Rarely do you have to be a member of anything to get in. All you have to do is pay your registration fee and the rest is up to you. If you do nothing else, be sure to get a program that has a list of attendees. Beyond this, there are two strategies.

One is to keep your mouth shut and listen for any morsel of information you can get as to who might be hiring who. The other is to tell everyone that you are a computer consultant with a client in their business or association.

I cannot teach you how to glad-hand yourself around the lobby or the bar. But the convention approach can yield great results. A friend of mine says:

> My specialty is designing and programming work-in-progress systems. So, whenever some manufacturing association has a convention, I go to the hotel and sign up. I usually don't attend the sessions, but I wear the badge and look as if I fit right in. More than a few times I have been sitting at the bar and have heard some people at a nearby table arguing the merits of their particular computer system. I simply walk over, tell them that I overheard their conversation, and let them know that I am an expert in the field. All they can say is, 'get lost'. They never do. I sit down, listen to them, don't commit myself to anything, and make some very valuable contacts. Twice, actually, I have been asked right then and there if I would be willing to fix their system so that it did what they wanted it to do. The next morning, I am in their shop, being introduced to the foreman. I tell him what I can do and leave. Two days later, I get a call from the MIS manager who has heard what a miracle worker I am, and will I accept a two month contract. Not bad for the price of a few drinks.

This may not ever happen to you, but consider that fact that a lot of top talent attends conventions these days. As I said before, marketing is a crap shoot.

I'm On Your List

The last avenue of marketing research that you might want to investigate is getting a mailing list. Get out the phone book and look in the Yellow Pages for several firms that specialize in supplying local mailing lists. You might also contact some of the local advertising agencies as they use lists all the time. They might be able to point you in the direction of a list vendor with whom they have had dependable results.

You might be surprised to see just how many stratified layers there are in American society. If you want, you can obtain a list of all plumbers in the U.S. who own mountain property and attend the symphony twice a month! For a very reasonable fee, you can probably purchase a list of all the DP managers or CEO's in your area.

It is important to determine the accuracy of the list. Nothing announces your letter as a "cold-call" faster than when it is addressed to a manager who left the company six months ago.

One other word of caution. Lists are usually supplied for one-time use only. To protect themselves, vendors will sprinkle the list with some dummy names and addresses. If the list vendor gets two letters from you at his dummy address, he calls his lawyer.

This is Great(full) Data

Up to now I have discussed the process of marketing *research*. It is nothing more than finding out who does *what*, in your area. Through the process, you might get offered a contract. However, don't expect it. Be happy to acquire a good list of fifty to two hundred names and addresses that you know can use your services.

It goes without saying that this research should be an ongoing process. Keep a shoe box of clippings from the paper and the trade magazines of who is moving where. It is your market, so keep abreast of it. Use a good database program and enter the data once a week.

If you think keeping abreast of the technical changes in our business is hard, wait until you see how fast people play musical jobs. If at any given time, you have ten good contacts out there in computer-land, consider yourself a marketing marvel.

> **COMMENT**: Even during the last recession, the music didn't seem to stop. My database of some 150 names was constantly out of date; and I live in a small city!

But research alone won't do it. You have to *advertise*.

A Walkin', Talkin' Billboard

I have indirectly mentioned a very powerful marketing strategy - word-of-mouth. It is imperative that you tell anyone and everyone that you are in the market to acquire a new contract. This goes even beyond your immediate friends and family. Everywhere you go, you must be a walking billboard.

But, please, don't carry this to an extreme. When you go to a party and meet someone for the first time, try to have a little tact. Somewhere in the conversation let it be known that you are a computer consultant. Remember that computers are fascinating to the average person and more than likely you are bound to hear for the ten-thousandth time about how their hard disk crashed, or how they got a check sent to them for zero dollars. Smile as if you were hearing this for only the hundredth time.

It won't be long until you are asked who your clients are. Try not to release the name of any client as you never know if the person you are talking with just got fired from that company and will take an instant dislike to you. Anyway, nobody really cares who pays you. They are just being polite and trying to make conversation. Just tell them that you have done work for some of the major firms in the area. If pressed, try to find out where they work and then name some other company.

> *TIP: When engaged in conversation with someone who hates computers, never, never, defend the computer. In this age, people have to have something to take out their frustrations. When we were an agricultural society, everyone blamed the weather. Today it is the computer. We've come a long way (baby)!*

Keep in mind that you are an advertisement for yourself and not a defender of the faith. If the person you are dealing with hates one of your clients for some reason, don't come to the defense of your customer. Change the topic. Walk away. Spill your drink on them, but get out of there. This is not the time to act as the chairman of the local debate club. One of my consultant colleagues from Washington tells this story:

> I was at a dinner party and was seated next to a young woman who went bananas when I told her that I

worked at a local defense contractor's office. She bent my ear for twenty minutes, telling me how anybody who even drives by the plant is somehow responsible for the arms race, destruction of the environment, death, destruction, and dismemberment! I really felt that I was in a jam, as I knew that I could not argue with a closed mind. I couldn't just leave the table! So I told her that I did consulting on the design of the new payroll system and was responsible for cost-of-living adjustments getting into the pay cycle. But I resolved then and there never to tell anyone who my client was, unless I was sure who I was speaking to and their politics.

Word-of-mouth will never get out unless you plant the seed. If you are between contracts, don't hesitate to say so. This may be contrary to everything you ever read in those books on how to get a job. But this is consulting... a totally different animal. If people don't think you are available, they are not going to pass your name along to the movers and shakers in your community. Even if they do, and the president of Ardvark Manufacturing is led to believe that you already have a lifetime contract with Platypus Industries, he is going to be hesitant to call.

There is no disgrace about being between contracts, unless you make it disgraceful. It is part of the game. Everyone knows that consulting is either feast or famine. Why the hell do you think that most people remain full-time employees. In reality all you need to do is let people know that you are searching for a new contract, and ask for their help. The key word here is to ask. If you come off sounding like you will have a new contract signed by 10 AM tomorrow, nobody is going to take the trouble to keep you in mind the next time they hear about the need for a top-notch computer person. They will think you are so big and important that you don't need their help.

> *TIP: Stories abound about consultants who on Saturday night attended some social function and simply asked all the people that they met to let them know if they heard of some opening somewhere. By Thursday they had two or three prospects. Remember, you are not begging. You are simply stating the truth. One simple fact: if you don't ask for the business, you are not going to get it.*

I cannot overemphasize the importance of word-of-mouth marketing. It is the one strategy that costs nothing (beyond the price of attending a boring party) and can reap huge rewards. Yet, I find that this form of marketing is almost never employed by the majority of consultants, especially people wanting to enter the field. Perhaps it is understandable. We all belong to a work-oriented society, and many feel that it is demeaning to be out of work, much less having to ask for assistance. If you cannot overcome this feeling immediately, don't worry, as all is not lost. There are other marketing strategies. but, if you can get your act together and by this I mean that you know precisely how you are going to present yourself as a walking advertisement to those you meet in everyday occasions, you might never have to employ any other marketing strategy.

> *TIP: As a consultant, never underestimate the power of some polite conversation, a handshake, and a passed business card. Empires have been build on just such events.*

For First-Timers

People always ask me what they should say when they are just starting out. The answer is simple. Don't lie.

You would not believe the stories would-be consultants concoct to try to make themselves seem "bigger" or more experienced that they are. Some tell people that they have just moved their business from out-of-town. Others make up fictitious clients and have friends "cover the phones" for them. I even know one guy who actually set up a dummy business in order to serve as a reference.

Don't be stupid. You don't need to make up the great American novel in order to get your first contract. Simply tell people that you are an entrepreneur struggling to start a consulting business. Explain that you have great references from your previous (or current) full-time employer or from your colleagues. And tell them that you are probably crazy for trying to start a business, but it is something you have always aspired to and you are taking the plunge.

The corollary to all this is your rate. To get your first contract you will probably have to work for much less than the going rate. Once you "are" a consultant, you can charge consulting rates. Until then, you will have to give a discount to get started. Let people know this. Hell, if need be, tell them you will work for food!

Word of mouth is more important for the new-comer than for the established consultant because the entry person does not have a referral base. It is absolutely a must that you tell everyone (and I mean everyone) what you are doing.

Here is how the process works for new-comers. You mention to Dr. Pane, your dentist, about your new consulting venture. That same day Jones comes in for a check-up. During the procedure, Jones mentions how the computers at work are all "screwed up". Dr. Pane mentions you as a possible savior to Jones (Pane wants you to do well so you can pay your dental bill... he knows you no longer have dental insurance. The next day, Smith calls Jones and says he is looking for a consultant to do such and such. Jones tells Smith that he could call Bill, John, or Mary. But he also tells Smith that there is a new kid who seems to have good qualifications and might work cheaper (and faster). And the new kid is definitely available. Smith calls all four of you but only you and Bill are available. Bill can't close the sale, so you get the contract.

Look, I know this sounds overly simplistic. But it is true. You have to trust me on this. It is definitely true. During my research for this book hundreds of consultants told me similar stories about how they got started. If your story turns out to be much different, I would be very surprised.

Deliver The Letter, The Sooner The Better...

If word-of-mouth is the most overlooked strategy, then letter-writing is the most often-used methodology that consultants use to market themselves. Maybe "abused" is a better word.

There are countless consultants out there who have dashed off two dozen letters and have sat endlessly next to a silent phone. There are three reasons for this. First, they had no idea how to write a good sales letter. Second, their letter never got to the right person. Third, they did not employ any other form of marketing strategy. Most of these consultants are now happily employed full-time.

We have all received promotional mail selling everything from insurance to funeral plots. Some of it we respond to positively, while the rest ends up in file thirteen. To keep your letters out of the trash, you have to know how to write a good sales letter. The problem is that most sales material crossing your desk is geared to a product or service. You are not really selling either. You are selling *you*!

The usual line that is fed letter-writers is to "sell the sizzle, not the steak" Big, big, big mistake. A manager or owner is going to contract with *you*, not some image that your create. The old concept of having to capture the reader's attention in the first line also does not apply for the simple reason that it has been so overdone that readers are just about immune to all the so-called contagious first-line hooks.

Managers get a ton of promotional mail from every vendor under every rock in the land. And you know where most of this ends up. So I've never understood why consultants try to emulate the style of a sales letter that would be used to sell a new magazine or software product. They think the hype is going to work. It doesn't. If you have never written a sales-type piece before, you are probably going to be more successful than the person who used to work in an advertising agency and supposedly knows all the ropes.

All you are going to do is present your availability on paper. Dignity is the key word here. You will end up in the circular file if you attempt any hype at all. You might be able to leap over a thirty foot stack of 386's in a single bound. Nobody cares at this point. Keep it simple and keep it dignified. You are a "professional", and your letter must show it. When you start a letter by saying "Wouldn't you like the services of the best analyst in the area...", you are sounding just like the last letter the manager received asking him is he would like to have the "best" word processor on the market. He has seen all of this hype before, and didn't believe it then. He won't believe it now.

Sample Sales Letter

As an independent Computer Consultant, I should like to introduce myself to Pine Tree Lumber, Inc. Having recently completed a project with National Widget, I am available for immediate assignment for projects lasting from three to eight months.

The basic rate for (programming, analysis, network design, etc.) is from $30 to $50 depending upon the length and complexity of the work. All information relative to my professional training and experience is contained in the enclosed resume. I have also enclosed a reference sheet for your investigation.

Having a list of reliable consultants to call upon is a valuable resource for any company. Can I take a few minutes of your time to acquaint you with my abilities?

Most sincerely

There are many variations of letters that you can use. The one presented here may or may not fit your purpose. However, I shall use it as a guide, and you can tailor each paragraph to fit your own objectives. Basically, a consultant's sales letter should have a minimum of three paragraphs.

The first paragraph must detail something about what you are and what you do. The title that you choose for yourself should be consistent with the local slang in your area. For software professionals, in some regions we are simply contract programmers or analysts. In others we have reached the level of consultants or consulting (software/hardware) engineers.

Whatever, don't leave the reader with any doubt about what you do for a living. It is also good to let him know who you have just finished working for. Even if it is your current or past full-time employer, I think you should mention it. Anyway, the client will find out sooner or later, and if the firm is well-known, it surely won't hurt.

> *TIP:* And if it is the competition, so much the better. Companies love to get consultants who have worked at their competitors office because they think they we will be privy to some inside information.

If you don't feel like telling them who you just finished with, it is imperative that you mention the fact that you are either available immediately, or at what date. This is also a good place to let your prospect know the type of project and length that you will consider. However, many consultants prefer to leave this out in order to not automatically disqualify themselves.

The second paragraph simply contains some information about yourself or it points the reader to an attachment. Whether or not you want to go into any detail about your experience is rather moot, so long as you keep it short. Do not make the mistake of putting your life story into this paragraph (or any other). Remember, you are simply stating the bare facts about yourself and your availability. We have resumes or brochures to tell our personal story.

I believe that it is important to mention money. The classic books on the subject of getting a job always advise us not to mention bucks.

For consultants, I think this is bad advice. You have a price for your service - right? Well, guess what is uppermost in the mind of the person who is thinking of signing for your services? It is not the color of your eyes!

In my view it is absolutely important that you be up front about money. You provide a service and you expect to be paid. so why beat around the bush? There is nothing worse during a client meeting to find that the manager loves you, but had no idea that you cost so much. It is a sinking feeling to have established a terrific rapport with a manager, only to have to haggle over money. If your prospect knows up front what the cost is going to be, and you get called to meet, all you have to do is sell yourself. There will be no sticker shock when he hears about your rate. You gave him a figure or a range in the letter so he is mentally prepared.

I will talk more about money later, but for now, simply decide on what an acceptable range would be and write it in.

> **COMMENT:** There are a lot of inexperienced managers who have no idea what consultants cost. It is no fun having to revive a young, recently promoted MIS manager from shock when he hears your rate just before the two of you go to lunch!

The third paragraph is sometimes referred to as the action or "do something" section. There are many variations on this and you should use one that you are comfortable with. If you plan to warm-call the manager, this is the place to put in that message. If this is not your aim, it is a good idea to end with a question. You want your reader to do something. Actually, you want him to rush to the phone and burn the wires to get you. But asking for this can sound too much like a hard sell. By ending with a question, your reader will subconsciously be answering it. You haven't pressured them into anything. You haven't asked for a million dollars or their first-born child. You only asked to get together. They may feel a "no", but their subconscious will probably answer a "yes". I'm not sure why. Perhaps they have nothing scheduled tomorrow and you can fill up some time so that they can at least look (and feel) important. Maybe they really have a hot project and need a body fast. You never know. The truth of the matter is that you really don't care. What you want, more than anything else, is to get into the office so that you can sell.

> *TIP: If you are on a wild-goose chase and the manager is just polishing his/her ego by having you in for a walk down memory lane, so what? You have a chance to make a contact, do some selling, plant some seeds that might germinate into an assignment; if not with this company than perhaps with one of his/her associates at another firm. Never turn down a client meeting, even if you are booked for a year!*

Who Is Running This Railroad?

As long as you keep your letter short, simple, and low pressure, you are bound to be effective. All you need to know now is who to write to. In the research stage of your marketing efforts you probably where able to come up with a list of companies and perhaps some names. The only thing worse (though not much worse) than writing to the wrong person is writing to no one. Writing a "Dear Sir/Madam" letter is simply a waste of time. Don't do it. It is very easy to find out precisely who to address your sales document to.

> *TIP: Knowing who to write to is actually more important than what you write.*

Here is what you do. Call up the company you are interested in and ask for the MIS or computer department. Be prepared for an endless wait, as the switchboard operator will probably have never heard of the department and will connect you with the company nurse!. But be patient and when you do get through, nine time out of ten the department secretary will answer. Say something like this:

> Miss, I'm a [programmer, analyst, integrator, etc.] and I'm interested in working for National Widget. I want to bypass the Personnel Department - you know how disorganized they are down there - and I want to get my resume to the people who count before the colonel runs out of chickens! Could you give me the names of two or three managers who hire and whom I could write? I don't want to talk to them now, as I'm sure they are too busy and I'm not free to speak, if you know what I mean. Maybe you could pick out someone who would be particularly good to work for. By the way, what was your name again.

> *TIP: Don't tell her you are a consultant. She may hate consultants worse than the plague. Let her think you are a working-stiff like her.*

A phone call like this takes some practice, but it is not difficult. What you are doing is playing right into the hands of the secretary. First of all, she doesn't want you to talk to anyone, as it is her job to protect her people from pests like you. Second, she hates personnel as much as you, as they are always creating needless paperwork for her. Third, she has her favorite people in the office, and by asking for her choice, you get her mind off of whether or not she should give out names over the phone, and on to which manager she likes the best.

> *TIP: While you are on the phone get their titles, and company mail stops, as this will speed your letter. Also, note her name down on your data base.*

This strategy will work most of the time, but it is not foolproof. One of two things might happen. First, she might say that all employees must be referred to the department by Personnel. If this happens, then just ask her for the name of the department manager and ask to speak to him or her. She will be just a bit intimidated and will probably tell you who this person is, but will say he/she is in a meeting. If this doesn't work, call back tomorrow and announce that our are a new assistant producer for Channel 3 and you need to know the name of the director. Tell her that the station is interested in doing a "piece" on her company and you need to send some preliminary material to whoever is in charge.

> *COMMENT: This of course is a total lie, so don't do it in you don't think you can handle the guilt. However, you will learn that nobody ever turns down the electronic media .*

The second thing that might happen when you call is that you might end up talking to one of the managers right then and there. The best way to handle this is to play it safe unless you are a super-salesman. Don't give your name, but simply tell the person what you told (or would tell) the secretary and emphasize that you are not free to talk. This universally implies that you are calling from work and you don't want to be overheard or for anyone to know you are "looking".

> *TIP*: Much of this can usually be avoided by calling at lunch time. Everyone but one secretary will be out of the office and the secretary will not be pressured for time. But you might get a temp who doesn't even know the name of the company much less the movers and shakers. Call back later.

Talking to secretaries can be very instructive, if you have a pleasing phone personality and they don't feel intimidate by you. You might even be able to find out if the company uses consultants. But don't ask this until you have the names you are after. Remember, secretaries often resent consultants for the money they make, as much as full-time employees do.

The important thing to remember is that you are looking for at least one name of a middle line manager who makes hiring decisions. Getting the director's name is better than nothing, but very few directors initially hire consultants. They may approve of the final deal you make with the middle manager, but by and large the ball game is between you and the staff.

> *TIP*: I advise that you don't give your name if you can avoid it. You never know if one of your enemies of a few years ago might have joined the company. If the secretary gossips that you called, you could be downed in the backfield before the play even unfolds.

The Friendly Folks In Personnel

When it comes to full-time employment, personnel people have found more ways to keep good people from getting jobs than there are stars in the sky. When it comes to consultants, they really outdo themselves. You see, personnel people keep so many charts and graphs about more irrelevant data concerning the people who work for the company that they usually forget their real purpose.

Consultants do not fit nicely into their charts or graphs. In fact, personnel people see clear and present threat. They seem to feel that when a company uses a consultant, it somehow reflects badly on the personnel department, in that the consultant reflects a job order that the department was unable to fill. They feel it is a slap in the face when a manager calls down and tells them to cancel a job requisition because a consultant is going to be used instead. The personnel people are afraid that this might become a bad habit. Let's fact it. Where would any self-respecting personnel Department be, if it didn't have a whole file of job requisitions to fill? Forget the fact that the really good people get hired in spit of the personnel department, in that they usually bypass the bureaucracy completely. There is nothing the department can do about that except sigh and hope it does not happen too often.

But when a letter from a consultant pops up in the mail, the personnel department can take defensive measures by trashing the letter right then and there. If they direct the letter up through channels to the MIS department, the personnel people would be in effect saying "We can't fill this job, so here is a consultant."

Personnel people believe that there is a body for every desk, no matter what the talent market is. They think that if there is a job, then there is someone to fill it. And they are not about to admit to their own failure in this endeavor by passing along the letter of a consultant. *Personnel people are the pallbearers of the consulting industry.* You have noting to gain by submitting a resume to them, so be wise and let them go on about their business of keeping meaningless statistics, while you go on about the serious business of marketing your skills.

> *COMMENT: One day some enterprising young personnel manager is going to set up a special division of his/her department simply to handle consultants. It is doubtful that contractors would respond in droves, but it would be a step in the right direction.*

It's Cold Out There

Here is a strategy that everyone hates: cold-calling. I consider cold-calling as either an unannounced visit or a phone call to someone who has never heard of you or your company.

> *COMMENT: If you were paying attention, you noticed I used the term "warm-call" earlier. This is a follow-up call after sending your prospect a letter or brochure. They still don't know you, but at least some contact has been made. It is not a cold-call.*

In the old days (whenever they were) it was common to see hoards of young eager job seekers converge on an office building, go to the last stop on the elevator, and start knocking on doors. It was one of the rare instances that one could start at the top and work their way down! The saying was that if you knocked on enough doors, one was bound to open sooner or later. Later was much closer to the truth.

I know a few successful consultants that have made a list of businesses and have visited each one trying for an opening. There is nothing inherently wrong in cold calling except that it takes too much time and people hate do it. If you were once particularly successful as a door-to-door book salesman, you would still be wise to spend your time learning how to write a successful sales letter and resume. Cold calling is just not an effective sales marketing method.

This is because anyone you are going to want to see will be either in a meeting, on the phone, or traveling somewhere. Another and more important reason is that you really do not have a product that you can demonstrate easily. You are going to be selling yourself. It is a curious fact of human nature that people have an extremely high sales resistance to buying a service when it is presented to them right off the street. How would you feel if someone rang your doorbell and offered to be your housekeeper, or lawyer, or auto mechanic. You would be a little stunned standing there on your doorstep. Well, technical managers are the same way. They want to know something about you before you come in. Indeed, they want to know *when* you are coming in! Whenever someone just shows up and waits in their office, managers feel that they don't have control of the situation. They don't like surprises. They actually feel intimidated.

Even if they are waist deep in computer alligators and really need an expert to come in on a short time basis, they are not likely to offer you a contract right then and there. It is just not the way things are done. That is all there is to it.

> *TIP: If you have an hour or so to kill before an appointment, go into the lobby of some big office building, look in the building directory, pick out some company that sounds like it might have a need for a computer consultant. Do a cold call at least to drop off your resume or brochure. You never know.*

Call Other Callers, Sell Other Sellers

There is one exception to cold calling. This is calling on other salesmen. The men and women who sell hardware are people in your community that you want to get to know. True, you can send them a letter, but they are too busy trying to make a sale and earn a living to give you much of their valuable time. The only way to catch them is by chance. These people regularly visit the same companies that you want to do business with. Court these people. Get into their office and let them know that you are available.

More than one computer system has been sold by a salesperson who could guarantee of competent people available to come in and make the thing cost effective by the programming and analysis of new systems.

One particular breed of salesperson to seek out is the in-store retail salespeople. Often these people can be a good source of leads and referrals.

Another good source are the software reps. This is especially true if you are a consultant in their product line.

There is a very effective way to approach salespeople. Give them a call and tell them that you are an independent consultant and that you are regularly approached by clients who want to know about the possibilities of using the reps software or hardware product. When they ask "who", tell them you are under non-disclosure. Mention that you would like to come to their office and explore what the costs and benefits would be to your client.

These people are not stupid. They need business contacts, just the same as you. And they are not about to miss out on a potential sale by telling you to kiss off. They will have you in their office that week and will fall all over you as a source of potential sales. They may suspect that you are bluffing, but they won't know for sure (they use the same tactic).

If you meet up with a rep you like, do your best to drum up business for him/her. They will do the same for you. Even if there is nothing in it for you, the favor will not be forgotten. When the rep has an opportunity to use your skills, they will know just who to call.

> *TIP*: If you haven't had much experience with sales people, then you may be in for a surprise. These are not glad-handing, joke telling, polyester clad flakes who go door to door. They are usually sharp individuals who have an intimate knowledge of their market and the computer business. Many earn big bucks for both themselves and their company. You can't be too nice to these people, and under the right circumstances, they can keep you in bread for a long, long time.

Does Advertising Cost, Or Pay?

You can invent a better mousetrap, but if people don't know that you have invented it, and don't know where your door is, nobody is going to beat a path anywhere. So this brings me to what I think is the single most important contribution this country has made to commerce and trade - advertising.

In researching this book I have found that advertising will either be a boom or a bust proposition. For some consultants, it has worked quite well, and for others it has served no purpose other than to generate a ton of junk mail; mostly from insurance companies. There is no reliable method that you can use in order to learn if advertising will work in your area. If you have never seen an ad for a consultant, then one of the following assumptions is true: either nobody has tried it, or it has been tried and it does not work.

I think the first assumption is probably closer to the truth because I could not find a large population of consultants who had ever given advertising a try. They said it wasn't necessary, were convinced that it would not work, or they claimed it was too expensive.

> *TIP*: If you see an ad for a consultant, give the party a call and ask if it has been effective. If you see the ad regularly, you can assume the ad is effective. Smart business people don't throw good money after bad advertising.

Unless you are positive that advertising is a waste of time in your area, you should give it a try. This does not mean that you take out a full page in *People Magazine*! The general consensus among consultants is that there is only one type of ad and it should only appear in two places.

The style is loosely termed "dignity announcements" in advertising jargon. You have seen these type of ads placed by doctors when they are announcing the opening of a new practice or when they are trying to get their name associated with a new procedure. For example I recently saw an ad for a doctor who was trying to drum up business with patients wanting varicose veins removed. You might have also seen the ads placed by lawyers, especially when they hire a new associate who has a specialty new to the firm, such as computer law, or environmental litigation.

For your ad to be effective it must be low-key and dignified. It should not be large or splashy. One of the places it should be placed is in the financial section of the best read daily paper. The people you want to reach *may* read the sports section and they *may* read the entertainment section. But they *always* read the business section.

I have seen ads that were nothing more than reprints of business cards. I've also seen ads with pictures of the consultant(s), similar to ads seen for real estate leasing agents or big-time insurance brokers.

There are many variations on the theme, but the key is not so much to sell your reader as it is to inform. If a manager does not have a project right now, you at least want him/her to cut out the ad and keep in the top drawer as if it were a business card. The next time an urgent need arises in the department, he/she says to him/herself, "I think I will call that ad I saw in the paper last month."

The other area that has been effective for consultant advertising is in what I call the "program" media. These are small ads placed in the program guides for the symphony, ballet, opera, various charity functions, and any other one-time and one-event publications. The rates for these insertions are not high, but the visibility is. Next time you go to your child's high-school play, or a local cultural event, look around and see how many people look through the program before the show and during the intermission. Often the price is very, very low and the quality of the readership is quite high.

> **COMMENT:** I can't predict just how your ad is going to play but there are two possibilities mentioned to me by clients I talked with. The first and most hoped for is that your readers are going to think that advertising is a great idea as you made their job easier the next time they have to find a consultant. At least they have a place to start looking. The second response is gong to run along the lines that you must be desperate if you have to advertise.

If you are going to give advertising a try, get in touch with the display advertising salespeople of your paper and tell them that you want to run an ad and have never done so before. They will be very helpful and will give you suggestions about print-style, size, and costs. However, don't let them oversell you. All you should go for the first time is a small 2 X 3 or 3 X 5 box in the business section on Sunday and Tuesday. Do this for three consecutive weeks and see what happens. As I said before, it will either fly high or sink fast. But, if you don't try, you will never know.

> **COMMENT:** George Hill, the well known commentator and former president of American Tobacco said that fifty cents of every dollar spent on advertising was wasted. The problem was that he could never figure out which fifty cents it was so he continued to spend the whole dollar!

The Write Way To Publicity

If the jury is still out on the value of advertising, the value of public relations is indeed real. You want a simple definition of public relations? Here it is. Advertising costs money, but PR is free. The definition is probably not adequate but I'm sure you get the picture. By incorporating an active strategy of public relations into your marketing efforts, you will not only get the satisfaction of seeing your name in print, but it may indeed help create a market for your services where no market existed before.

There is only one skill that you need in order to do your own PR - you have to know how to write well (or know someone who does). Unless you are able to get yourself interviewed on a local talk show, the written word will be your PR vehicle.

The strategy is to get your name in the local print media as often as possible. If would be nice if you could, through consulting, do something newsworthy, such as solving a computer crime case. But the chance of this is slim. So you are going to have to put on your reporter's hat and hit the keyboard with articles about your craft.

I am not talking about *Gone With The Wind*; just some human interest pieces on computers and software.

The world might hate computers but it is fascinated by them. You are in a dynamic industry that few outsiders really know much about. You can write about almost anything in the computer/human relations area and can count on getting someone to publish it.

> *TIP: When you see what passes for good writing these days, you will see how easy it is to write an article.*

Get an idea for an article and simply write it. It doesn't have to be very long or very detailed. Keep it simple and interesting. When it is done, send a letter to the editor of the local paper or local magazine detailing your story. This is called a "query letter" in the literary trade. You will collect a few rejections slips along the way, but sooner or later you will find a taker for some article.

> *TIP: In your query, let the editor know that he can have it for a small sum, such as $20 to $50, but don't offer it free. Things that are free are usually only worth their price.*

After you get your first piece published, keep coming up with ideas and getting them on paper. Keep submitting them and it will not be too long until you will be recognized as the local expert on affairs in the computer industry.

There is one important point to remember. You must get a by-line and a blurb about who you are and what you do. After all, this is what PR is all about. If you were trying to earn your living as a freelance writer, you would simply be in it for the money. But what you want is the publicity. You want to be able to send a copy of an article to a prospective client or present it as an "after-thought" during a meeting. The potential clout of this marketing tactic is enormous if diligently employed.

Where do you get ideas? Listen to how one well published consultant from Boston does it:

> I read *Computerworld* as well as the other trade publications and find some new product or application that can be the basis of a short article. I re-write the article, cutting out all the technical crap and I put it into simple "8th grade" reading level style. I once rewrote an 8,000 word article on word processing and came up with 900! The publisher of the paper cut it down to 600! Anytime I come up with an idea for an article about computers that everyday people will find interesting, I jot it down. I sit down on Sunday morning, pick out an idea from my little black book and write it the way I think a sales clerk can understand it. I am not looking for a Pulitzer Prize or even a big check. What I get for my efforts is a string of short articles which gives me a great deal of publicity and credibility. I am not just a "lone-ranger" consultant but a so called "computer expert. The articles don't cause the phone to ring off the hook with assignment offers and I don't expect them to. But when I enclose a copy of an article with an introduction letter to a client, I know it will be read. There is something mysterious about being in print. People are eager to meet you.

There is another tactic that you should employ here. Create a market for yourself. Get as many pieces published as you can about how computer consultants save their clients money, are more efficient, harder working, etc.

> **COMMENT:** *There are whole sections in this book that you can rewrite!*

What you are aiming for here is to educate a manger or business owner who has never even considered using a consultant into calling you up and asking about the possibility. You know they are out there. Surely you have met the narrow minded manager types who are absolutely positive that using a consultant is just not cost effective. Here is your chance to get to these people. There no better way to reach these folks than to send them a clipping of your article with a good "let's get together" letter.

> *TIP: You won't convince every one of them. But then again, it only takes one.*

If I seem to emphasize the simplicity of all this it is because it really is easy once you get the hang of it. It would be worth your while to invest in one of the numerous books on magazine writing. You can find them in either the business section or the reference section of your book store. Bypass all the stuff about how to write and concentrate on how to get published. You might also want to pick up a copy of *Writer's Digest* magazine. Besides being interesting reading, it gives valuable insights into how to get your ideas into printers ink.

If it comes down to the fact that you really can't write at all, you can always find a ghost. Get in tough with the English or journalism department of your local college or university and ask them to recommend one of their students or faculty who would be interested n doing ghost articles. You might also try a local advertising agency, as they use ghosts all the time. The rates vary by region, but it is not too expensive. An experienced ghost can turn out an article on almost anything in a matter of days.

> *COMMENT: If you think this is unethical, just who do you think writes most of the books by so-called famous people? Well, maybe it is a bit unethical, so you will have to decide for yourself. Anyway, as someone said, nothing is illegal if a hundred businessmen decide to do it.*

Join In And Speak Up

The public relations game does not end with getting into print. Getting active in your community is another good method of getting publicity, as well as making good contacts. There are organizations for every conceivable purpose which business people like yourself join. Sure they do it out of civic pride, but if they can make a few good contacts on the side, so much the better.

Find out who the leaders of these clubs are organizations are and offer to be a guest speaker for one of their meetings. Of course, this is predicated upon your having a good speech. Again, if you can't write one, get a ghost.

> **COMMENT**: *You say you can't speak? If you can't give an interesting twenty minute speech on how computer consulting can be beneficial to the business community, then you should not be in the business!*

If you can find speaking engagements where you can talk about your type of business, so much the better. However, it would be wise to have a good talk prepared on some amorphous topic such as computers and society or the office of the future. Really it is not hard. Just sit down for a few hours on a Sunday and decide you are gong to write a speech; then do it! Nobody is going to take your speech as "words to live by". They are not going to pass the gems of wisdom that you espouse down through the generations. All you have to do is present an interesting and humorous twenty minutes about that fascinating machine: the computer. You will have a fifteen-minute question-answer session and you will be out of there. Talk about your interesting experiences, or why machines will never replace people. It does not matter. People are fascinated by computers and will be eager to hear you, so long as you don't get into a long winded explanation of structured design or relational methodology. A young consultant from Virginia told me:

> I talk to many business groups about simply what a computer is, and what it isn't. I spice the talk up with every good computer joke I have ever heard (Ed: there are very few good ones] and I talk about the wonderful data processing goofs that have occurred. I found all the information I needed in about ten hours of research. I have used the same twenty minute speech about thirty times and it actually gets better as time goes on. I not only enjoy speaking but I get to meet some pretty influential people in my city. At my age, I would never come into contact with these people without speaking at their meetings. Nobody offers me a job on the spot, but you'd be surprised how many ask if I am available to help solve their problems.

> **COMMENT**: If you always thought that the civic association was simply an excuse for a businessperson to take a long lunch, think again. More good deals have been started over tablecloths than over desk tops.

Market Timing

The ultimate goal of marketing is to get your name known to the people who count and to get your butt into their office so you can make a sale. It does not happen overnight. Sometimes you just have to sit it out until your strategy pays off, or until market conditions get better. I believe that because marketing people were never able to get the courage to tell the boss that results take time, they invented the term of "market timing".

I don't believe there is such a thing. While some times of the year are better than others, there is no absolute period that you should do your marketing. The sheer nature of computing is such that projects are started (and canceled) almost every ten minutes! While the period between March 1 and June 1 is usually the best time to harvest a new contract, there is no hard-fast rule that says the summer is a dead period. In our business the machine cranks on around the clock, every day of the year. So don't believe those who sound like they are in the know when they give you a lot of bunk about when is and when isn't the best time to market yourself.

Covert Interviewing

No matter what time of the year it is, it is always a pain to have to sit and wait for the phone to ring. Alas, there is one other strategy that many consultants employ during the slack times. For lack of a better term, most consultants refer to this tactic as "covert interviewing".

This name has been applied because there is an implied deception that takes place between the prospect and the consultant. To use this strategy, you have to fabricate a small illusion. No, it does not mean we tell an outright lie, but instead, we lead the prospect to believe something that might not be the whole truth.

The first thing you do is get the Sunday paper and make a short list of companies that are seeking computer skills on a full-time basis. If it is a small company and the personnel department is not involved, then give them a call. Otherwise, send a letter and a resume.

In your call or letter it is important that you tell the truth, or at least not lie. You state that you have seen their ad and that although you are an independent consultant, you might consider working full-time if the situation was right.

Okay, on the surface this probably sounds like an outright lie, but in reality it isn't. After all, you haven't defined what the situation is. Wouldn't you take a full-time job if the price was right, if they made you the proverbial offer that you couldn't refuse? What if they made you head of the company? What if they gave you a boat and a Rolls? It is your fantasy, so come up with your own situation!

Also, we all have our price. The fact that you are a consultant bears this out! (Remember, you are in this mainly for the money). Many consultants have been brought back into the corporate game by companies that valued their consultants so much, that some pretty good offers were made.

> *COMMENT: Are we actually causing a deception? Remember, we are semantically telling the truth. We only said that there are conditions that might cause us to consider full-time employment. We haven't said what they are. We are letting the prospect believe what they would like.*

The objective is to get in the door. Once in, you will have the opportunity to at least gain some exposure. If you really sell yourself, you will get a full-time job offer. As with any offer, you are under no obligation to accept. Thus, you will tell them that you prefer to remain in business for yourself.

One of three things will happen. First, the company might take you on as a contractor for the run of the project. This is exactly what you are shooting for. Many times they will hope that they can recruit you during the project to accept a full-time position. (This could happen no matter how you get a contract, and I will address this later).

Second, they could say that they have no use for you now, but will keep you in mind if an opportunity for a short-term project develops. No problem here, as you never know when this opportunity will develop.

More than one consultant has used this strategy only to be told that the company does not and never has used consultants. Then bingo, the phone rings a week later and they offer the consultant a contract.

> *COMMENT:* What probably happened was that they couldn't find a full-time person and some manager's butt was on the line to get the project rolling.

Third, the company will be ticked off and will never have anything to do with you again. Some firms get real touchy about anyone, consultant or employee, who turns down a job offer. They take it personally. It is a risk that you take and a lot of the outcome depends on how you carry off the interview and the job offer, if it comes.

No matter what happens, this strategy is geared to get you off your butt and take some direct action to get a contract. It will not work for everyone, everywhere. However, if you are a skilled interviewee, you probably will have little trouble carrying it off and getting several good contracts.

I interviewed a consultant from San Francisco who said:

> As I figure it, if the company is looking for a full-time person, then they must have a need to be filled. I come along and offer to fill that need. I tell them that I might consider a full-time position, but when an offer is made, I decline it with a great amount of appreciation. I do tell them that I would like to come on board for a short time, and leave it at that. I don't put a gun to their head. They can take me or leave me. I've been taken on board many more times than I've been left at the dock!

I'll make him an offer he can't refuse.

Mario Puzo

The Godfather (1969)

TOOLS OF THE TRADE

The Name Game (Banana-Banna, Bo-Banna)

You have heard the expression that clothes make the man (and woman)? Well, in American society, just looking like you are in business is almost more important than actually being in business. Why do companies house themselves in sleek modern buildings with plush interiors? Out of some motive of philanthropy toward their employees? No way! They want to appear successful.

When a company hits hard times, what is the first thing they cut back on? Landscaping, expensive cars, expense account lunches for their clients? Wrong again. They cut back on people. If the medium is the message, in business, the image is the medium. If you are going to be successful you are going to have to create an image (hopefully not an illusion) of success. To do this, you are going to need some simple tools.

The first item you will need is a name. That's right, a name. While it's true that some consultants do upwards of $100,000 of business under their own names, by and large the majority of consultants have some sort of business umbrella that they stand (hide?) under. There is no law that says you have to have a business name, and it is "easier" to do (not get) business under your own name.

There is one important fact that you must take into consideration. For better or worse, companies like to do business with companies. They do not like to do business with individuals.

> **COMMENT**: *Try this simple test. Call any company and say you are whomever you are and you want to speak to the head person. Then time the minutes that you are put on hold. Call back tomorrow and tell them you are president of Amalgamated Consolidated and see how long it takes you to get through.*

On the whole, the name you pick is really not that important so long as you feel comfortable with it. There are several favorites among consultants. One involves the use of the word "associates" on the tail end. Another well-known formula is to use your initials in front of the words "systems", "technology", "solutions", etc. A third is to take a shortened form of two words and combine them into one word, such as "Systec". A fourth favorite is to name your company with some environmentally pure image like "Blue River Consulting".

> **TIP**: *I suggest that you keep you name short and simple. You will repeat your business name countless times over the phone and you want something that the average person can spell without assistance.*

At one time, the rule was to get a name that accurately described what you did for a living. Thus we see General Motors, American Tobacco, etc. The trend today, with big conglomerates owning everything under the sun is to have a name as general as possible. It is even a plus if you can come up with just some initials as your business banner so that nobody really knows what you own or even who you are. There are probably not too many of us left who know what ITT or 3M stand for.

> **COMMENT**: *The absolute best name I ever heard for a consultant was a guy who was a big-time Grateful Dead fan. He named his one-person company: Grateful Data.*

Form vs. Substance

There are three forms your business can take: sole proprietorship (prop), partnership, or corporation. I'll talk about each very briefly but if you are really unsure what form to take, either consult your lawyer or find one of the million books on how to start your own business. They usually treat this subject in great detail.

The corporation is the most complex business form because it is actually a separate legal entity from you. In other words, it has legal status. It can buy things, sell things, sue, and be sued. To be a corporation you have to file papers with the Secretary of Sate of your state and "do" business as a corporation. This means keeping separate records for the corporation, keeping minutes of meetings, and paying corporate taxes. One of the variants is the Subchapter S corporation in which profits (and loses) flow to the owner(s) of the corporation much like a partnership. There are many, many tax advantages to being a corporation but most people do business as a corporation for the "implied" limited liability. In other words, they don't sue you, they sue the corporation (which may not have very deep pockets).

> **COMMENT**: This has been taken to an extreme. First of all, the chances of you being sued as a consultant are very slight. Second, any lawyer can take an action called "piercing the corporate vail" and sue you personally.

If you really want to do business as a corporation, find one of the books on how to do it yourself (NOLO Press puts out one for several states). Also take a look at *Inc. Yourself* by Judith McGowan. These will give you some guidelines. You also should consult a lawyer and an accountant. The lawyer will give you further help and can do the paperwork for you if you desire. The accountant will get you set up with the federal and state bureaucracy's for taxes, and the like.

> **COMMENT**: It seems that a lot of consultants are forming corporations because some larger clients wont' deal with sole props. Clients want their consultants to be an employee of some corporation so they so not have to send a 1099 or be liable for possible workers comp claims.

Being a corporation is kind of neat in that your are taken a bit more seriously by the business community. After all you are paying the same kind of taxes they are and putting up with the same massive amounts of inane paperwork that being a corporation entails.

> *TIP: Starting out I strongly urge you not to be a corporation. It is too much work to maintain and will divert you from other more important activities. I started as a sole prop. You can always become a corporation later.*

A partnership is a business relationship between two or more principles, all of which usually own an equal share of the business. There are no special filing requirements and taxes are figured on the percentage of each owner. One very important thing you must know about partnerships. While one partner may own 90% and the other may own 10% under the law, they are equal. This is known as the concept of joint and several liability. Not only can any partner enter into an agreement which binds all partners, all partners are legally liable for the acts of any individual partner.

A good partnership is not based upon agreements but upon handshakes. If you don't trust and/or like your prospective partners, don't enter into the agreement. Think about doing a "joint venture" where you remain independent but cooperate with another sole prop on a project. The possibilities are endless. Talk to a lawyer.

Well over 70% of independent consultants are sole proprietorships. This means that you have proclaimed to the world that you are doing business under another name... but it is still you. If you enter into a lease for a car under you business name, you are still liable for the payments, even if the business goes under or you stop doing business under that name. A sole prop is just a facade. Behind the business is the full faith and credit of *you*!

Once you pick out a name you should make sure nobody else has it. If you decide to be a corporation, each state has procedures for determining if the name has been used. (In California you write the Secretary of State and they will do a name search for you). For a sole prop or a partnership you will go through the records at the county recorder's office to see if the name is available.

This is a simple process where you (or your lawyer) goes down to the recorder's office and either looks in a large book or on microfilm for your business name. If it is not there, it is available.

You then file what is called a fictitious business name statement which tells the world that you are doing business as some entity name. This is known as the DBA form. Usually it takes three minutes to fill it out and you pay a small fee and walk out with some papers declaring you and your business name to be one. It is very easy to file. Just go to the recorder or clerks office and they will be glad to help. Usually there are signs all over the place instructing what to do.

> **COMMENT**: *Most counties do not enforce the requirement that each business name be different. They really don't care. The recording is done so that people won't be infringing on someone else's name or have their name infringed on. If you use someone else's name they may sue you. If there is a dispute over who "owns" the name, usually whoever recorded it first, wins the name.*

In some states you have to "advertise" the fact that you are doing business under a fictitious name in a so-called "newspaper of record". You send one of the copies of the form to the newspaper along with a fee and they do the rest. In most county offices there are drop boxes for the various newspapers (usually they are called the Legal Reporter or something like that) for you to deposit the form and your check (in my county is it $30). The paper will write the "ad", run it the requisite number of times, send you a copy, and file the copy with the county clerk. Again, if your time is limited, you can have your lawyer do it for you.

You might ask, why bother doing the filing at all? Besides the fact that it is the law, you will need evidence of the filing (one of the copies with the county recorder's stamp) in order to open a business checking account at the bank.

Also, in some localities you have to get a business license. However, check to see if there is an exemption for being a home based business.

> **TIP**: *Your recorded name is usually good only for a specified number of years. Be sure to re-record it or someone may pick it up. Often the paper that you advertised in keeps a database and will remind you to re-file.*

Paper, Paper, Paper

The next "tool" you will have to acquire is some business stationery and business cards. For the cards you will have to deal with a printer. Most of the quick-print shops can give you a very good rate on business cards. These orders are shipped out to a large printer that specializes in doing business cards. You select the style of card you want from a catalog and in a week to ten days, they will be delivered.

The style is completely up to you. Your card is how many people are going to first see and remember you. If your card is passed from one manager to his or her friend, that card is going to be your first introduction to the potential client.

I used to tell beginning consultants to spend money and have a logo designed. Logos have been overdone such that everyone has one and nobody will remember your logo from the next person's. A better idea is to use the money for a better quality card, maybe two color. You also might check out The Stationery House, 1000 Florida Avenue, Hagerstown, MD 21741, (800) 638-3033. They have a large catalog of printed items such as business cards and stationery at very reasonable prices.

> *TIP*: Stay away from cards that are double size and which fold in the middle. These tend to be very bulky and people will either tear off half of the card (and half of your message) or they won't carry the thing altogether.

There is no ego booster quite like a good looking letterhead. Unfortunately, a good looking letterhead can set you back a serious number of bucks. This does not mean that you should opt for a poorly done letterhead. There are two simple methods to get a really nice letterhead.

First, find yourself a desktop publishing person (DTP) (look in the phone book or call a mailing house for a referral) and have them throw together something using a nice type font. They can even draw or scan a logo. Have them print out a few copies on a standard 300 dpi laser printer (use 600 dpi for a letterhead with heavy graphics). Take one of the copies to the quick printer, pick out a nice paper, and have them printed.

The second method is even cheaper and yields a really nice letterhead, but takes some time. Find yourself a really good stationery or business supply store and ask for some "touch lettering". There are many bands - Chartpak Velvet Touch Lettering is one. These are sheets of letters which, when pressed with a stylus or the end of a pen, transfer to paper. Pick out a style you like. Put each line of your address on a piece of white bond and then cut the line out and position it on what will become the master. This is called the "paste up". By doing it this way, you can change each line around until you get it the way you like it. Then, with a small drop of rubber cement, glue the lines in place. Use a tiny drop of glue, as you don't want the glue to seep over the edge. The nice thing about rubber cement is that you can easily peel up the line if you change your mind. As for the letters, the transfer process takes some effort in order to get them lined up in a word, but after a few words you will get the hang of it. If you screw it up, the letters will peel off the paper by scraping it with a razor blade. Besides letters, you can buy little designs and pictures which transfer the same way. When you are done, go to the quick printer and have it printed. You can get a hundred copies for under fifteen dollars and the letter sheet costs around five dollars. So, for under twenty dollars you can get a really good looking letterhead.

As for envelopes, cut out your copy (either from the DTP person or via the transfer process above) and let the printer position it for you.

By doing the work yourself or using a DTP person you can get a really niece letterhead at a very reasonable cost. If you go to a trade printer, you could spend some big bucks for stationery. Because it is not too expensive to create your own, you will have no hesitation in changing designs whenever circumstances dictate or when the mood strikes.

Send Your Resume For Our Consideration...

You are faced with a decision. Are you going to use a resume or a printed brochure? Both have their advantages and drawbacks. If you go the resume route, you can type it up yourself and get it cheaply reproduced. It is easy to keep current and most managers are used to reading resumes. A brochure, on the other hand, must be well-written the first time as they are usually more expensive to produce and thus you will not want to update it until you have exhausted your stock. A brochure, however, can have a very professional appearance and could serve to really impress your prospect (remember what was said about image?).

If your technical specialty is in one or two areas and you are going to actively limit yourself to these areas, a brochure might be the better choice. For example, if you are an expert in managing conversions, a brochure that describes the "before" and "after" of one of your previous projects might be very effective. Brochures seem to lend themselves to the specialist and tend to be used as marketing tools for those who work in narrow areas. If you know just what your reader wants to hear than the brochure is probably the route that you want to take.

> *TIP*: If you plan to use a brochure, hire a copy writer and graphic designer to help you. It will cost you several hundred dollars for their services but you will end up with a better product than if you try to do it yourself. Ask your printer for referrals.

The resume route is the most popular, especially for entry level consultants. I am not going to tell you how to write a "basic" resume. If at this point in your career you can't write an effective resume, then there is probably no hope for you as a consultant. Get yourself a good headhunter and a full-time job!

Resumes for consulting are just a little bit different than those used for full-time employment. Look over your current resume. It is probably several pages long and describes in pretty good detail what you have done over the past several years. This is fine when seeking full-time employment because the firm is going to be stuck with you and will want to know as much detail as possible. As a consultant, however, your resume must make you seem as broad based as possible without going into great detail. The reader is not looking at you as a permanent body. All they want to know is if you have any experience in their area of interest. If it looks like you do, you will get called in for an interview. If hired you will have a week or so to prove that what was on the resume can be backed up by results. If it can't, you are out the door.

Take a look at my resume. Notice that it only tells the reader the types of systems I worked on. If that had been a resume for full-time work, each system could have been a separate paragraph. Instead the resume tells the reader just the highlights without boring them with endless details.

You can use a chronological approach if you like but I prefer to use a functional methodology. I try to group my one hundred years of experience into three main areas and still sound as flexible as possible. It works for me.

Conventional wisdom says to keep your resume short. I disagree. Can a client make a business decision to interview you based upon one short page of information? I don't think so. By the same token, avoid sending out War and Peace.

Alan N. Canton

123 Maple Street
Any Town, CA 99999

(999) 999-9999
auto   888-8888

QUALIFICATIONS:

- Twelve years consulting on IBM mainframe, UNIX and PC-DOS platforms.

- Broad experience in data communications, LANS.

- Extensive knowledge of database methodology.

- Multiple computer programming language fluency.

ENVIRONMENTS

- Language: SQL, COBOL, C, BASIC, IBM 370 ALC, 8086 ALC, FOXPRO2

- Operating System: MVS, VM, UNIX/SYSTEM V, MS-DOS, VAX/VMS, MACINTOSH,SUN-OS

- Interface: CICS, TSO/ISPF, CMS, MS-WINDOWS, X-WINDOWS,UNIX /C SHELL, REXX

- Database: DB2/QMF/DB2I, IDMS, ORACLE, PARADOX, EXCEL, CLIPPER, INFORMIX,

- Network: NOVELL LAN, 3270 SNA/SDLC, MICRO-MAINFRAME, 3780 RJE

- GUI: EASEL, OBJECT VISION

RECENT CONSULTING EXPERIENCE:

IBM Mainframe

- Analysis, design, and programming of Legislative Bill History System using client-server methodology via CICS running under OS/2 gated through token ring to mainframe - IBM and Legislataive Data Center: 1992

- Analysis and programming of Fleet Inspection processing modules using COBOL / CICS and ADABASE - CA Bureau of Automotove Repair: 1991

- DB2 / SQL analysis and programming for Personnel Resource System - DLM, Inc.: 1991

- CICS, SQL maintainance programming in COBOL of various health care reporting modules - Quality Medical Adjudication: 1990

- Normalization analysis for large IBM DB2 eligibility database - Quality Medical Adjudication: 1989

- CICS programming of Fire Protection System - CA Department of Forestry: 1988

- Design and implemention of micro-mainframe 3270 and 3780 remote communications - Quality Medical Adjudication: 1989

- Research and presentation to management of new software development methodologies (CASE) as well as advanced communications and networking technologies - Quality Medical Adjudication: 1990

- CICS/IDMS programming for Job Search System - CA Employment Development Department: 1989

- Consultant / Project leder for creation of schema and entity normalization for large hospital certification / licesning system: CA Department of Health Services: 1986

- Communications consultant to integrate 911 emergency system into Fire Protection System - CA Department of Forestry: 1988

- Converstion of Non-Enterprise Accounting System from HP-3000 Image/Query to CICS/VSAM - Sartorius, Inc.: 1986

UNIX Systems

- Responsible for design and installation of TCP/IP UNIX network - Quality Medical Adjudication: 1990

- Installation, configuration and Shell script programming for 3780 RJE Claims Receipt System - Quality Medical Adjudication: 1990

- Analysis and design of ORACLE in-house master database - Health Management Systems: 1990

- C programming of Insurance Claims Price Conversion programs as well as analysis and design of various modules of the Claims Batch System - National Medical Enterprises: 1988

- Responsible for benchmark and procurement of UNIX hardware (Pyramid 9825) - National Medical Enterprises: 1989

- Design and development of communication poller between central UNIX mainframe and multiple remote DOS PC's using UUCP - National Medical Enterprises: 1989

- Network consultant for development of digital imaging applications linking high speed engravers over an IEEE 488 LAN on both UNIX and MS-DOS hardware - Computer Identification Systems: 1985

Micro Systems

- Analysis and programming of hospital claims billing system for electronic submission via CHAMPUS, Foundation Health Care, using Foxpro2 -Primus Healthcare Consulting, Inc. 1992.

- Installed twenty user Macintosh network for executive/administrative services - Health Management Systems: 1991

- C Programming of on-line modules of the Emergency Command Console system - CA Department of Forestry: 1988

- Design and programming in BASIC of Check-It-Out bookkeeping system - Computer Programming Associates,Inc.: 1988

- Installation of first Novell Netware network in CA state government - CA Department of Health Services: 1986

- Analysis, design and programming of prototype modules for Nursing Home Licensing System in BASIC and C - CA Department of Health Services: 1985

- Programming of Employee Skill Tracking System written in Paradox 4GL - Proctor & Gamble: 1985

- C Programming of Loan Number Assignment system - Bank of America: 1985.

- Analysis, design and BASIC programming of Real Estate Analysis system - Computer Programming Associates, Inc.: 1985

DATA PROCESSING EMPLOYMENT EXPERIENCE

Systems Engineer

ELECTRONIC DATA SYSTEMS • San Francisco, CA.1974 to 1978

- Graduated from intensive two year System Engineering Development program .

- Responsible for company RFP solutions on large Medicaid contract bids.

- Programmer/Analyst for health care and banking clients using IBM 370 ALC.

Programmer Analyst
INTERNATIONAL BUSINESS SYSTEMS, INC. Richmond,VA.1971 to 1974

- Legislative advocate on government data processing contracts.

- Completed   IBM Programming/Analysis in-company training program .

TEACHING EXPERIENCE:

- Taught entire 8th grade in rural poverty area school system - Webster Springs, W.VA: 1969-71

- Obtained CA Community College Teaching Credential in data processing: 1980

- Evening instructor in IBM 370 ALC, COBOL, system design and communications - College of Marin, Kentfield, CA: 1980-81

- Evening instructor in introductory programming and database. - National University, Sacramento, CA: 1984 to 1985

EDUCATION:

- Master of Arts, Government, - College of William and Mary, Williamsburg, VA: 1974

- Bachelor of Arts, Economics/Government - University of Virginia, Charlottesville, VA: 1969

ABILITIES:

- The ability to understand and explain in simple, clear language the latest technologies.

- The ability to translate relevant technology into company-relevant business objectives.

- The ability to network widely into non-technical company sectors... sales, manufacturing, finance.

- A strong track record of putting new technology successfully into practice.

Thats The Phone... I'll Get It!

Now that you have all the paper taken care of, there is another tool of the trade you will need. This is your phone.

While you can get a phone number from an answering service that you rent and have them answer it, most consultants find this to be too cumbersome. Your best bet is to have another line installed at your house. This is usually quite simple and won't cost much. In my area the line costs $35 dollars and any wiring needed to put in a new phone jack is about $100. (The wiring you can do yourself). This way you have a personal phone (for you and the rest of the family) and a business line which is a tax deduction.

> **TIP**: When you call the phone company do not tell them it is for a home business. Tell them you need another line because you are "on call" from work and your boss requested you put the line in. This way you will not pay 'business' rates. However, you won't be able to advertise in the Yellow Pages unless you pay 'business rates". Don't worry, the Yellow Pages is worthless for consultants, according to my research.

You must have some method of having it answered when you are not in. If you have a friend, spouse, or "other" who stays home all day, then you are covered. Otherwise you have two choices.

The first alternative is to get call forwarding and route your calls to an answering service. For forty to fifty dollars a month you can get 8 to 5 coverage. Some of them have a hefty one time hook up fee, and you will have to pay the first and last month's service in advance. They will answer in your business name, take messages, and give you voice mail abilities. An answering service is more personal and will not break down when you are waiting for that important call. However, they are expensive and have been known to lose messages that you don't find out about until your prospect wants to know why you didn't return their last three calls. Answering services are inflexible so that if you move you have to be re-hooked up again.

Answering machines are your other alternative. When I first started out in the business my machine cost about $250. I recently bought a terrific AT&T for $70. Machines today are a snap to hook up and have a crisp clear recording and playback capability. You can also get your messages remotely from any phone in the world. (This is really an advantage for me). The down side is that many people don't like talking to machines. A machine really tells the world that you do not have an office with a secretary. At least with an answering service a client might think they were calling a place of business instead of your living room.

My recommendation is to get a machine. Most clients know you are a small business and there is not much of a stigma attached to having a home based business anymore.

> **COMMENT**: Did you ever consider that the President of the U.S. runs much of his business from his home?

Record a message something like "Thank you for calling XYZ Consulting. We pick up our messages hourly so leave one at the tone." Notice it is short and to the point and does not give your life story. People hate long winded messages telling them where you are, when you will be back and what the weather is!

As a consultant, you are on-call all the time. As one manager from the brokerage industry said:

> Sometimes when I am looking for a consultant, the first one that gets back to me is the one that gets the job. Some projects are just too hot to wait around on. The first guy I get on the phone will most likely get the best shot at it.

Just The FAX, Sir!

I am a nut on the fax machine. I recently put one in my home office and I saves me tons of time. It is especially handy when I want to get my resume into the hands of a prospect quickly. Also, I find that faxed letters seem to have a 'sense' of urgency and have a better response rate.

A lot of consultants like to have a fax board in their computers but I have not heard good reports on these things. Also you have to leave your computer on all day. You will find that a good deal of the stuff you fax is not computer generated and having a conventional fax machine makes life easier. The boards are cheaper, but so is their flexibility.

If you are going to get a fax, make sure it has a fax/phone switch built in (almost all the new ones do) and look for a feature called a TAD interface. This lets the machine work in tandem with your answering machine (again most new ones have this). I use a Brother Intellifax 600 which cost me $350. Works great.

Your Computer

It was interesting to find that many computer consultants do not have a personal computer. Many of these people work only on mainframes or do project management and have no knowledge of micro computers.

I don't see how anyone can run any kind of home based business without the aid of a computer, but it is done all the time. If you have a

PC you will agree. If you don't you are in no position to disagree since you don't know what you are missing.

So, if you don't have a micro, consider getting one. I also urge people to spend the extra money and get a laser printer as well as a modem. The computer is the tool of the 90's and with a good computer, modem, printer, fax machine and perhaps a cellular phone, you can compete with any large company out there.

> **COMMENT**: *I am always asked by consultants and non-consultants alike what computer I recommend. I have a Windows based PC, a Macintosh, and a UNIX based machine. Far and away the most versatile system is my Macintosh. The software and hardware hang together well, it is a piece of cake to learn, and the reliability has been terrific. I have never found anything you can do on the PC that you can't do on a Mac. I run my business on the Mac, but often make a living programming on a DOS based or UNIX based machine.*

Human Resources

So much for the hardware. Let's take a look at the human resources you will need. First, and most important will be an accountant. More specifically what you need is someone to give you sound tax and financial advice. This should also be someone who can relieve you of the paperwork of doing your taxes at the end of the year. You can do our own taxes, but the word on the street is that the IRS is less likely to question a tax form done by a professional.

Finding an accountant is no easy trick. In the first place, you don't need a CPA. As a small business, you just will not need the experience and price tag of a senior partner. A 'public accountant' or experienced bookkeeper will probably work out quite well as long as they know tax law and keep up with the latest rulings and changes. Like finding a doctor, ask your friends and others you do business with. When you get a few names give them a call and go see them. Find an accountant with whom you really have a good rapport and with whom you will have no doubt as to which side of the tax fence they are on. Be prepared to pay a hefty hourly rate. Good advice does not come cheap.

I can't emphasize enough the need for a good tax consultant, unless you happen to be an expert in small business tax matters. And even if you are, you are not going to want to spend the hours in March doing your federal and state forms. When your clients want computer help, they get a pro. When you need financial advice, get a pro.

> **COMMENT**: It is said that a doctor who treats him/herself has a fool for a patient. With consultants who do their own taxes, it is truly garbage in - garbage out!

It is getting to the point where people can't even say hello anymore until they have consulted their lawyer to see if their action might result in a lawsuit or what the possibilities are should the other refuse to answer! It is no fiction that our society is simply over legalized. The more lawyers there are, the more complex things seem to become.

> **COMMENT**: The old saying is true. One lawyer in town starves. Two lawyers in town clean up!

Like it or not, you will have to have a lawyer. You may not need him or her for some time it is wise to latch on to one in the early stages of your business life. Fortunately most of your legal work will be mundane so you will not need the services (nor pay the expense) of the legal superstar in your community.

Most of your work will involve the drawing up of contracts between you and your clients. This does not mean that every time you get a client you will have to use a different contract. Many consultants don't use a contract at all. However, if you bid fixed-cost, there will be penalty clauses to apply. It will be absolutely necessary that you have good legal advice before you get into a fixed-cost contract.

> **COMMENT**: You will need a lawyer going in... hopefully you won't need one getting out!.

Besides contracts, you might need specialized tax advice that is beyond the scope of your accountant or bookkeeper. If you make it big and decide to incorporate, you will need the advice of a tax attorney.

If you don't have a lawyer now and are not in immediate need of one, or are not sure how to go about getting one, here is a simple method. In many areas of the country there is a surplus of legal brains. A lot of young graduates are hungry for a new client. Call your local bar association or a local law school and tell them you want a young lawyer who practices general business law. Or, ask what firms might have some very junior members that have just been hired. If reports are to be believed, the bar associations, the law schools and even law firms will fall all over themselves trying to help you.

Many people are scared to death to visit a lawyer. Perhaps this is because in the past lawyers did their best to foster an elite image that made ordinary people feel inferior. With young lawyers out there scratching for clients, you need not fear any of them.

> **COMMENT**: *For the first time in your personal history, you might make more money than your lawyer. ("The times they are a 'changin'!").*

their

Don't be afraid to talk money right up front with the lawyer. Find out what the hourly charge will be for a service and if you fee it is too high, say so and look for another. There are always others out there who can handle your business.

Whether or not you like lawyers, you will feel more secure knowing that there is somebody out there who will rush in to protect your butt should you somehow screw things up at a client's office.

> **TIP**: *When you think you need your lawyer's advice, get it. An ounce of prevention is cheaper than a pound of litigation!*

Insurance: Covering Your Butt

A good insurance agent is an important resource. If you don't have an agent, ask some of the people you do business with... you banker, lawyer, accountant etc. By and large you will not be doing that much business with the agent, but many clients are going to want you to carry a certain amount of insurance and sometimes name them as co-insured. You want an agent who can get you a policy quickly (like in 24 hours).

your

Clients sometimes make you carry insurance because they don't want to be liable if you trip over some coax cable and break your arm. Even though there is probably no way they can escape responsibility if they don't take proper precautions in the work areas, they still make you get a liability policy. The cost of these policies is not too high and you can always cancel it after the contact is up.

Remember all those medical benefits you had when you were a fill-time employee? They are gone now, so you will have to purchase them yourself. You might investigate getting together with some of your friends or other consultants an form a "group" so that you can get a lower rate.

Unless you have been living under a rock, you know about the health care crisis and the stratospheric insurance premiums individual's have to pay. Your only defense is to settle for a policy with a high deductible.

> **TIP: With respect to medical coverage, do not go naked! I have seen it happen to a number of consultants over the years. They figure they can get by without medical insurance. Then "it" happens and they are busted. It is terrible to see. I carry a $2,000 deductible for myself and my wife. I can take a two grand hit. I can't take a two hundred grand hit! I'm serious. Make sure you and your family are covered! Notice that this is one of the very few text items in bold type! Why do you think that is?**

Your last insurance consideration should be your car. If you plan to carry clients around you might need extra coverage. Anyway when (or if) your insurance company finds out that you are self-employed, they may raise your rates by a few dollars. But this increase may be adjusted by the fact that since you are no longer commuting you could be eligible for a reduction. If you do most of your work in your home office and only go to the client's for meetings, you should receive a substantial discount from the rate you paid as an employee driving forty miles round trip a day.

> *TIP*: Your best bet is to find a client close to home, buy a bike, write it off as a business expense (with an investment tax credit), ride to work and save gas!

You Can Take It To The Bank

You are going to need a checking account for your business. This will help you keep your personal money separate from your business income. As far as the tax people are concerned, there is no difference between you and your business (if you are a sole prop), but banks and others that you might want to borrow from do see a difference. They want to see how your business does as a separate entity from you and your other investments. It is a subtle difference, but then again, banks were never number one in the use of sophisticated logic!

You will find that while your personal account might be free, the bank will probably charge a service fee on all business accounts, no matter what balance you keep. So, shop around for a bank. You will find that they all offer different services at different rates.

Many consultants believe that since they are in business they should deal with a large commercial 'business' bank. However, many of these institutions are not going to be interested in you until you can keep some sizable balances. Don't overlook the small boutique banks. Their fees will be the same but you will get a modicum of personal service that the large banks are unable to provide.

> *TIP: Unless you have an enormous vanity, just order the plain, cheap bank checks. If you ever write checks to either employees or subcontractors, they will not be interested in the pretty paper or design.*

If you bank at the main office of a small bank you will get to know the executive staff as well as the loan people on a first name basis. When you need to give a client a bank reference, you can give out the president's name.

> *COMMENT: I bank at The American River Bank in Sacramento, CA. You can call the president and ask about me. Try it if you like. If I were your prospective client could I call the president of your bank and find out about you?*

Book 'em Danno!

You probably use an accountant now to do your taxes. You might consider looking for a bookkeeper to keep track of your income and expenses. This may seem like a needless expense, considering all the accounting software out there that you can buy to keep the books, but it is not.

A bookkeeper will keep everything in tight order each month so that you don't have to run like a chicken with the colonel behind him during tax season, gathering up all your figures and printing the reports to give the accountant.

Most consultants that do not have the time or discipline to keep their own records, contract with a bookkeeping service, usually an independent who works out of their home. They send all their receipts and check stubs to the bookkeeper who sorts it out and sends back nice looking profit and loss statements.

A collection of financial reports are great to have when you need to obtain credit for yourself... house loan, car loan, etc.

> *TIP*: A few years after I started consulting I incorporated. I started using a bookkeeper who I liked very much. I soon moved about a hundred miles away. I continued to use the bookkeeper by mail. This worked out very well. I sent a big envelope of "stuff" and she sent back beautifully prepared reports, as well as the various payroll and other b.s. forms I had to fill out. If you incorporate and become an employee, use a bookkeeper. You will be glad you did.

MAKING THE SALE

I Sell, You Sell, We Sell

We are all salesmen. Those of us that can sell better than the rest usually make more money. True, we may not sell a product or perhaps even a concept, but business is the process of convincing another person that either you are right or they re wrong. Just look back over your career and think about all the situations that required you to be persuasive. How many times did you have to sell the user on an idea? How many meetings have you been in where you had to convince some manager that what was desired just couldn't be done? Business is salesmanship, pure and simple. Those who succeed at it are usually cognizant of the best methods to make sales in their particular situation.

There was a time in American history when the salesman was held in high regard and little boys and girls saw an image that they would like to follow. The salesman was a trusted friend to a business person, one who could be counted upon to give good advice and deliver a good product at a fair price. There was a time that the person who sold you a suit or a dress was the son or daughter of someone that you knew, perhaps grew up with, perhaps a neighbor.

There once was a system of trust between the sales people of this country and the consumers they sold to. Yet today, this is all changed. Perhaps it is due to mass market advertising. Or more likely, it is due to the fact that too many sales people neglected to uphold their end of the trust and sold out to the pursuit of the quick buck. Whatever the cause, we Americans have an extremely high sales resistance. We are just about taught by our parents not to believe what the salesman says. We expect to be cheated and lied to. Perhaps that is why we are.

In spite of the above, more of us are salespeople than at any time in our past. Unless you are a factory worker or a civil servant, the only way you are going to advance up the corporate step ladder is by accomplishing objectives and making sure that you get the credit due you. To succeed, you not only have to be proficient at your craft, you must also have a degree of salesmanship to sell the merits of the objective you want to accomplish. These are often called "political skills", which is nothing more than a euphemism for being a salesman. Even though we don't hold the salesman in high esteem or want to be considered in the same light as the guy who pushes played-out cars down on auto row, in our own working eco-systems we too must sell.

The reason I dwell so long on the concept of everyone being a salesman is that many computer people refuse to go into consulting because they don't want to have to sell themselves in order to get a contract. What they don't realize is that they are already salesmen in their full-time jobs. If they want to really advance, they have to come up with ideas and sell them to their superiors. No only do they have to sell the idea, but they have to sell their own skills and abilities. Many a young employee has come up with a terrific idea to save or make money, only to see it put into practice by someone else who eventually got the praise and promotion. The idea was great; it might have sold itself. However young people fail to sell their own skills and qualifications and thus lose out on the opportunity to carry out their own plan. An old friend of mine, with twenty years of consulting experience told me:

> When I worked for General Motors as an analyst, I
> continually came up with great ideas. I put them
> down on paper and sent them "upstairs". Two months

later a new project was unveiled to implement my idea...but I wasn't on the team! It was not until a few years later that I learned the importance of not only being able to be creative, but also the value of simple salesmanship. I learned to not only pitch the idea, but to pitch myself along with it. A valuable lesson early in life.

Marketing Is Not Selling

It is one thing to be able to market yourself; it is quite another to sell. Marketing is much more impersonal. You are usually dealing with printed matter or you are on the phone. The whole objective of marketing is to get you an opportunity to sell face.

Selling is what is going to separate the successful consultants from those who get a lot of phone calls but very few contracts. It is a simple fact of life. If, as a consultant, you can't sit directly in front of a seasoned technical manager or business owner and actively convince him or her that you are the one for the job, then you have little chance of being successful. Unless you are some well-known local computer genius who has a wide reputation, the business is not going to come to you. You are going to have to go out there and get it.

I have told you how to go about putting together a marketing strategy. Now you are going to learn about actually selling yourself to another person. You may not like the term "selling yourself", but that is exactly what you are going to do.

> *COMMENT: At today's rates, your potential client can get anybody they want by simply putting an ad in the paper. One of the reasons they don't advertise is because they don't just want anyone. They want someone who simply won't turn out to be a waste of their time and money. If you are that person, then you will have to convince the client of it. You will have to sell. Your good looks alone are not going to get you a signed contract.*

The First Phone Contact

At this pint you have practiced a marketing strategy similar to what has been presented earlier and you are now sitting near the phone waiting for that next (or first) contract. If you have done your work well, the phone will ring. It may take a few weeks, but you will get calls. I promise.

Ring!

Unless you are very adept in selling over the telephone, do not let your prospect conduct an interview with you over the wires. You will be at a severe disadvantage in that you will have to overcome a sales resistance to an unknown voice and unknown face.

You have little or no way of seeing "between the lines", as it were, when you are talking with the prospect over the phone. Everything you say can and will be used against you. Used incorrectly, the phone will only screen you out, not invite you in.

You have two objectives in the initial phone contact. First, you want to let the prospect know that you are interested and that you want to come in and sit down as soon as possible (even today, if time permits).

The second objective, although far less important, is to get as much information as you can without getting in to an interview situation. You want to get as many details so that you will be ready for he interview appointment. The kind of questions you will want to ask should concern the technical aspects of the project such as type of machines to be used, software packages, deadlines, etc. You will know what is important to your specific consulting practice, be it programming, design, management, troubleshooting etc.

Don't linger too long or you might be faced with an interview situation. The manager might say, "Now that I've answered your questions, please answer mine." Don't let this happen to you. Do anything you can to get off the line. Tell him you have another call, or that someone is at the door, or the house is on fire.

> *TIP:* Do not pitch over the phone! Selling over the phone requires a special technique and it is usually not suited for selling a service. You may market yourself over the phone or through the mail, but you sell yourself face to face.

Are They Interviews or Sales Meetings?

There are as many interview strategies as there are employment categories. We have all experienced interview situations that were much to our liking, where the management was cordial and receptive. We have also endured interview situations which became ego trips for some petty tyrannical middle manager who enjoyed putting us through stress. You are also probably familiar with the inquisition interview in which you are screened by a panel of team members, some of whom think they are on the FBI terrorist interrogation squad.

Interviews are here to stay. No matter how many computer job matching programs are run, mangers are still going to want to have a face-to-face interview with their potential employees. Some people hate to interview and some really enjoy the challenge of it. To succeed in consulting you just have to be good at it. You must be able to present yourself well in a face-to-face situation.

There is one twist, however. While I have used the word "interview" up to now, so as not to confuse you, you will not be "interviewing". You will be in a "sales situation". No, I am not playing word games with you. There is a big, big difference.

Many consultants make the mistake of thinking they are interviewing for a full-time job. This is a basic mistake. During the full-time employment interview there are, at all times, well-defined lines between both parties - one person is clearly the superior and the other the subordinate. Not so in consulting.

From the minute you set foot on the client's property, you are an *equal*. Many consultants do not understand this and fail to come across in a strong, forceful manner. There is a distinct difference between walking in and asking for a job, and walking in and selling a service. It is important to understand the client/consultant relationship. It is simply the combined efforts of two people working together for a different reason - the client to get his work done, the consultant to earn a living.

We Are All The Same; Just Different!

The sales situation is just the opposite from the full-time employment interview situation. In the full-time scenario, the potential employee enters the meeting as a subordinate, but if hired, *might* one day become an equal of the person doing the hiring. The consultant, on the other hand, comes in to the meeting as a complete equal. He runs his own business and is responsible to only himself for decision-making. The hiring manager, likewise is in a business situation somewhat similar to the consultant. The manager has broad authority to make decisions concerning the enterprise as a whole. Both the consultant and the manager are on equal footing during the sales situation phase.

You must understand that you are not asking for a job. You are there to sell your services. You come not with your hand out, but rather, with your hands full of solutions. You come to the meeting (not "interview" anymore) as a complete equal to the client. For the moment the both of you are on equal footing. But a change will take place.

Remember, the full-timer starts out the meeting as a subordinate, but if he gets hired, he may - in a day, week, or year - be considered on a level equal to the person who hires him. Look at the difference here. The consultant comes in as an equal during the meeting, but if he gets the assignment, the consultant becomes subordinate and will remain so without the chance to ever be considered otherwise.

As soon as the ink is dry on the contract, the consultant is a well-paid whore to the client.

The first mistake that many consultants make is to confuse the roles of who is who during the sales process. Yet it is an important distinction to understand. There is no way that you can effectively sell yourself if you have a mental attitude of your position being subordinate to the manager/client.

> *TIP*: You must recondition your thinking from the days of being a full-timer looking for a job, to the reality of being a businessman making a sales call on a client.

Not Salesmanship, But Closemanship!

There is no book, course or individual that can *completely* teach you how to sell yourself as a consultant. You will master whatever technique you develop by simple experience. This book will give you pointers that should make the sale go somewhat easier and will provide information on techniques that you can use. Understand that you will have to develop your own style, your own pace, your own pitch.

You probably know that ninety percent of salesmanship is the detailed application of the obvious. You have heard them before - things like: maintain eye contact, be a good listener, know your strong points, do your research, ask leading positive-type questions, etc. If you are not familiar with the techniques of basic salesmanship, there are books on the subject. You can find them at the library.

> *COMMENT: I don't cover all of this sales material because there are a million books already on the subject. I like the Tom Hopkins material, but most of the literature on the subject is much the same.*

Instead of selling, you are going to learn closing. There is no more important aspect to selling than being able to close your sale. It is the one aspect that leaves consultants very confused. Just how do you get the prospect to sign the contract and get the purchase order cut? This is the prime objective and you must never forget it.

When you were out there looking for full-time work, all you really had to be was a good conversationalist. You had to be an "all right" person, non-threatening, civil, and perhaps interesting. So long as you possessed some of these qualities and had some knowledge of computers, you could get a job.

From now on, you will have to rely less on your conversational skills and instead, learn how to be a good closer. If you can't close, you can't sell. I you can't get the name on the contract, all that good conversation you had with the prospect becomes nothing more than a bull-session.

Closing is not hard, it just takes a good sense of timing and some courage. It is where you come face to face with the prospect of rejection. This is why so many consultants can talk up a storm when they are in the client's office, but they don't seem to come up with as many contracts as they should. They lose out to someone who might be less of a conversationalist or less even less technically qualified, but who is an astute closer. They lose to the person who actively makes the client want to sign the contract. They lose to the person who leaves the client feeling like they just made the deal that is going to get their name in lights. They lose to good closers.

Establishing Control Of The Situation

Every sales situation is different, yet every situation is the same. Sooner or later you will have to "go for it". You will have to close the sale... you can't b.s. with the prospect forever. Maybe you will get lucky and the client will "close" for you by offering you the assignment. However, this is not likely.

No matter what type of pitch you use, or how you present yourself, you must understand the importance of controlling the meeting. Whether you want to come off as a whiz kid, as a helpful uncle, as a pal, or as God, you must keep in mind that you are in a *selling* situation and *you* must control the direction that gets taken. When you run the show, the sale is yours to lose!

It is important that from the minute you walk in and shake hands with the manager, you are in control and you take the lead. The reason this is so important is that *you* have to do the *selling* so that the manager is able to do his/her job... the *buying*. You must be in control so that you can deal with, or overcome, extraneous factors.

There is the possibility that the manager is so desperate for some help that he/she would sign an elephant as a consultant. On the other hand, he/she might have interviewed ten consultants in the past three days and may have already decided on one or two of them as finalists. Whatever the case, *you* are in the office now and you have only one chance to get the assignment. You can't do much about outside forces except recognize them and try to work with them.

Most clients are pretty adept in interviewing potential full-time employees. But when faced with the choice of selecting a consultant for an important three month contract they do not have the experience to determine the selection criteria. They don't know what questions to ask. They often have little idea as to what qualities they should be looking for. They don't have a set procedure for signing a consultant, like they do for hiring a full-time person. For many, this is a new experience.

So, you must lead the prospect by the hand through the selling and buying procedure in order for you to get the contract. To do this, you must have your pitch down pat. You should know what you are going to say, maybe not the exact words, but at least by subject matter, before you go in. Too many consultants try to wing it and don't end up with a contract they could easily have obtained if they had controlled the selling situation.   By planning your presentation and working your plan, you control the outcome.

> *TIP: Before every sales call I go through a dry run of the first ten minutes, out loud, in the car. When I walk in, I am ready! At least for the first 10 minutes. Work on your own "first 10 minute" play book. That is how the pro's do it. The odds are that if the meeting starts right, it ends right.*

The Prelims

A sales situation is something akin to a title fight. Before the main bout, there are several prelim bouts that have to be endured before the main attraction.   If the *final close* is the title feature, here are the preliminaries you will go through.

THE GREETING: This is the so-called important first moments when the first impression is made. This is where you give the "I'm glad to be here" speech and talk about how nice the office is, the weather, etc.

You want to avoid those awkward first moments where each person is waiting for the other to get started.

Practice these first two to five minutes over and over again. Use a friend as a role player. Get this down pat. You will be glad you did.

THE BILLBOARD: After the initial greeting, you must not let the client take control of things and start asking a lot of questions which are best "asked" and "answered" by you at the proper time.

As soon as the two of you are seated, start right in describing your background and experience. Start out by saying something like "Sue, before we get to your project, let me quickly go over some of my qualifications... ."

Most consultants simply sit back and let the manager gaze over the resume and ask questions. Some clients go right to the project and the consultant misses out on an important selling tool - his/her own background and qualifications. Jump right out there and take the initiative. Because most prospects have no idea how to hire a consultant, they will be very relieved to have you take the lead.

THE TALE OF WOE: This is where you sit back and let the prospect describe the project to you. If you can't remember everything, take notes. Don't interrupt. If the client starts getting off the subject, let them wander. If they ask you a direct question before you have determined that you have the "full story" try delaying you answer.

Let the client tell the story and get the steam out (if a disaster is pending or has already occurred). Keep our mouth shut and your ears open. If you don't understand something, make a note and ask later.

This part may take two minutes or two hours. Don't day-dream. Keep alert and start thinking of solutions.

THE RECAP: Your job here is to recap the problem or reiterate your role in the project as best you can. You can ask questions, but make sure you get the answers and not some long-winded non-answer.

You must came across as a person who understands the client's problems and can solve them Or, you must restate the "mission" so that the client is convinced you won't screw up.

THE QUICK INTERMISSION: Up to this point a lot of information has changed hands and it has been all business. You have done a majority of the talking (selling) and it is now time to slow things down before the closing activities.

You want to get the client as completely at ease as you can. The best way to do this is to start asking about the data center, the products of the company, about the client's background, about anything. While you are giving the manager a chance to get his mind off the project, you should be listening with one ear and coming up with some trial solutions or soft closes that you can use next.

While the client may be doing most of the talking, you must stay in control and bring the conversation back to the project when you are ready.

Some clients will not want to change the subject, but it is important that you take their mind of things for just an instant so that you can get your closing strategy together.

THE BIG PITCH: The client will probably go on forever talking about whatever you asked in the INTERMISSION phase, so you might have to interrupt them by directly changing the subject and getting back on the business track. This is where you have your head together and have come up with some possible solutions or reasons why you should get the assignment. Any solutions you come up with don't have to be the most plausible ideas in the world, or even possible. But you must present some evidence that you understand the problem and that you can handle a solution. You need to explain why you are the one to do the work.

What you are really demonstrating is that you have had some background in the client's technology and that you have several possible solutions in your bag of tricks. Even if your "solution" would cost more than the company is worth, mention anything you come up with to the client. Sell your competence. Make a real pitch and a real impression.

Remember, all the consultants before you got to this point and simply aid, "Yes, it is a big problem (or project) and I'd like to look into it."   The client obviously thought "big deal" and decided to call one more candidate. That is you.

Don't be afraid to hedge your answers. There is nothing wrong in stating, "At first glance, an on-line inquiry for the product file could be set up and..." by all means tell the client that you are not a magician and that you are only presenting possibilities to them. This is more than any of the previous candidates sitting in your place has come up with and the client will be impressed.

Even if you are tossing the bull, and the client realizes it, the impression will be that at least you have the ability to come up with high-quality bull!

Whatever you say, remember that this is the *most important* part of the sale. If you blow the BIG PITCH you might be able to correct yourself in the FINAL CLOSE, but it will be much harder.

It is important that you have total control during this phase and that you do most of the talking. If asked a question which does not fit into your sales pitch just say that you will get to it later, and continue. You must look the client clearly in the eye, talk coherently, and impress the hell out of them. You have all the information from the client and you have had a chance to digest it. You should be able to put what you have learned into the context of your pre-planned sales pitch and come up with an impressive five to ten minute speech outlining as many methods as possible that can solve the problem and why you are the person to do it.

This is not the time to be modest. If you have experience in the type of project at hand, don't be afraid to toot your own horn. The client *wants* to be sold. They called *you*, right? They *have* a problem, right? They *need* it fixed, right? If you have your act together and have controlled the situation, you should have them ready to jump up out of their chair and beg

you to take the project. It is true. You have to
believe me on this. I've been there and I know what I
am talking about.

The Final Close: It's A Wrap!

This brings us to the FINAL CLOSE. The little outline above is
fairly representative of any consultant client interview. You take the
bull by the horns and lead the prospect through the sales "experience"
until you are pretty sure that you can go for the final close. This is the
point that so many consultants are not able to get beyond. They sell
themselves beautifully. They answer all the questions and really impress
the prospect. But they don't get a contract because they don't know how
to go for a close. The client may want to hire the consultant but does not
know how to go about it. Instead of showing ignorance, the prospect
simply says, "Thanks for coming and we will get back to you".

These are the worst six words that a consultant can ever hear. "We
will get back to you" is a statement by the client that the consultant has
failed to make a sale; most often because he or she failed to go for a
close. Technical people, trained in logic always feel that once the
"merchandise" is on the table, the buyer will see the impeccable logic of
making a purchase.

I talked earlier about how high sales resistance is in business today.
You may have sold the client on the idea that his problem can be solved.
But unless you go for a close, you are leaving it up to the client to
overcome their own resistance to making an actual commitment. Unless
you learn to close the sale, you are going to hear a lot of "we will get
back to you" refrains.

You are going to have to be a one-call closer. You might have a
chance to get a second shot, but most often you will either persuade the
client to contract with you right then and there, or you will thank them
for the privilege of the meeting, and you are history.

There is no *sure-fire method* that I can give you to close a sale.
There is just no one close that will always work. There are eight that,
used at the right time in the right manner, to the right person, by the right
consultant, cannot fail to get the consultant a contract. The key is
selection and timing.

Again, like your sales pitch, the wording is going to have to be up to you. The style will have to be yours. The timing and selection will come with experience as well as instinct. After you have been in several sales situation, you will just know what to say. It is uncanny, but it is true.

Your Objective: Conquer The Three Big Fears

One of the main objectives of the CLOSE is to overcome the client's fears. Once this is done, the rest of the sale is a piece of cake. Your prospect will have one or all of three common fears.

The first is the money fear. Clients are often afraid that they will not get their money's worth by hiring a consultant. This is another way of saying they think they will get cheated. In your close, you must emphasize that the money they are going to spend is going to be small compared to the value that they are going to get. When you deal with owner-clients who are extremely bottom-line oriented you must demonstrate that this money will be well-spent. You should make use of all the information that I presented in earlier chapters about the value of consultants. You should hit on points like:

- No benefit payments (medical, etc.) to the consultant

- Consultant not on payroll

- Consultant billed as a vendor (deductible cost item)

The second fear that you may have to overcome is one that you might create yourself. They may not feel you can do the job. In the early part of the CLOSE you must, again, state your qualifications and how you have the necessary experience and qualifications to do the job. If you don't have the actual experience, you must create in the mind of the client the idea that you are the closest they are going to come to finding the candidate they are looking for. You should dwell on the idea that, as a consultant, you can do a better and faster job than if the client goes out and hires either a full-timer or another consultant. You should impress upon them the fact that they are not taking a risk. If you can't cut it, then you will be history.

TIP: You might mention to them your agreement to the "whore principle". I often tell clients that I become their personal slave and that there will be no management problems or policy disputes. When they say jump, I ask 'how high'! (You start out equal, but when they sign, you become subordinate).

The third fear that might be present is more esoteric in nature. This is the fear of what the manager's peers will think by bringing you onboard. The client wants to know whether hiring you is going to bring credit or discredit to him and/or the department. You must assure them that, by signing a consultant (especially you) they are not only doing the right thing for the company, but perhaps for his/her own career. You must mention the fact that many companies have used your services and have been the better for it. You must assure them that you will not run the company or the department into the ground. Let them know that *you* are the best insurance they have for a successful completion of the project or resolution of the problem.

Eight Final Closes: Use One or Some!

Do not forget the objective: to get the client to sign your contract or at least shake hands on a deal. This is what it is all about. The FINAL CLOSE is the 'final frontier' (for you Star Trek fans). When you get a firm handshake or the signature on the contract you have made a sale. If neither of these occur, you have lost a sale.

It is precisely at this point in the sales situation that most consultants are completely inept. They cannot do a FINAL CLOSE. They might lead up to it, but they don't really have a closing strategy in their mind. Most consultants get to this point and simply ask the manager, "Well, Mary, what do you think?" They are going to let the manager close the sale! Obviously, this works some of the time. More often it is the consultant who *has* a closing methodology that *makes* the sale. The others receive a "we will get back to you" reply.

Take a look at eight possible closing methods that are used by consultants. Remember, some are better than others in certain situations or with certain client personality types. Another thing to remember is timing. Close no sale before its time! If you maintain control and follow the sales situation sequence presented earlier, one of the following CLOSES will work for you.

THE TAKE-IT-FOR-GRANTED CLOSE: The secret to getting contracts is to expect contracts. In this close you communicate to the client that it is not a question of "if", but a question of "when" you are supposed to start.

All you need say is that you are available on Monday, as soon as the contract is signed. You are leading the client into accepting the fact that you are obviously going to be the consultant for the project.

You can get out your calendar from your planner and check through it, saying that you can be in the office five days from now, ready to start.

If you are positive, absolute, and confident, you will create these same feelings in the client's mind and you will make a sale. In using this close, you are simply taking it for granted that both of you have 'covertly' agreed that you are the person for the assignment. All that is left is the signing of the contract... a mere formality.

This is a really simple close to do, and if it fails, you can fall back and try it again later.

THE SUBORDINATE QUESTION CLOSE: This a slight variation of the previous close. However, here you get the client to make a decision on a relatively minor matter which helps them make up their mind on the major matter (of using you as their consultant).

You might say, "Well, do your consultants bill you every week or every two weeks?" They will then tell you to submit *your* bill whenever they want it.

You might ask if they want you to wear business attire or if casual clothes are okay. If they say "You can wear jeans if you like" you've done it. Agree on a start date and get out of there.

The client is not afraid to make a *minor* decision, and using this close will help them make the implied *major* decision. Like the previous close, this is an easy one to use and little is lost by trying it.

THE TAKE-ACTION CLOSE: At the point that you are ready to "go for it", you get the client to take some physical action that will cement the arrangement.

Most often this is a contract signing. You show the client the contract, go over it point by point and have them sign it. The contract should be simple (I will talk about contracts later) and should be filled out in advance.

Say "Sign here and we are partners!". You want to treat the signing as a mere detail. The TAKE-ACTION close has many variations.

You can simply say "Bill, why don't you give me a tour of the shop?" Or, "Why don't you introduce me to Mary Smith who you mentioned earlier?"

By taking some action the client has confirmed, perhaps not in so many words, that you are going to be their person.

This is a very powerful closing method, so find the words that go with it, the "action" that will work for you, and use it.

THE TOMORROW-IS-TOO-LATE CLOSE: This is a simple one that can be very effective when the client has a really hot project or big problem and needs to get off the dime. You merely bring this unpleasant fact to their mind and you may have the contract.

You have to impress on them that you are available right now (or in a week), and that if they want to take longer to decide, you just might have to take a contract with that other company that you are going to see tomorrow afternoon.

You also might say that the available talent pool out there is slim and getting slimmer. If they want you, then now is the time to say so.

By using this close, you have established a sense of *urgency* in the mind of the client as well as the fear that they may not be able to find someone as good as you for a long time.

I *always* use this as my first closing attempt. If they reject the reasoning, I try to establish in my mind "why" and start planning on another close.

THE FREEBIE CLOSE: This close should be used when you think all else is failing. You should hold it in reserve. The object is to offer some inducement to the client so that they think they are getting something for nothing.

This is when you tell them, "I don't charge extra for system documentation. It is part of the deal." All along you assumed that you would provide good documentation to your client. But they have probably been stung by consultants who did poor documentation. Thus, you are offering something for nothing, or so the client believes.

If you are a technical writing consultant, you might also show them fancy binders with their firm's name lettered in. You "deliver" these at "no extra cost".

Most consultants say that they find this close hard to use and is best utilized as a last-ditch effort.

Most high-tech clients know that nothing ever comes free. However, some consultants in the survey say they have gotten contracts by saying, with a humorous smile, "And John, if we can come to terms, the end-of-project party is on me!" Seasoned data processing managers find it hard to tun down the inducement of eating free food and getting a good buzz on!

THE LIFEBOAT CLOSE: This is a simple and crusading method to get the client to decide on you as their choice. You want to let them know that you have done work for people or companies that they admire. You let the client know that other firms have been in the same "boat" that they are in now, and that you have been a "lifeboat" to the rescue.

This close consists of telling a relevant business story so that the client can see him/herself in the same light of another client's experience. We all like to imitate the actions of people we respect.

Say to the manager, "Mary, your problem sounds much like the one Jim Smith had over at Armadillo, Inc. Jim reminds me of you - young, dynamic (pick some good sounding traits)... and he had the same type of project that you have.... So he and I did... and did ..." etc. When your client realizes that others have been in the same fix and that you have bailed them out, they will hunger for your contract.

In this close you can effectively utilize a well-put-together reference list. Even better, you can ask to use the phone and call one of your best references right then and there. If you can't get one on the line, no matter. Your prospect is going to admire a consultant that has the confidence to call a reference during a sales situation. This close and variations of it may be the only tools you ever need to make sales.

THE SEEK-AND-YE SHALL RECEIVE CLOSE: This is also a weaker type of close than the others, but it does work with certain personality types and under certain sales situations. With this close you simply ask the manager for the business. That's right - simply ask.

One situation where you might want to employ this is when you are in the middle of an inquisition with two or three company employees. When the conversation finally hits a lull, you should say something like, "Okay, ladies and gentlemen. I think it is time to get down to it. In understand your project. I think I'm the best person for the job. Can I have the contract?" If they say no, you can backtrack and find out why, and try another close.

This also works on the client who has a "suspicion complex". They have an inferiority complex, are unsure of themselves, and feel that you are trying to trick them into signing. By simply asking for the business, you can put them at ease and give them a sense of self-worth.

The type of prospect who has a terrific ego and wants to be asked for everything is also a candidate for this close.

So is the exceptionally bright manager, who was once a sales person and may know the manipulation that goes on with the other close techniques. Just asking for the business makes these types of people feel important and can close sales that other consultants could not make.

THE LOGIC CLOSE: When you are dealing with the technical heavy type, you can often employ logic with great effect. These people try to stay so open-minded about everything, they often have difficulty in making up their mind about what shirt they should wear in the morning!

The logic close will appeal to them. Here you summarize to your prospect all the pros and cons about bringing you on as a consultant. This can be very effective if done on a blackboard *and* you know what you are doing. You can admit to certain negatives, so that you can knock them down by positives. "John, it may cost you a few dollars to use me, but when you consider the type of experience needed, and the fact that you won't have need for me when the project is done, you really are better of in using a good consultant."

You go through the pros and cons of making a decision. This client wants evidence to help them make up their mind. If you give this evidence to them correctly, you close a sale and have a new assignment. On the other hand, if you do this close poorly, you can talk your way right of the door. Be careful with this one. It may sound easy, but it isn't. Be well-rehearsed before you try it out on a live prospect.

Drop Back and Punt

You can get any contract you want if you know how to close. The trick is in knowing *what* type of close you are going to use. You should be figuring this out during the phase of the sale that we called the QUICK INTERMISSION. If you size up your prospect correctly, and understand what is happening during the sales situation, you should be able to pick the type of close that will work.

If there is still sales resistance on the part of the client, either you have not done a complete job of selling, or you picked the wrong close. All is not lost. You just have to drop back into one of the previous sales phases and try to make up for what you didn't accomplish the first time around. Then try a different close.

There are going to be those sales situations where things just do not go right. You know that you haven't convinced the manager that you are the one, and you can see the six pallbearers of consultants coming at you ("we will get back to you"). There are several techniques that you can use to rescue a sale. Sometimes they work, sometimes they don't.

You can try to change the subject. Get to talking about anything other than the business at hand. Maybe you can get the manager to be interested in your personality so that while he/she may think that someone else is more qualified, he/she will feel that working with you will be more pleasant. Get back to a close when you feel that the air has been cleared.

Another technique is to admit you have not convinced them. Put everything on the line and ask them point-blank what it would take for you to be the consultant they are seeking. If they come back with the "we want more experience" response, you have to come back with a sales point - be it that you are cheaper than some heavy that they saw yesterday, or that you are a harder worker, or that you love the company and might consider a full-time job after the project, or whatever.

Another technique that has worked for consultants when they hear the death-knell is to express extreme remorse in missing out on a chance to be allied with such a good firm, and that now they will have to accept that offer with their competition down the street.

> **COMMENT**: *It is not an outright fib - you never know if the competition down the street is going to call you during the next day or two!*

There is another situation that is going to happen to you. The company may have a project, but they don't plan to staff it until a month from now. They are simply interviewing to see what kind of talent is out there and what it will cost. You are the merchandise and they are the window shoppers.

It can really level you when, at the end of forty minutes, they say that you are really impressive but that they don't expect to be getting the project under way for thirty or sixty days. (Of course, if you had done your homework earlier, this would not come as a surprise.) When it does happen, just shrug it off. Continue to make a strong close. You never know when you will be able to change their minds; they have a live one here and it might be wise to get going on the project earlier than planned. Hell, they can always find something else for you to do until they firm up their plans. Suggest this and you might just get on board.

If, when you hear their plans for a delayed start, you give up the ghost, you don't even have a chance for fate to intercede; as happened to one consultant from Chicago:

> I was interviewed by a project manager and his technical heavy. Every time they told me about their plans to start the project to revamp their work-in-progress system in two months, I kept trying to get them to start now. During my third attempt, a woman walked in and told the project leader that she was fed up with the "damn system", the inventories didn't

balance, and the accounting was all screwed up. "I want it fixed and I want it fixed now" she said, not too sweetly. They signed my contract right there. It was the vice-president of operations and when she wasn't happy, "wasn't nobody happy!"

As a final word, do understand that there are going to be sales that you don't close. It may be your fault or it may not. It may be that the manager did not feel well and decided that today was not the day to buy a consultant. Whatever the case, never get angry and never apply any heavy pressure. Sure you feel rotten! It is going to happen many times in your business life so you might as well get used to it instead of fighting it.

Win or lose, you must always write a follow-up letter. If you win, express in the letter how you are looking forward to being allied with their firm and that you have absolutely no doubts that the project will be a success. If you don't get the contract, write a warm thank-you letter and remind them to keep you in consideration should something else develop later. You may not have made a sale this time, but you have at least opened a door.

> **COMMENT**: *Sales is the name of the game and closing is the most important thing in sales. It is not easy. It is hard work in developing a good sales presentation. It takes a good deal of experience to get it down right. But you can do it. Tens of thousands before you have and thousands after you will too. Though I said it earlier, it bears repeating: If high-tech consulting were easy, every technically literate person in the country would be one.*

Willy was a salesman. And for a salesman, there is no rock bottom to the life. He don't put a bolt to a nut, he don't tell you the law or give you medicine. He's a man way out there in the blue, riding on a smile and a shoeshine. And when they start not smiling back - that's an earthquake. And then you get yourself a couple of spots on your hat, and you're finished. Nobody dast blame this man. A salesman is got to dream, boy. It comes with the territory.

Arthur Miller

Death of a Salesman (1949)

10

CONTRACTS AND MONEY

Should You Use A Contract?

Believe it or not, most consultants do not work under a contract with their clients. Beyond a simple handshake and an agreement of what the rate will be, there are no other formal understandings between the majority of consultants and their customers. The reason for this is that most consultants do not know what to put into a contract and once they have a verbal offer of a position, they are simply afraid to bring out a contract and take a chance that it might frighten the client into reconsidering the whole thing.

This all goes back to the fact that consultants just do not know how to close a sale. It is too bad, too, because the contract can be a very powerful sales tool, if used in the right manner. It can serve as a perfect lead-in to the final close.

Picture yourself in a prospect's office. You are ready to go for a close. While you are talking about how great you are, you reach into your brief case, pull out the contract, and say something like, "I took the liberty of filling out a contract before I came, so let me quickly explain how it protects you." Before you even give the client a chance to breathe, you start explaining the terms while they are looking at the form.

If they object to contract talks at all, you know that you have not properly sold them and it is time to drop back and do some more sales work. If they start quibbling over some point in the contract, you know they are sold on you and all you have to do is get the signature.

> *TIP: Contracts can become sales aids for the consultant as well as provide an important means of protection and understanding between the consultant and the new client.*

In God We Trust; All Others Pay Cash!

Another reason so many consultants work without contracts is that they trust their clients and the clients trust them. While this sounds all well and good, I have problems with the concept. Originally (say ten years ago), the ranks of the consultant army were thin; not too many people in the business, and those that were consultants were good people who knew what they were doing. Nobody was going to get ripped off. Today, however, with so many new people deciding to take the plunge into consulting, there are many people who really are not quite ready for it. This undermines all the good will that has been built up during the past decade. It is sad, but true.

In the 1990's there is going to be a proliferation of computer consultants as well as an increase in fees, such that the client companies are going to have to take some precautions against the rip-off artist. It is one thing to do business over a handshake for twenty dollars an hour. But, more and more companies are reluctant to do the same business over the same handshake for sixty dollars an hour.

There was a time when a person was hired to simply do whatever he was told. Then along came the personnel people and the "job description" was invented. Well, the same thing is happening in the consulting field. More and more firms want a clear-cut written understanding of what their money is buying. It won't be long until contracts are going to be used as instruments of performance evaluation.

During the 1990's it is likely that our contracts will get longer and more explicit as to just what is supposed to be accomplished and in what time span.   Of course, there are going to be court cases and some lawyers are going to have a field day!

> **COMMENT**: When more and more people who are less and less qualified enter into contracts with companies to do harder and harder tasks, well, you might just think about giving up this game and getting yourself a law degree!

Don't Leave Home Without One!

Working without a contract gives you absolutely no advantage and actually puts you in a slightly legal disadvantage. It is true that if there is no contract between you and the client, there is no record as to who is responsible for what. This is all well and good, if the client is satisfied.

But, what happens when a dispute arises?   The answer is simple. Your check is going to be held up until things get ironed out. If they are not ironed out, the check might be withheld permanently.   That is all you need! What if some user decides that he doesn't like the reporting system of the project (even though he signed of on it two months ago!) and the manger, in order to placate him, hands you your hat. The hat is one thing. but what happens when they owe you for three or four weeks of work?   Try taking a sob-story like that to a lawyer. You will be laughed out of the office, and they will still charge you a hundred dollar consultation fee.

A contract is not really going to protect your position with the client because there has never been a contract that could not be broken. In fact, one of the important terms of the contract is that it can be broken. Your contract will probably serve three substantive purposes.

The first purpose that it legally establishes you as an independent business person as far as the IRS is concerned. If there is ever a question as to whether you earned some income as a contractor, or as the IRS might claim, as a pseudo-employee, you have proof through a signed document that you are considered as a consultant by those who pay your fee. This might seem like a small thing now, but wait until you are called down for a audit because the government thinks that you are a wage-earner and, thus, not allowed all the business deductions you took! With a contract (and good documentation) your butt is covered.

The second purpose is that the contract seals the rate of pay that you will get. It is not left to a handshake or a gentleman's agreement. There is nothing worse than receiving a check for a bundle less than what you were expecting, simply because when you said "forty" they heard "fourteen".

The third function is that your contract projects from being dragged into court, and perhaps having to pay a lawyer everything you own or hope to earn! Outside of a few sensational computer crime cases that have been committed by consultants, very few of us have been taken to court and sued for negligence. However, it is bound to happen sooner or later. By having a clause that everyone agrees to some form of binding arbitration, you can at least avoid a long and costly court case. Nothing is going to protect your butt from a negligence suit. If some client is out to get you, you better get a lawyer. However, your contract can specify the mechanism for solving disputes, short of a ten-year court case (which means ten years of legal fees).

A Sample: Use At Your Own Risk!

The sample contract that I present is one that is used by many consultants. You will notice that it doesn't read like the fine print on the backside of your mortgage papers. If you really do want to scare your prospect into reconsidering, just hand them some long drawn-out contract pages written in complicated legal lingo. The first thing they will want to do is have it reviewed by the firm's legal department. In reality they will throw it out and look for another consultant! You want to present to the client something they can easily understand. This is the prime strength of the sample presented here. It has all of the things that you should put into a contract, yet it is still easy to understand.

> *TIP: I have seen many contracts that (probably) provide "better" legal protection and cover a wider variety of issues. However, this contract is simple, straightforward, and, understandable by the average client manager. Don't use this contract on my say so because I have no legal background. I like it, but that does not make it right for you! Take this to your lawyer for review as it may not be applicable to your particular situation!*

SAMPLE CONTRACT

TERM

_____, herein referred to as the Client Company, contracts with _____ herein referred to as the Consultant, for a period of _____, beginning _____ and ending _____, to perform various computer related consulting functions.

CANCELLATION OR MODIFICATION OF CONTRACT

Whereas both the Client Company and the Consultant agree to the length of the contract, both parities understand that unforeseen business situations can develop and, as such, the actual length of the contract can be reduced or the entire contract canceled by either party without notice or penalty.   The term of this contract can be extended only by mutual written consent of both parties.

CONFIDENTIALITY AND OWNERSHIP

All programs or systems developed by the Consultant either alone or jointly with Client Company staff, remain the sole property of the Client Company and may not be given, divulged, or sold to any outside party by the Consultant without written permission of the Client Company.

COMPENSATION

The Consultant will receive an hourly straight time rate of _____ for each actual hour worked.

Unless otherwise agreed via a separate amendment, the Consultant will submit a statement of hours worked to Client Company on the _____ (and) _____ of each month. The Client Company agrees to pay the Consultant in a timely manner. Consultant will receive only the straight time rate and will not bill for overtime rates.

The Client Company agrees to pay for any transportation and travel expenses incurred at the request of the Client Company with exception of travel costs to the Client Company's office located at

_____.

STATUS

Consultant shall not be deemed to be an employee of the Client and Consultant will exercise all tasks in an independent manner including, but not limited to, arrival and departure times, format of finished product, and location of work.

LOCATION OF WORK

Work may be performed at either the Client Company's usual place of business, or the Consultant's place of business, or both. It is not to be assumed that work it to be performed only at Client's place of business.

STANDARDS AND ETHICS

The Consultant , although independent, will make his best effort to abide with any/all usual standards of business practices requested by the Client Company including, but not limited to, dress codes, attendance at meetings, entertainment functions, secrecy of Client Company's business, etc.

The Client Company will not request or in any way expect the Consultant to perform any action contrary to the laws of the United States, or the State of _____, or any of its local jurisdictions.

DISPUTES

Both parties agree to summit all disputes arising from the business relationship entered into by this contact to binding arbitration via the American Arbitration Association and to abide by its decision. Both parties agree to evenly divide any costs of the arbitration process.

ENDORSEMENT OF TERMS

Both parties enter into this contract in good faith and agree to all terms as stated. Any alterations are stated in a separate amendment initialed by each party. This contract can be amended or altered from time to time by written mutual agreement of both parties..

(Signatures and dates)

Analysis Of The Contract

There are a few items that you should notice. Right off you can see that there is the proverbial "Catch-22." It is probably due to some human flaw, but we tend to always write contracts which state that we can get out of the contract we are entering. This makes the contract little more than a handshake in writing! The fact that either party can terminate the contract without notice, puts the client on notice that you can get your butt out anytime you want. It also tells them that they can easily fire your butt any time they desire. In reality, both of you know this when entering a consultant/manager situation, but it is nice to have it in writing. The section actually goes to the advantage of the client. They know that there is less chance of you walking off the project, at least if you value your reputation. However, they also know that they would not suffer the *least hesitation* about dropping you if the need warranted.

The section on confidentiality and ownership of the work is another one of those business-like kisses. You are telling the client that you will not run off with all the software and/or solutions that you write or design and sell it to their competitors. First of all, you wouldn't do such a thing. But if you did, the client knows that you are probably smart enough to do it without ever getting caught!

The section on standards and ethics states that you are not a crook and that you have no intention of working for your client's in-house Mafia.

> **COMMENT:** *Didn't some famous person once say to the nation, "I am not a crook, I am the president, make no mistake about it"?*

The section on location of work is put in for your friendly IRS. If they ever claim that you are not an independent contractor, you can show the contract which declares your independence to work wherever you wish. The section on status also is put in for the same reason.

With respect to the term of the contract, it is the usual practice to contract for a fixed period of time (your lawyer will tell you that a legal contract must have a beginning and an ending.) When the deadline is nearing, and there is still work to do, most consultants use some type of contract extension form. Of course, if you are going to re-negotiate your rate, you will probably want to write an entirely new contract.

A Few More Words On Lawyers

I am not down on lawyers. I think they are terribly necessary for consultants, especially those who are new to the business. You just never know when some client is going to file a complaint.

> *COMMENT: I tell the following story in my seminars. It seems that a minister, a doctor, and a lawyer were adrift on a raft. After several days, land was sighted, and although there were signs of human habitation, no persons were in view. Since the drift was away from the island, the lawyer volunteered to swim ashore and get help to the stranded men. Just as he was about to dive into the water, the minister urged a word of parting prayer. So, a brief religious service was held. Then with great anticipation, they watched their companion jump in and start to swim toward shore.*
>
> *At once they were horrified to see a huge shark heading directly for the lawyer. At the last moment the shark veered away and the swimmer was saved. Two minutes later another shark came into view and he, too, veered sharply away when he came close to the swimming lawyer.*
>
> *"There!", said the minister, triumphantly. "Observe an answer to our prayers. Because of our service, the Lord has preserved our friend from the hungry sharks."*
>
> *"Well, that may be,", said the doctor, dubiously. "But, personally, I'm inclined to think of it as professional courtesy."*

Shark or not, you should have the name of a good lawyer on a card in your wallet. You are a business person, and as such, you are fair game for anyone to pick on(in a legal sense). Someone just might sue you when you slightly scratch their fender. Who is to say some client won't take you to court fro screwing up their accounts payable system? Trust me on this (I have been there)... an ounce of prevention, along with a good lawyer, can help you sleep better at night.

The most important function that your lawyer is likely to serve is to help you draw up contracts between you and your client when you do fixed-bid work. The sample contract presented in this chapter is quite adequate for simple time-and-materials contract programming. but when you get into the complexities of doing fixed-cost work, there are many contractual considerations that you must take into account.

Contract negotiations can be difficult, especially for computer people. If you are going to take on a consulting assignment where you provide project management, or perhaps complex design work, you will need a lawyer to help draw up the papers as well as negotiate.

A well trained attorney can keep the negotiation phase on track by keeping both you and your client from getting bogged down in technicalities. The lawyer can answer all of the "what if" type of questions, and this can really help speed the process along.

Also, many clients will have one of their company lawyers present during the talks and it is imperative that you also be represented.

Finding And Using Your Hired Gun

Years ago I didn't advise so strongly about having, needing, and finding a lawyer because I (wrongly) assumed that all consultants had one. And, I get asked all the time about finding the right attorney. Ask ten friends for the name of their lawyer, and it is a safe bet that eight of them will not have a name to give you.

> *COMMENT: Just because a lawyer is right for your friend, is no indication that he or she will be right for you. You also might end up with a lawyer how has a "name" and, thus, could be beyond your price range and/or not have the experience you need.*

Look for a lawyer who has a background in corporate law and who understands the ins and outs of what is called "intellectual property". Most of the larger firms have an attorney or two who keep up on this facet of legal study.

With the growing glut of lawyers you probably won't have much trouble finding one who will be happy to work for you. Lawyers like working with technology consultants because we often come into contact with more "important" people in a given year than would an average owner of a small business. And if we like our lawyer, we refer them. They know this.

As I said in the chapter on Tools Of The Trade, interview several lawyers until you find one you can work with.

When you bring in a lawyer to help with a contract matter, there is one rule you should always follow. No matter how much or to whom you throw the bull with during the negotiations, with your lawyer you must be perfectly straight and honest. It makes no sense to misrepresent yourself to the person who is being paid to represent you! Don't tweak or manipulate your lawyer. Let him/her know what your "real" bottom line is and what you will accept and what you won't. Tell your lawyer what you *really* want and what you are *willing* to accept. Let them do their job and follow their advice.

Many large clients will have boiler plate agreements or contracts that they will want you to sign. These have been drawn up to protect *their* interests, not *yours*. Pass these by your lawyer and if they say not to sign, don't sign!

> **TIP:** *This is especially important when dealing with brokers (I'll talk about them later). Anytime you are presented a contract to sign by an agent or a broker, have your lawyer read and approve it. I have seen countless consultants get burned by contract language they didn't understand and didn't have reviewed.*

If someone files a complaint against you, (this is usually for breach of contract) do not try to settle it yourself. You can do more damage to your position. Unless you have a legal background, don't do what you don't understand because you could lose your house, savings, and possessions. Let the lawyer handle it and follow his/her advice. Again, I've been there. I'm telling you the truth.

Finally, do not hesitate to use your lawyer to enforce your contract. More than one consultant has had to have their attorney write a letter to a client in order to get a final payment sent out. Again, I've been there!

> **COMMENT:** *Lawyers get a bad rap and maybe it is deserved. I don't know. All I know is that it is a big hard mean world out there and my clients have and use their legal resources for their advantage. I'd be stupid if I didn't use mine for the same purpose. And you would be too!*

Finding The Prevailing Rate

You will not work for free. You will have to establish a billing rate, even if you plan to work fixed price.

In a previous chapter we talked about calling other contractors to get information about the local market. As I reported, you will probably be able to obtain this information since most consultants are not hesitant to exchange information in the hopes of being able to call on you later for the same information. But, rates are an entirely story. Consultants do not like to reveal their rate, even to those whom they know well, much less to a stranger. So you can save some bad feelings all around by not asking directly.

The key word here is "directly". It will not take you long to find the prevailing hourly rate in your specialty if you simply ask other consultants what the *range* of rates are for any particular area or skill. You will get a pretty wide range, but you can narrow it down.

> **COMMENT**: *Often two consultants with similar skills doing almost exactly the same work, will get different rates. One of them did not know what they were worth to the client, or was a poorly informed abut the rate structure in their area.*

If there is a body-shop agency in your area, you can easily get in touch with them and make an inquiry. A rough rule of thumb is that most agencies take from 20% to 30% of the total billing. So, if they say they will pay you $30 an hour and you assume that this is, say 78% of the total billing (they take 22%), just divide what they pay you by your percentage of the billing to get the prevailing rate. In this case the going rate would be in the area of $37 to $42 an hour. ($30/.78=$38.46). (There is an entire chapter devoted to brokers.) Work with the numbers and you will get a pretty good idea of what to bill.

Another method is to call the managers of several firms in your area and flat out ask them. Don't give you name if you can help it, and tell them you are doing some survey research. Most will cooperate, in fact they will be flattered that you called the to ask.

> **COMMENT**: *I know one consultant who uses this as a marketing methodology. He calls managers asking for rates. He starts "shmoozing" with them on the phone and often ends up going in to meet them. I don't like cold calling, but it works for some.*

You have to figure out where you are (or are going to be) in the rate picture. You have to remember that the higher you price your services, the more responsibility you are going to have in giving the client their money's worth. It is one thing to take a 15 minute coffee break at $20 an hour, and quite another to do it at $60. In the first case, the client has staff people at more than $20 an hour, and they take breaks, so he probably won't think much about it. But he probably doesn't have anyone earning close to $60 an hour and might kick your butt to the food-stamp office if you try to bill for a coffee break.

My advice is to simply be honest with yourself. If you have extensive experience and the assignment calls for this, then you can command a good price. Go for the gold. You have to earn it when you can. The same goes for the case where you have a high degree of expertise in a particular application, even if you are not a technical wizard.

But face facts. If you are simply a programmer, with three or four years of experience and not a lot of exposure to some of the more advanced computer concepts, you cannot justify charging $80 an hour.

Your rate is a statement about where you see yourself in the hierarchy of high-tech consulting. You can set your own position. But if you get into a sales situation and the client finds out that you are not "hot" enough to charge what you want, they are going to send you back to the street. And they will tell their friends. So be realistic.

> **TIP**: Do your first contract for 15% under the lowest prevailing rate. Do the second one for 5% under.

The "Interest" Rate Method

Unlike full-time employment, where you can usually expect a salary adjustment only once a year, in consulting you have the opportunity to raise (or lower) your rate every time the contract expires. For some consultants, this can be six or seven times a year, even if they stay with the same client.

You can use this fact to help you make up your mind what you should charge. For example, say you are considering taking a project that might bore you to tears, one which you really don't want. but since you don't have anything else cooking, you figure that you might as well take it. In this case you might give yourself an extra five dollars (or more) an hour to give the project some incentive. If you don't get it, well, something will come along. If you do get it, at least you will be paid well for it. (So what if it will be the 10,000th time you have designed an accounting system.... you can cry all the way to the bank!)

On the other hand, if a project comes your way that you really have to do, either because the application is really interesting or the experience will be invaluable, then you can cut the rate for the opportunity to get on a project that will be fun and challenging.

The Short Rate-Long Term Mistake

Many consultants are quite willing to trade long-term contracts for a short or lower hourly rate. It is analogous to a volume discount a manufacturer gives to a large customer. On the surface it makes sense.

Don't do this. You will be, in effect, averaging down your income. The objet of this business is to make money. You should do the things that make you the most money, not the least.

Your four alternatives are (from most money to least money):

- Charge a high rate all the time.

- Charge a high rate for long term, low rate for short term.

- Charge a low rate for long term, high rate for short term

- Charge a low rate all the time.

There are only so many billable hours in a year. Every hour that goes by cannot be replaced. Thus, you must look at hours as your "inventory". You want to price your inventory as high as possible to maximize your return. If you sell most of your inventory at a low price (long project, lower rate) you will be making less than if you reverse the pricing structure and try to dispense as little inventory as possible at the low rate.

The only way you can price most of your inventory at a low rate is if you make a tremendous return on the little bit of inventory you make a high rate on. Thus, if you can work for three months at $100 an hour and the remaining nine months at $30 an hour, you are better off than if you work the whole year at $50 an hour.

Try to average up. You do this by working longer at a high rate than at a discounted rate. Almost every consultant you meet will do just the opposite (unless they have read this book).

> *TIP*: Don't be like a software vendor friend of mine who was not quite with the program. He told me that he lost money on every sale, but he made it up in volume. Think about it.

Change Rates As The Market Changes

When you were employed, you would never take a cut in pay. The consulting game is a bit different. Just as there are business cycles for every industry (as well as the economy as a whole), there are going to be ups and downs in your business year. Do not get yourself into the psychological trap of thinking that the rate always has to go up and that taking a project at a lower rate is a sign of failure or setback. It isn't.

Some companies will only pay so much at any given time. If you want $50 and hour and their policy is to pay only $40, consider taking it for a short time. Keep abreast of the market; as the demand factor for consultants changes, so do the rates.

If you are one of those eternal optimists, who always feels that something better will turn up if you just wait, this is fine. Just remember that you could "wait" yourself into mild starvation and acute bankruptcy.

You have to walk a fine line between maximizing your income (see above section) and the old consulting maxim that says that any work is better than no work at all.

During the 1991-93 recession many consultants cut their rates drastically in order to keep working. Thus, you hear the oft repeated phrase that "rates are going down". However, my research shows that the large majority of consultants kept their rates at pre-recession levels. In isolated markets there has been some rate erosion, but nationally, the averages seem to hold rates steady.

If you work for less than you are worth for too long a time, you are going to wake up one day and realize that you would be better off financially as a full-time employee with benefits. This is *exactly* what has happened in some of the hard-hit areas of the country, like Southern California and New England.

> *TIP:* Other consultants will tell you that if you take a contract at a low rate, not to worry, because you will find one later on at a higher rate and everything will balance out. You don't want balance. You must keep "beach time" to a minimum, but must maximize your available hourly inventory. So don't drop your rate before you have done some market research into what is happening in your local economy. Don't sell yourself cheap!

11

A DAY IN THE LIFE
(Keeping Out Of Trouble)

The Guest In The House

You used to come into the office, pour yourself some pretty horrible coffee, chat with your friends for a bit, go to the machine and check your e-mail, call your stock broker, and maybe by around 10:30 or 11:00 you settled down to get some work done - only to get up again at noon to get some lunch. Are you really sure you want to be a consultant?

It is all different now. You are in business for yourself and you are a guest in the house. You don't have the security of the corporate umbrella anymore. You screw up and you are history - plain and simple.

What I am going to present in this chapter is some down-home advice to help keep you from screwing up.

Try to keep in mind that as a full-time employee you have to go a long way in most companies before you even get any notice that you are in trouble, much less fired. You can really go the limit in some large companies, especially those that are growing rapidly and who are terribly short-handed. You can come in late, goof around, and leave early. If you work for some government agencies (not all), the only important factor is that you get to work on time and not leave too late! Survival isn't that hard if you have any technical or managerial skills at all.

If your brother-in-law comes to your house for a visit, sits around all day drinking beer, expects you to pick up after him, is rude to your dog, eats you out of house and home, and comes on to your sister, you are going to kick his butt out. Guests are supposed to act like guests (even if they are family). Your client feels the same way; and as a guest you are going to have to behave differently from the rest of the corporate family that is housing you.

Be A Clock Watcher

Time is money and it is *money* that you are working for. You must keep one eye on the clock at all times. This is especially true if you are working under a number of different purchase orders for the same company and they want you to bill your hours to several different projects. Project managers get a sincere feelings of paranoia when they take on a consultant. They feel that the top brass is watching them to see if all that money the company is spending for the consultant's services is being put to good use. The manager may act as if the bucks are coming out of his own pocket (they do come out of his budget). They may never say it, or even hint it, but paranoia is what they feel. They will be watching the clock, so you should too.

The one sure-fire absolute screw-up that will always get you fired is to bill them for hours you did not work. Now, you are saying to yourself, "Why is he telling me this? I wouldn't do a thing like that!"

If you are thinking that you would never bill false hours, then think again. It is very easy to rip off your clients. They know this. It is very easy to add an hour here or an hour there and get away with it. In many companies it is not necessary for you to even keep a time card or have an invoice signed by a manager. You simply turn in a bill to accounts payable and in due time (usually overdue time) you get a check. Adding an hour or so is easy to do because it is easy to get away with.

I am not saying that most, even many, consultants actively engage in a conscious effort to rip off their clients. It is simply that you can easily become seduced into what I call "stupid think".

Your client expects you to put in eight hours, but you only work seven and a half. On a weekly invoice you bill for forty hours with the rationalization that you round to the nearest hour; and get paid for it. Ninety-nine times out of a hundred you may get away with it. Even if discovered, nothing will be said to you...until it can be proved.

What will happen is that the manager and another employee will start "clocking" you and compare their findings against your bill. If the figures don't compute, you are going to get your butt kicked out. You are going to get a reputation so bad you may never be able to work in that city again.

The simple advice here is just don't do it. No matter how easy it might seem, nor how foolproof the scheme looks, ultimately you will get burned. When they get on to you, they may wait until the project is just about complete and then fire you. Or, they may let you finish the project and murder you with a terrible reference without ever saying a word to your face.

If you ever get the reputation that you have to be watched because you can't count the hours, you can just about kiss your consulting career away. After all, would *you* hire *you*?

> **COMMENT:** *No matter what the extra bucks are, it is not worth the risk. OK., you are saying to yourself, "All this guy is preaching about is that I should be honest. I knew that without buying the book!" I am sure you did. But I have seen many consultants just get plain greedy. We are all human and are led easily into temptation. It can happen to you too.*

Above And Beyond Suspicion

You should not put yourself into a position where a client can even question the accuracy of your billing. Translated, this means that you should stay the hell out of the coffee room! It means that you damn well should not be discussing the state of the world or the stock market with the full-time staff, or even worse, with other consultants.

Don't become one of the "boys". The last place you want your manager to see you is with a group of other consultants, standing behind the printer and gossiping about the company and its employees. If you waste time, you are just asking for trouble.

Unfortunately it doesn't make a difference whether you bill for the time or not. The staff are going to believe that you bill for every minute you are in the client's building. Sure it is nice to take a break and chat with one of the staff about the relative merits of one Club Med over another. But, when the conversation is over, the employee is gong to think it must be nice to be able to engage in a bull session and charge $40 an hour. No, he won't figure what it is costing his company while *he* tosses the bull. It will all come down on *you*.

The bottom line is that you will have work to do, so you should get on with doing it. You are not being paid to crap around. Even if you make a big announcement that you are "off the meter" you will still be under suspicion. And if you are suspected of wasting time, you can really end up in hot water. Okay, I know you are not a workaholic. You have to come up for air sooner or later. Even pizza-codas have to come take a break sooner or later.

> **COMMENT:** *Pizza-codas, for those of you who never worked for IBM or EDS were the guys who would stay in a windowless room for days on end. Every seven or eight hours their manager would slide a pizza (with everything) under the door for these troglodytes to feed on. I guess today it is chips, salsa, sushi, and Jolt Cola!*

When you take a break, you should do it so that you are not noticed. Leave the building and walk around the block. Find an office or conference room where you can get away and have some coffee. You can sometimes get lost in the crowd milling about in the company cafeteria. Find a spot and retreat to it.

Don't pour yourself a cup of coffee and sit at your desk and read the morning paper. You know that you are not going to charge for the time, but the image that you create is that of the high-priced consultant who is getting rich by goofing off.

Of course, if the manager asks you to accompany him/her for a short snack, you have no problem. But make sure you, somehow, mention sometime in the conversation that you are "off the meter".

> *TIP*: If the manager says it is O.K. to bill the time, then bill it. Remember you only have so many hours in your inventory.

In conjunction with the above, may consultants, in order to avoid the suspicion of overcharging, never bill more than 36 or 37 hours in any one week. This is not to say that they work forty and give away three or four hours. They simply bill for the time they work. Yes, you could bill forty hours, take three or four hours a week in break time, and compensate by working an extra three or four hours to balance things out.

However, there is a trap that you fall into. When the manger sees your bill for forty hours and did not see you hang around for the extra time (either before they came in or after they went home), many of them are prone to question your figure of forty hours. Remember, you are a consultant. To some, that means you have a license to steal, and no matter how honest you are, there will always be those who will suspect otherwise. It is always these folks who have the loudest voices. You will always be guilty until found innocent. And you are not likely to find a jury of your peers!

> *TIP*: If you do a lot of work off-site (at home) for your client and are on a time-materials billing, keep an accurate time sheet. You can buy a nice pre-printed one at the stationery store. Enclose with your bill.

Who Loves You, Baby?

Just who are your peers? You were one of them at one time. If you had trouble getting along with your high-tech brethren before, you better work damn hard to getting along with them now.

When you were a full-time employee *and* the shop super-tech, you could be an arrogant SOB and get away with it. In fact, it was probably expected of you! Your peers would tolerate you because they knew that you were a "heavy", and if approached in the right way, you could teach them quite a lot. And when they really got to know you, they found out you weren't such a "bad ass". Well, if you are still strutting around as the "great one", you better get off your stage because your full-time peers are going to drop the curtain on you.

The staff will be looking for any excuse to dislike you, and if you come on as an obnoxious slob, you are going to give them all the reason they need. Many of them will resent even the *concept* of a consultant entering their ranks. If you compound things with an arrogant or insulting nature, you are going to wind up as a very lonely person. If you come on like a superstar, you are likely to get the troops so angry that they may go to the manager and demand your expulsion.

So how should you come on to them? There are two paths you can take - the "safe" one and the "better" one. The better one is to be friendly and act much as you would if you were an employee. You have to play down the fact that you are a consultant and be able to answer the usual barbs (i.e. "You consultants sure make a bundle for doing nothing I can't do...."), in such a way that you disarm them without putting them down ("but we do it so much *slower!*"). It requires a very unique personality, usually one who is really self-confident in his/her own ego. You sort of need to play the role of the wise old father or the gentle giant. You have to be a good salesman and a good politician. In short, you have to be one of those "nice" people that we all know and strive to be. If you have this gift of personality, you should use it to the best advantage. Don't hide it.

Then there are the rest of us! Let's face it. We consultants have large egos and down deep we are probably something close to "rotten"! We know we are good and we tend to show it off. We are aggressive and want to be the "best". If we didn't have this aggressiveness, we probably would not have joined the dog-eat-dog world of business. Our egos serve as a buffer between us and rejection. But it is not likely to help us win friends and influence people. If I have described you, then you better take the "safe" path in working with the full-time staff.

This means keeping a safe distance between you and them. In short, you have to be a little bit stand-offish, without being a snob. It comes down to speaking only when spoken to, but still observing the usual social amenities, like saying "good morning" or "hello". The real keyword here is "polite". You should think of your full-time colleagues as people that you met on a short plane trip. You should be cordial and polite, but at the same time, you should keep your distance.

This is the "safe" approach because by keeping to yourself, you don't give them anything to "pick" at. If they dislike you because you are a consultant, there is little you can do about it. You will just have to accept this as one of the facts of life in the consulting merry-go-round (at this client, anyway). The important thing is that you give them no ammunition to dislike you personally. We all dislike the IRS agent, but we do not dislike him or her personally (unless they have offended us). However, wouldn't it make you feel better if the agent *did* say something to offend you. It would really serve as a rationalization for real antipathy. Well, it is no different with your esteemed peers at the client's shop. To them, you are the IRS agent.

If I am sounding a bit paranoid it is because I want you to take a reality check. You are going into a difficult situation with people you don't know and you are going to be expected to pull off a hat trick. It could be a hornet's nest you are entering, or it could be the land of milk and honey. You will not know until you have been there for a few days. So, it is wise to just play it cool and not get yourself off to a bad footing with the staff.

You may think you are the sweetest, kindest, most lovable person in the world. Others may perceive you as a horse's ass. An old friend of mine from Los Angeles said:

> I used to be employed by a company that only hired what could be called the best and the brightest. We were a pretty aggressive lot and had pretty thick hides. We engaged in a lot of good-natured kidding in the office and to those who didn't know better, it would seem that we were all a group of impudent snobs. Since that was my fist real exposure to the business world, I assumed that every shop was that way. Boy, did I suffer some culture shock when, after five years, I decided to become a consultant. I was let go from my first three assignments because of personality problems the staff had against me. Hell, I treated them like I was back at the old office. Big mistake. I didn't get straightened out until I met a manager who used to also work for the old company. He recognized the symptoms and gave me my reality check.

Kissing Up

While it may be good and prudent policy to remain aloof from the general staff, the management staff is another matter.

With these people, you should be as close as you can get. These are your potential customers. They are not going to be with the same company forever. When they move on to other firms, you will want them to remember you when you come calling. And, you must remember that good managers are a results-oriented people. Even if they hate consultants, they will still admire a true professional who can come in off the street and quietly perform a miracle or two.

You should also remember that you are on a more equal footing with a manager. You are a business person and so are they. You run a business (albeit, rather small), and they help to run theirs. The problems only differ in degree, not necessarily in complexity. The client/consultant relationship should always proceed on the illusion of mutual respect for each others autonomy. You can't tell them how to run their company, and they really can't tell you how to do your project. (However, we both know who is really in charge...if you don't, please see the chapter on sales).

It may be self-serving to tell the general staff what they want to hear, but with management you should try to be as up front as possible. While I will go into this in greater detail later on, for now it is enough to say that even here you must use some foresight. It is one thing to be forthright and honest with the manager. But you were not brought in to be a company spy. If you realize that someone on the staff is totally incompetent, it is not your job to enlighten the management. If the management is competent, they will already know. It they aren't, you are not going to be able to make them competent.

Of course, if you are asked for your opinion, and you believe the project is in trouble, then you damn well should say so; but *only* if asked. If you know nothing about management, at least learn these two facts. First, managers often mistake the bad news with the bearer of the bad news. The second is that most managers can't stand anyone coming in from the outside (even outside the department) and telling them either stuff they should already know or advice about what to do about a known problem. The last thing you should do is take your own initiative and walk into the manager's office and give a candid critique of the project, the staff, or anything else.

> *TIP*: *Wait until asked. Nobody gave you the "Oprah/Donahue Award", so you have no mission to run your mouth and get involved beyond your professional capacity. Wait until asked (I say it again because it is important) and then use caution.*

Be A Pro

You are going to hear the term "professionalism" thrown abound by lots of consultants. Yet, most have very little idea what they are talking about. It is more of an image that an entity. The word "professional" is easy enough to define. As one starving writer put it, "The difference between an amateur and a professional is that the professional gets paid." That about sums it up. If you do something "on the side", such as write books for a hobby, then you are an amateur. But, if just one person gives you a dime for your work, then you become a paid amateur. However, if you do nothing else for a living and still only receive the same dime, you then become classified as a professional.

I shall define "professionalism" as a standard of conduct that conforms to a code of ethics. When you say that so and so is not acting as a professional or seems to lack professionalism, you are really talking about that consultant's conduct, not their technical abilities or whether they get paid. You are saying that the conduct does not conform to the standards you think should be adhered to by those in the consulting business.

The best code of professional ethics I have seen for consultants was drawn up by the Independent Computer Consultants Association. This organization of computer consultants is about fifteen years old and has played an important role in promoting the concept of professionalism within the industry as well as in increasing the awareness of the general business community to the services of computer consultants.

If you are going to be a consultant, you might as well be a good one. You might as well be a professional. There are six areas in which you can judge yourself:

COMPETENCE: *A professional consultant does not knowingly take on a consulting assignment which they cannot reasonably expect to complete with competence.* Of course the key word here is "reasonably". If you don't know the very first thing about network design and you contract to put up an enterprise wide-area network, you are not acting in a professional manner, unless you truly, honestly, and sincerely believe that you can bring it off. Competence means being able to do what you say you can do.

Unfortunately, there are many in our business who think they are superstars and take on projects that should be passed up. They are just not qualified for the project. And I am not just talking about technical skills, but also business skills as well; being able to commit to a schedule, on-time attendance, making milestone dates, etc.

You have to get the work done when you say it will be done. If your client wanted haphazard or slipshod work, he sure as hell would not be paying your rates for it. You shouldn't be taking the money if you can't do the work.

INDEPENDENCE: *A consultant shall not express an opinion or make a recommendation in any professional situation unless he or she acts independently with respect to such opinion or recommendation. Independence is considered impaired if a member has any interest in a client's decision that has not been disclosed to the client.* For example, if you are asked to evaluate a new database product that the client is thinking of buying and if you just happen to be a very close friend of the sales person (who might have helped you get business in the past), you have a real obligation to tell the client about this conflict and politely decline to do the evaluation.

You are just asking for a charge of conflict-of-interest and perhaps a law suit if you do otherwise. Sure you might lose a contract here and there, but think of the alternative. When the word gets out that you have trouble expressing an independent opinion, your consulting days are numbered

You and *I* both know that just because you are friends with the software vendor does not mean that you could not make an independent decision. But nobody is going to believe that you can, so don't be a fool and leave yourself open to a conflict-of-interest charge. A professional wouldn't.

INTEGRITY AND OBJECTIVITY: *A consultant does not knowingly misrepresent facts nor in any recommendation does a consultant subordinate his or her judgment to others.* You just can't misrepresent facts or tell half-truth's to your client. Sooner or later you are going to be found out and you are going to be washed out.

Your client is used to getting half-truths and sugar-coated projections from the regular staff. From you they expect the full truth. They expect you to be objective. When asked for a direct statement, you are supposed to tell the truth. You can't look at things through those ever-present rose-colored glasses. If things are going to hell and your client wants a status report, you will have to tell the facts. Sure you might get the blame. In fact, that may be what you were brought in for! But even if you get the blame and the boot, the client will admire your integrity. It will be passed along in what will probably become a good reference.

Integrity and objectivity may have short-term dangers, but they always have long-term virtues.

What man, (who was not a crook) who, had he told the truth about a small break-in, would not have had to resign a high office in disgrace?

CONFIDENTIALITY: *A consultant will not disclose any confidential information obtained in the course of a professional engagement without the consent of the client. The rule will not be construed to conflict with compliance with any valid subpoena or summons enforceable by order of court.* Keep you nose out of your client's business and keep your mouth shut about what you hear.

Confidentiality is a big deal, especially in companies that make high tech widgets. Nobody wants their trade secrets given to the opposition. As a consultant, you are likely to be privy to a lot of good poop about your client, the people who work for them, and the product they produce. Don't become a motor-mouth.

In the first place, believe only half of what you see, and none of what you hear. In the second place, keep it to yourself, since you probably received bad info from an unreliable source. You just cannot go from Company X to its competition and bring with you all the high-tech methodology that your former client uses. The word will definitely get out and there is a good chance that you will be hit with a law suit.

And you will have *deserved* it.

ACTS DISCREDITABLE: *A consultant will not commit an act discreditable to the profession. A consultant will not knowingly participate in any engagement where the consultant's professional skills might be used to violate the law.* It would not be a good idea for you to accept a project in which the manger wanted you to search the Personnel files for what could be called "confidential" information. Don't use your skills to break the law. Don't work for a company that is engaged in illegal activity. Don't take on a contract with the Godfather (because if you screw up they will take a contract - on you)!

Some consultants carry this further than others. I, for example, will not use my technical skills to develop offensive weaponry or on any product that I know causes the destruction to life or the environment. (I will do defensive weaponry). This is a value judgment that I and many others make.

Determine in your own mind as to what is moral and legal, and what you will or won't do. Just don't blame me if you are caught after committing the computer crime of the decade. There are not too many consultants working out of a prison cell!

EMPLOYMENT: This used to be part of the ICCA Code Of Ethics but it was dropped several years ago. I, however believe that *a consultant should not take part in the recruitment of client staff either to another company or into consulting.* You may get asked by clients to advise them of people in other firms that have been clients of yours, who might be willing to jump ship and join your present client. Stay the hell away from this trap. Even if you know ten people whom your current client could "raid", keep quiet. If you get into the "flesh" game, you are going to make enemies with everyone. The people are going to dislike you for giving out their name without heir permission. The former client is not going to be too happy about you helping your present client conduct a raid on their personnel. And the current client will believe that if you help them raid a former client, you will have no hesitation helping your next client to raid the people on this project.

This also goes for being the good Samaritan and helping one of the staff get into consulting. Your client does not want to lose people to our industry any more than to other industries. If you try to form some sort of syndicate with employees of your present or former clients, you face the risk of never working for any of these firms again. If the regular staff wants to get into consulting, they will find a way, just as you did. Sure, it would be an ego trip to help someone break into the business. But if you take this ego trip, you are taking a risk of hurting yourself. Don't play Santa Claus.

CYA (Cover Your Ass)

No matter how professional you are on the job, your butt is going to be in someone's gunsight at one time or another. More than ever, you are going to have to rely on the time-honored CYA memo. A great way to get yourself in the paper shredder is to make substantial changes in your client's production systems and not tell anyone. After the first crash, you are liable to find yourself sitting in the parking lot asking for spare change!

To prevent this evil, as well as others, it is very important that you keep your client appraised of what you are doing. Most consultants who are working independently, usually write a weekly status memo to their client letting the good folks who pay the bills know what is going on. This is just as important in dealing with the users. Nothing is worse in a consultant's life than, at the end of the project, finding a glaring misunderstanding between what the users wanted and what they got. First the users yell at management and then management yells at you.

By keeping a file of all your memos to the client, you have an audit-trail, as it were, of what actions and progress has been made on the project. When a dispute arises, all you have to do is reach into your folder for the memo of April 4th. You can relax. Your ass is covered.

These memos also project you from the charge that "those consultants never do any work". Remember, the regular staff will always have the inside track to management's ear. If a lie is repeated often enough, the management may start to believe it. Shooting a memo to them every week will help them (and you) sleep easier.

Users vs. MIS: No Choice

Dealing with the users is probably the most often overlooked area in the literature on computer consulting. This is probably because there are not too many problems that consultants have with users. In fact, research seems to point to the conclusion that users get along better with consultants than they do with the regular staff. The users have been ignored by the MIS department for so long, when a consultant comes in, the users just fall all over themselves to help. But when the regular staff go downstairs to meet with the user, the users feel that it is just another smoke-blowing session.

> **COMMENT**: Did you ever notice that users are always downstairs and MIS is always upstairs? Think about it. Are we really closer to God? What do you think the users think?

This is not to say that working with a user is always a bed of roses. You have to be just as careful with them as you do with the full-time staff, but in a different way. When you are asked to go downstairs and meet with the user, you really have to watch yourself. You have to remember that the users are not paying your invoices. It is all too easy to please the user and anger the information systems management people. List to this story as told by a consultant who works in St. Louis:

> I had been at the company for several months, working on a inventory system. When it was done, I was asked to stay on and help do some work on the AR system. The manager said to run over to the user and find out what they wanted. In an all-day meeting, I found they wanted an on-line data entry capability. I told them it was quite feasible. Big mistake. This was not the first time they had asked for this, and they had been told that it was impossible with the existing configuration. This was a lot of crap, but the users bought it. Now they had it on good authority (mine) that an on-line capability could be installed. The war of the century ensued. I lost!

My friend fell into a trap that many consultants find themselves in if they are not careful. You have to know what to say to a user as well as what not to say. Good intentions can get us into big trouble. It makes sense that if the user is behind a project, the MIS department will not have to do a sales job on that user. But what happens when the user wants more than MIS wants to (or, indeed, can) give? Corporate politics, back biting, departmental infighting, and general chaos ensues.

As consultants, we want peace and harmony between the users and the MIS moguls; it is the surest way to get good references. So, when we meet with users, it is not easy to be less than enthusiastic about their desires. *Their* projects keep *us* in groceries. And in our desire to be good citizens, we often give them just the opposite information they have received from MIS. Another midwest consultant said:

> I was often approached by several user groups to answer questions. I might be down in the cafeteria having lunch, when a division manager would come up and ask if it was possible to have a report sorted differently or include new data. I soon learned that they were seeking ammunition from me to throw back at the information systems department.

Users are important people, and they deserve to get good (if not better) service from their data processing budget. But it is always a mistake to get involved in a corporate struggle between a user and the MIS people. You must never allow yourself to get yanked around in this type of fight. You must not take sides. Sometimes it is very hard to resist. What do you think happens when the two groups are evenly balanced and are depending upon your judgment to tip the scales for one side or the other? One side will lose and will not forget your role in it.

It is not easy to keep our objectivity. In a perfect world the advice would be to pick the side you think is right. But this is not a perfect world, and if you take the side of a user, you might win the battle and get to do the project, but you have a good chance of making an enemy of the people who cut your checks. When the project is over, it will probably be your last.

The best advice is to stay the hell out of this type of situation. If you can't help being brought in, then you better take the side of the technology department. Of course, you should stress to both sides that you cannot possibly be objective since you know who is buttering your bread. But, if they still insist on a definitive ruling from you go with the technology group.

All things being equal, you really have no choice. You are their agent and you do owe them first loyalty. More importantly, they are going to be the ultimate winners. In your whole career, how many projects have you seen completed that the technology people were adamantly opposed to? Damn few.

Taking the side of the data processing group can be hard for many consultants because we have seen too many user-supported projects go down the tubes by narrow-minded MIS management. All too often it is the MIS department that tells the users what systems they will have and how they will work. Many users feel that "if it weren't for the system, things wouldn't be so complicated."

We know better than anyone how users have often received the shaft. Shooting down another user can be a difficult task for a consultant who has been around for a while. But, as I say, this is not a perfect world. If you come up against your client, you are bound to lose. It may not be fair, but that is the way it is. So, be careful what you say to the users.

Users: Care And Feeding

Be careful how you treat them. In the long run, it won't make much difference if the regular staff likes or dislikes you. But you do not want to tee off a user. You are of no use to your manager, if his user group will not let you in the door. The way you get along with the users can determine whether or not the project sails smoothly down stream or hits every snag in the river. It is really important to court these people. They might know next to nothing about data processing but they know the right people. They know who to talk to in the corporate structure and the more favorable it is about you, the better you are going to be for it. (The converse is also true). More than one consultant has been invited back because a user was so satisfied, they demanded the MIS department call the contractor for the next project.

There is another thing to consider. Techno-people (another made-up phrase) are very mobile. The odds are that three years from now, all the people in the systems engineering or MIS department will have moved on to other places. The users are a different breed. They are *company* people.

> **COMMENT**: *Perhaps it is because they don't have the mobility of a technical person. Every company has a technology platform. But in how many companies can an insurance claims processing manager find a suitable position should he or she decide to pull up stakes?*

The user staff is there for the long haul and they can be very valuable as a reference source. You should not hesitate to use them as references. In many places, a good user reference carries more weight than good words from the technical staff. After all, information systems management hired you. If they totally pan you, they are subtly implying that they screwed up by bring you on board. Since managers don't like to imply bad judgment, many are reluctant to give less-than-favorable references. But users are considerably more impartial. They didn't hire you; they didn't even ask for you to be on the project. When your next client hears from some divisional user manager that you are the greatest thing since RAM memory, you can write your own ticket. They will know that you not only have technical skills, but that you must also be a competent business person.

> *TIP:* The day of the "pizza coder" is long gone. If you can't communicate with a user, all the technical knowledge in the world will not insure that you or your projects will be successful. Keeping on good terms with users can be worth tens of thousands of dollars of work with that company in the next several years.

Play Me And Pay Me!

Billing is important. You should find out when the client would like you to submit invoices - and then try to change it to a greater frequency! Remember I told you how your bill is going to travel the length and breadth of the company and is going to take lots of time before it is turned into a check? The more invoices you have at the "cut off" period will mean a better cash flow for you.

Many companies will ask you to submit a monthly bill. This allows your client to have use of your services as well as a nice float on their capital, for several weeks, while you languish out there trying to keep the creditors from you door while at the same time living on the brink of starvation! There may be little you can do about it, but it does not hurt to try. Many companies who are experienced in using contractors know that their consultants are not Fortune 500 concerns and will allow them to submit invoices on a weekly basis. If the client does a weekly accounts payable cycle, you have a better chance of staying solvent. Of course, if the company only does its accounts payable monthly, you are not going to be much better off even if you do submit weekly invoices.

It is a good idea to have your invoices signed by your client manger. Many companies have the department secretary run around to get the manager's o.k. anyway, so you can speed up your own payment by alleviating the secretary of that burden.

Keep a hard copy. You'd think this is obvious, but so many consultants only keep their invoices on disk and then have a crash. When the IRS comes snooping around and claims you are not a contractor, but rather a full-time employee, you can show them a stack of paid invoices and close the case.

Many companies will have an invoice form they will want you to use to speed up payment. Don't use their actual form (it makes you look less independent to the IRS or anyone else) but include the same information on yours. A simple invoice form is all you need; nobody is impressed with invoices in three colors and engraved on parchment! When you finally receive the check, you should attach the stub to your copy of the invoice and place the invoice in your "paid" file.

> *TIP*: *Before you cash your first check, make a copy of it and frame it above the invoice in a nice frame. Hang it on the wall. It will be a source of pride as the years go by. To this day I wish I had a copy of my first check!*

The Golden Rule

The final word I have about keeping out of trouble is simple. Learn to be nice. You are a guest in their organization and you must conduct yourself accordingly. You must learn to conform to their way of doing things. You are not going to change their corporate procedure so there is no reason why you should eve try.

For example, you might end up in a shop that has the most haphazard method of distributing user reports. Maybe 30% of the data are lost every day. You are just going to have to grin and bear it. Look, everybody probably knows it is a bad system and you surely won't be the first to recognize the fact. But, there is a reason for every lousy system in every data processing shop. Unless you have been specifically given the task of fixing it, keep the hell out. You will only come off as some type of "high and mighty" from the outside who is there to "help"! Be nice and don't bitch about how your client does business.

Be nice to the staff. Sure, you might like to let some of their arrogant staff people "have it". Don't. It won't work. Be nice. You may not win friends, but at least being nice will keep you from making enemies.

> *The enemy of my enemy is my friend.*
>
> *Old proverb*

12

DIGGING YOURSELF OUT
(Of Trouble)

Crash And Burn

The last chapter concentrated on what you should do to *stay* out of trouble. Here I shall touch on some of the things you can do when you find yourself deep in it. The word "trouble" is defined as any time you find that being a consultant is a pain-in-the-butt. It is when you are not a happy consultant.

> *COMMENT: If you simply get fired, then you are in trouble. But if you get to the point that you wish you were fired, then you are really in deep trouble.*

We Regret To Inform You That You Are History!

Every consultant has been released from a contract against his or her will, a least once in their career. Most often it happens when the project is canceled in mid-flight, or when someone upstairs decides it is time to cut the budget. All of a sudden you find yourself with nowhere to go on Monday morning.

First of all, you should not find yourself in a state of shock. We have been telling you all along that consulting is no picnic. If you have been doing some on-going marketing, then you will at least have some idea of what firms are looking for consultants. Due to the lax nature of most consultants, however, when "Black Monday" comes the majority of them have no idea where to turn. Of course, the solution is found in the chapter on marketing. But this is only part of the solution. On your next client meeting you will have to tell your prospect why the project was canned.

Depending on the prospect, they may or may not believe that it was beyond your control. They may take the position that if the project was canned and you were on the project, the it was somehow your fault! To prevent this from occurring, you should make arrangements with the present (past) project manager to explain to anyone who might call, the whole story about why the project went down. It is even better if you can get a letter of reference which (besides glorifying you) gives details of the project and its cancellation.

If a project of yours is terminated, do not leave until you have button-holed all of the other department managers and users as to whether there are any other projects they might need you for. Remember, often there is little communication between managers, and it is not until you are gone that Manager A finds out that Manager B let go a contractor that could be used in a different department. After all, you know how your client operates, and also something about his/her business. You are actually more valuable now than when you came in.

It is also not a bad idea to ask other managers if they have friends in other firms that you might call upon. If they say no, you haven't lost anything, but many times you can make some good contacts this way.

> *TIP:* Make a "friendly" termination the springboard for getting your next contract.

Booted!

All of the above is fine when the termination is not your fault. But, when you are canned because you either couldn't do the job, or the manager did not like you, or you simply screwed it up, you have to take another approach. Again, you should not go into a panic. Everyone has been fired before and it is not the end of the world.

The age old advice is true, but hard to do: don't leave behind any enemies who an hurt you. Sit down with the management and ask why they think things went sour. This is not the time to argue. The die is cast. You are out. It is now time to look back in retrospect. More importantly, you are showing the manager that you arc a mature person who can accept criticism and adversity in a calm and cool manner. If you "bring off" the final meeting, no matter how badly you screwed up, what the manager will remember is that you acted as a person with dignity. When you get home that evening, write a short note to the manager, expressing your disappointment that things did not work out, and that you appreciate their frank and candid criticisms, etc. (lie like hell!). If you can neutralize the management, when they are called for a reference they will have something good to tell about you.

> **COMMENT:** *Acting cool, calm, and collected when you are booted is the hardest thing you will ever do. The advice I give is what I learned from research. I can't do it. The few times I have been terminated, I have blown my stack. It wasn't smart and it wasn't right. But it beat having a heart attack from keeping it all inside. Looking back I wish I had done things differently. But if you are a type "A" like me, your chances of acting rationally are not too good!*

The question always comes up as to whether or not you should mention your last contract. Many consultants, when questioned on this, said that if it was a very short assignment (under eight weeks), they would be hesitant to mention it. However, the general assessment of is that it is foolish to take the chance that a prospect will not find out about your misadventure. Remember, the computer community is a small one. With the mobility of full-time staff, you never know when one of the regular staff people from you last client will come and interview for a job with your new client. As Sue Mitzer from Palm Beach put it:

> When it comes to bad experiences, the truth might hurt, but it rarely kills, if presented in the right way. Getting caught in a lie, even one of omission, is always fatal.

You *must* have the ability to explain to your prospect why things went to hell in your last assignment. Again, honesty is your best policy. You could probably make up a ton of excuses of why you were booted. And they might play in Peoria! But sooner or later you are going to be caught by a prospect who does not buy your story and calls the last company to find out. It is to your advantage to be as honest as possible. Sure, you want to present yourself in as favorable a light as you can. And as long as you keep the facts in order, you should be able to convince your prospect that what happened before will not occur again. People can be very forgiving.

There is nothing else I can say on the subject of being terminated. You can learn how to deal with the hurt, pain, the rejection, and the fear from the many excellent books on the subject. Just understand that it will happen to you some time in your career. It has happened to some of us many times. Hopefully the preceding has prepared you mentally. Take it in stride and keep the faith.

We Need You, We'll Feed You!

On the opposite side of the scale is the possibility that you will become so popular with your client you will receive a full-time offer. While this will serve as a boost to your ego, it can develop into a very serious problem. The question is just how do you turn down the offer and still remain in the good graces of your client. Diplomacy is in order.

The approach depends a lot on your relationship with management. If you are really on close terms with them, you should level with them by letting them know that contracting is what makes you happy and that you can do much better on the independent route. Management has heard this before. They know what you get paid and they know you can clean up financially.

If you can't take the low road, you must go to higher ground by bringing up the (sometimes esoteric) argument about being in business for yourself and all its rewards. Sure your client is a fine company which anyone would be pleased to work for, you will explain. But for you, independent consulting is the only path to true salvation!

It is very important to take the time (or give the appearance of taking the time) to think it over. Nothing is going to tee off your client more than if they make a flattering offer to you and you turn it down cold a minute later. After a few days, let them know you agonized over the decision but decided consulting is your best course for the next six months or so.

You are always going to hear the argument from the client about an ever-present recession putting you out of work. This may be true in your locality. The important thing here is not to argue whether a recession is coming, going, or here. Just explain to them that you understand the risk and are willing to take it. Give them the "entrepreneurial speech" and you will be able to walk away from the offer and still have a client who wants not only your services, but also your name on a W-2 form.

The Golden Handcuff

There is also the problem of being of such value to your client that you are literally trapped in your contract. This often happens to consultants who do business with firms who use contractors much the same as they use employees. These are usually big, rich, outfits who like to buy their talent by the pound and when times get lean, they trim down by letting the consultants go. The firm not only gets superior service from the consultants and save money on benefit payments, they can also go through a recession and claim they never had a layoff. They just boot the contractors and leave their permanent staff intact.

> *COMMENT:* When a company has a large employee force in a geographical area where they must compete for bodies with a dozen other firms, just the rumor of a layoff can panic the workers into skipping out and joining the competition. Using consultants is a preventive measure against a massive exodus.

The Golden Handcuff is tough. There is no easy way out. When you have been with a client for a long time and you want to take advantage of a good opportunity with another company, you have to move very carefully. Remember, some day you might want to come back to this client. You cannot simply walk out. When word gets around that you took a powder in the middle of a project, you are going to have hell to pay.

The best thing to do is to give the client some form of notice, preferably as long as possible. If you go to management and tell them (politely) that you need a change and would like to wrap up your affairs in two months, you have a good chance of getting away clean. But as I said before, this is by no means a sure thing.

Many clients are going to think of you as an inconsiderate slob. Here they are, thinking you are happy as a clam, earning all of this money, and then you go and tell them you want out! You are likely to ruffle a feather or two. But so what.

It is important that you be true to yourself. What good is being a consultant and taking the risk if you can't be happy. This is the overriding message I got from consultants I talked with about the Golden Handcuff. One of the reasons you went into business for yourself is so you could call most of the shots. If you find yourself trapped in a project which never seems to end, it is imperative you take steps to get yourself on a track where you will enjoy your work.

> *TIP: If you feel you need greener pastures, then this is a risk you should take. There is nothing worse than to go into the consulting business and trade being stuck in a dead-end, full-time job for being stuck on a never-ending project. The money is better, but is it really worth it? Most don't think so.*

The Big Snore

Please note something that was mentioned earlier. Many consultants go into the business thinking they are going to work on state-of-the-art technology, only to find that they are doing the hack COBOL report coding that nobody in the shop wants to do. It gets to be quite a let-down. Many consultants have found that they are not immune from occupational boredom. There is no real cure you can effect, beyond getting the project finished as soon as possible. You can, however, treat the symptoms.

When involved in a boring project, you have to concentrate on your mental attitude. You must keep reminding yourself that the project will not last forever and that better things will come along. This is also a good time to extol to yourself the virtues of being an independent business person, and take a day or two off in the middle of the week. If all of this fails, now is a good time to buy something expensive, something you would or could not have afforded when your were working full-time. You have always wanted those mink-lined golf club covers, so now is the time to get them!

If you can make a positive mental image compensate for a boring work environment, you will be able to successfully complete the project without becoming frustrated and short-tempered. If you are not able to overcome the effects of working on a boring project, you might as well throw yourself into virtual memory.

If there is nothing about consulting that can make you happy, perhaps you should consider going back to full-time employment. It is no disgrace. Many people go into consulting to see if they will like it and find that they miss the corporate life. So, they chuck the whole thing and get a full-time position. You didn't sign a contract in blood, saying you were going to be a consultant until doomsday! If it isn't for you, do not let pride keep you in an environment where you are not happy. If you do, you *deserve* whatever unhappiness you feel. Anyway, it won't last long, because your work effectiveness is going to suffer and sooner or later you are going to be booted. Be true to yourself... and to hell with the rest of the world.

> *COMMENT: Some consultants actually look for a simple "boring" project after finishing a "death march" assignment. They use the project as a time to recharge as well as to study a new language or technology. It is hard to learn anything new when you are working 18 hour days. It is nice to have easy 8 hour days for a change.*

The In-House Butt-Head

The most prevalent problem that consultants face when they work on-site is the full-time staff member who is just plain rude and antagonistic to you. We discussed some of this earlier. You know that your presence may be resented by the regular staff. However, most of them will be polite enough not to make a scene. The really smart ones will welcome you and try to pick your brain.

But there is always one in every shop who carries some chip on his or her shoulder. They plain hate consultants. It seems that the prime mission of this butt-head is to make you as miserable as possible. Although more than one consultant has had his disk re-formatted by a resentful employee, most of the antagonism you are likely to feel will be verbal.

You are going to work with some personality types that, when you were a full-time employee, you probably didn't like, but got along with (you weren't a consultant, thus, no problem). It is not that easy now. You are going to have to walk that thin line between being diplomatic and keeping your own dignity. The most obvious advice you can receive is to avoid these people as much as possible. If you only have to do a limited amount of business with them, you should try to be as nice as possible and take your lumps. It is a bit different, however, if you have to deal with some jerk on a day-to-day basis.

Most of the literature on human relations in the business environment instruct you to turn the other cheek and attempt to win your nemesis over with kindness. This might work in marketing or finance, but not in the world of high-tech.

If you have been out in the world for any length of time, you know the kind of personality type being described. Surely you have met the arrogant super-programmer, super-analyst, super-network guru, who knows all there is about software/hardware and who isn't happy until he or she rubs somebody's nose in it. These are the people that always have to get their way and never, never admit to being wrong about anything. These are also the people who can and will do anything, no matter how ruthless, to win.

Dealing with these "fine folks" when you were a full-timer meant having to be nice. After all, you were part of the "family" and, thus, had to make the effort to get along. The old advice was sound. The best way to get along was to go along.

As a consultant, it is not quite the same. You were brought in to straighten something out. If you let a butt-head employee get in your way, you are only jeopardizing your contract. You must get the situation in hand. As sated before, the usual advice is to "make nice". The reality of the situation is that you will have to establish your *dignity* and your *autonomy*. You must make it unlawful for anyone to stray beyond the bounds of conduct which infringes on either. When you find yourself with your back up against the wall with an antagonistic employee that you must work closely with, you must establish a strategy and be on your guard. You will have to have a confrontation, but first you have to "woik a plan."

One of the best "plans" for dealing with this employee is to always try to have someone else present when you have to be with the jerk. You then have a witness to all the abuse your are taking. You should continue to take the abuse for as long as it takes you to nose around and get some background on the person. It is also wise to court some of the employees and try to make a few allies before the confrontation. Yes, this is politics, but only for a limited duration. The ends are simply to get this clown off your back. Kindness and logic is not going to work They need a swift kick in the ass. It could work something like this (compliments of a consultant from New York):

> "You contractors never do a damn thing", he said as I walked into the printer room. He'd been on my back for three weeks and was beginning to be a real pain in the butt.

> "I don't see why they keep you around. I never see you do anything. I don't even think you know what the application does. You contractors are all alike. You just rip us off", he continued.

> Well, I had about all I was going to take. The time had come to put this guy in his place. The stage was set, as several others, whom I knew would back me up, had wandered into the room.

> "You know, John", I said, "it is hard for me to understand you. You're one of the brightest analysts I have ever met. But you are a real pain-in-the-ass. " I had caught him off guard. Obviously, no one had ever spoken the plain facts to him like this.

> "It has come down to this. I don't give a rat's ass about how bright you are or how much you know. I was brought in here by your management to get some things done and I am not going to let you interfere. I don't care what you think of me or consultants in general. But from now on, I am not going to turn the other cheek to your remarks." He was really in a state of shock, so I continued at a rapid pace. "Now, if you

want to have a political war, that's fine with me. I've been in this business a long time and I am not afraid of a good fight. Either you are going to treat me with some dignity, or you and I are going to go to the mat. Starting tomorrow, the slate is clean. I am going to treat you as politely as I have in the past. Maybe, just maybe, we can do some business together. But, if you don't get off of my back, I am going to climb all over yours." I looked around the room at the hushed audience. "It is all up to you, and they are all witnesses. Tomorrow is another day. Let's try to get it together and bury the hatched." I looked around once more, turned toward the door, and walked out.

I hadn't gotten more than three steps past the doorway, when one of the guys in the room ran up beside me. "I've been wanting to tell him that for two years now. I'm glad someone had the courage to let him have it", he said. "In two hours, you are going to be a hero around here."

Unlike the bedtime story, we never became friends. But, he minded his business and I minded mine. I treated him with respect and dignity, and he did the same. When the project was over, I went my own way. Eight months later I was back at the company. He had been fired and the last anyone had heard, he was joining the Navy as a technician on a submarine.

This is a true story, as told to an audience of computer consultants at a recent West Coast computer show. The important thing to learn here is that very often a display of force is necessary to establish your own territory. It is the only thing that some personality types understand.

Of course, there are risks to this strategy. If you handle it wrong, you can end up making a real fool of yourself. But, most often you will have little choice. You have to establish yourself as someone the office bully damn well better not tangle with.

Hopefully, a bluff will be enough. If push really does come to shove, you absolutely must go to the management, lay it all on the line, and offer to resign. It is important that you tell the management you cannot fulfill the terms of the contract working in such a stressful situation. Either they will let you go or they will bring in the offender and read them the riot act. Either way you win. If they let you go, at least you will be able to find another contract where you will not have to put up with crap from an office moron. If they, instead, decide to take "administrative action", you have established your own dignity and self-respect to anyone else in the office who would seek to emulate your friend.

Business is much like life in the so-called "state of nature" - the strong survive and the weak get weaker. There is no use in trying to accomplish a contract if you are going to be thwarted every step of the way by an antagonistic employee. It would be wonderful if spreading "sweetness and light" around the place would neutralize your enemies. But the reality of the situation is that you have to put up your fists and be ready to go ten rounds. Otherwise, you might as well stay in your corner.

The Visitor From Planet Zardo

A few words should also be said about having to work with a "space cadet" employee. There is no adequate definition or comprehensive description of the guy from Zardo, but we have all run into them at some time in our work experience. These are people who just don't have "it" in order to keep up in the world of high-tech. They keep their jobs because they have either been with the company for a hundred years, or they are really "in" with someone important.

If it were just a matter of competence, it would not be that big a problem. You could lead them by the hand step by step and give them some valuable training and experience. But with the space cadet, it is more a question of ability. All the training in the world is not going to get these people up to par.

It is likely you will get one of them on a project, because they often wind up working with consultants on the short-term projects, since nobody wants to work with them on a long-term system development effort. Listen to my friend from Virginia:

> I was put on a team to come up with a better inventory system. The other members of the project were all first-rate. But with my luck, I got assigned to

a real dud. In ten years of programming, this guy still struggled with simple job control language (JCL). And Lord help him if he took a simple data exception abend. The rest of the staff were sick of trying to carry him, so he became my "responsibility". I ended up having to do his work, as well as mine. It was only through sheer luck that halfway into the project, he was assigned to another team.. as a manager!

> *COMMENT: This is one of the few times when there is little difference in being an employee or a consultant. When it comes to the Zardo Man, all you can do is complain. And little is likely to be done about it, no matter who you are.*

Here is one strategy. When you first suspect one of your team members is a "flake", get yourself a small notebook and start keeping a short journal. This might sound like a rotten thing to do, but it is your butt at stake and not his, if the project crashes. You should note down the failures your teammate makes and your assessment of why the failure occurred. You will know the errors they cause because they will probably run to you for help.

After about three to five weeks of note-taking, you should arrange a meeting with management and fill them in on your findings. No, you are not ratting on someone, as more than likely the manager knows about the space case. And even if you are, so what. You have a professional obligation to let your client know any time you feel the project is in trouble. Two weeks past the anticipated deadline is not the time to tell management that things went to hell because one of the team members could not cut the mustard.

> *TIP: If you are put on a project you feel cannot be done with the current level of team expertise, speak up. It is your ass that will be carved up during the post-mortem, so you may as well cover it now. Later will be too late.*

Pay Me. Now!

There only one money trouble you will have as a consultant - not getting it. As I mentioned earlier, it may be months before a check shows up in your mailbox. There are a few things you can do, but they are not too effective. The first is to find out about the paper flow of the invoice through the financial area. If, for example, your invoice sits on some director's desk waiting for a signature, you should hand-carry it to them for the sign-off. Tell them the truth, that you are having trouble getting paid in a timely fashion and that you are trying to expedite things. Either you will be thrown out of the office on your butt, or the manager may take a genuine interest and make an attempt to find out why there is so much red tape in trying to get a check to you.

Another tactic is to ask your manager to make a well-placed call to someone important who can grease the skids for you. This works only if you happen to be working for someone who is also important. If your manager is some top dog, the financial people are not going to risk getting this person upset. The word will be put out to get your invoices into the earliest cycle. You would be surprised what a well-placed phone call can do!

Another tactic is to simply withhold your services until a check is delivered. This is a drastic measure and obviously you should not use it unless all else has failed. But after all, you have to eat. John Riddick of North Carolina, a long time consultant put it this way:

> I just got fed up. Hell, I pay my bills every month. Why can't a big company pay theirs? The float, that's the reason. As far as I was concerned, they could float with someone else's money.

> I walked in to the big guy's office and said that I could not perform services until they had paid me for the last three months' work. I just wouldn't wait anymore.

> I slept late the next morning. The phone woke me, It was my manager telling me a check was on his desk.

> Why did I wait so long before I spoke up? It just didn't occur to me that it would really do any good.

It may not always work as easily for you. But it is possible. There is a little bit of "ruthlessness" in every big company. They will "push" you around as much as you let them. If you let them get away without paying more than once a quarter, so as to enjoy the float, then you deserve to go hungry. But if you establish a policy of "no pay....no play", they are more likely to take your seriously.

A third idea is to offer a discount for prompt payment. It sounds good, but don't do it *unless one of your colleagues tells you otherwise.* What will happen is that the company will take your one to five percent discount and still take up to three months to pay! Just try getting your discount back from your client. It makes for a very sticky situation.

If you have it on good authority from another consultant that the company will honor a discount, then offer a percent or two. In fact, while companies will not admit to it, many take their good old time in paying their bills, and in effect hold out for a discount. Why pay 100% when the can pay a few points less?

> **COMMENT**: *Take a company that normally pays out $300 million for goods and services. If they can get a 1% discount on everything they buy, then can save a quick $3 million.*

The final tactic which can be used by programmers, is one I mention with great hesitation because it is so controversial. Many times clients find it "hard" to make that final payment to contract programmers. Somehow, after you leave and they have already had the benefit of your services, your invoices seem to be forever lost in the system. Weeks turn into months and nobody seems to give a damn about your final payment. Do you drop a logic bomb or not?

Those of you who work on mainframes may not be familiar with the "bomb". It is used by consultants who mostly work for small business on micros and find that they don't get paid very often. So, they put some code in the program that locks the machine up and tells the user to call the consultant to fix the "problem". This is hard to do on mainframes, because unlike small businesses, mainframe shops have their own programmers who can "defuse" the bomb".

The bomb is not destructive. It usually is date activated and simply puts up a message saying there is a "fatal error" and that you should be called (your phone number is usually displayed). The consultant usually leaves a hidden program that will "defuse" the bomb (like changing a date file) that can be run by the user after they call you.

When you get your final payment, you call the client and have them run the "defuser" program, and that is that. They will never know what they are doing. (Tell them they are running a file-clean-up program that only has to be done once).

If you haven't been paid, when the call comes you will have to tell them that you cannot extend credit any further. Believe me, they will have a check waiting for you when you come in. When you get there, you run the program and leave. (I've actually known some consultants to send a bill for this... kind of a penalty payment!).

There are some real *ethical* as well as *legal* issues here and it is a hot topic among consultants when they get together at computer shows and user groups (as well at ICCA meetings). You have to make up your own mind on what you are going to do to insure that your final payment is made.

COMMENT: Here is what I have done, but it is not a recommendation. I never activate a bomb during a project or upon leaving. However, I have code in some startup program that can be activated by changing a file. I wait six months for payment. If after six billing statements there is no satisfactory reason as to why I have not been paid, I call the client and tell them that a bug in the program has been discovered by a client with a similar program, and I need to come in and fix it. I activate the bomb. I won't debate the issues here. This is my way of 'repossession' of my services. The bank will take your car if you don't make the payments, and the mortgage company will grab your house. Like them, I want' to be paid and the only thing I can do is bomb the system until the client pays up. Fortunately, in fifteen years of contract programming I have only had to turn on a bomb twice. Both firms deserved it. Both paid promptly. Make your own judgments and hit me with your best shot. But I have no regrets.

Stick 'em Up

Getting a raise is not quite like it was in the old days. You just can't walk into a managers office and say you are increasing the rate five dollars an hours. As long as your are on the project you started, don't ever try to raise the rate. It is considered highly unethical to hold a gun to the manager's head at mid-project demanding more money. You may get the raise, but as soon as possible, you will be booted. No amount of money is worth getting the reputation of being a "highwayman".

However, when the project is finished and they want to keep you around for another one, it is perfectly acceptable for you to negotiate a new fee. In fact, you are really more valuable to the company, since you now know something about their business and their systems. You have proved you can do good work. But there are some companies that are really "money tough". Raise the rate on them and they will boot you, and go looking for another boy or girl.

> *TIP*: Don't jeopardize a good situation by being greedy. As they say on Wall Street, "Bears make money and bulls make money, but pigs never make money." And in real estate, it is said you make your money when you buy, not when you sell. Get the right rate when you first sign, not later on.

Help, I Need Somebody...

Sometimes all the money in the world will not help if you get yourself in too deep. More than one consultant has had to leave a project because he or she wasn't technically competent to do the job. If usually happens when you try to bull your way into a project by saying you know more than you actually do, and find that you can't learn it fast enough. Thus, when you have to dance, you have trouble with the steps.

The obvious answer is to get help. And you should get help from other consultants. Let's say that you are weak in database concepts and you have to deal with the client's data base. Instead of spinning your wheels and trying to make sense out of manuals, get on the phone and find the name of a consultant who can help you. Call an agency, or another company and ask for a referral. When you get a name, give them a call and be honest. Tell them you are in a jam and you need help. Be ready to meet with your savior after hours and offer to pay a reasonable fee.

Many consultants will be so honored you called them for assistance, they won't charge anything more than a dinner and a drink. If it does cost you some money, so what? Whatever you pay will be less than what you would lose if you had to leave the project. My friend in Phoenix reports:

> I was a real lightweight in on-line programming. So,
> I called a lady who probably invented on-line systems

and I just asked for help. The next two weeks we met for an hour after work at her client's office and she gave me some of the best training I had ever had. She really helped me out. And she wouldn't take a dime. She made no money on the deal, but she made a friend for life. Over the years I have sent her enough business to pay her back over a hundred times what I would have paid her.

You should not be ashamed to turn to your colleagues for help. What do you think doctors and lawyers do? Don't ever refuse to offer assistance yourself. What is ten or twelve hours worth in return for that good feeling of knowing you really helped out someone? And when you help out a colleague they are in your debt. The next time they hear of a contract they can't take, guess who they will call first?

Hung Down, Brung Down, and Burnt Out.

If the economy is good, and you are good, you are going to burn out. You probably are saying that it won't happen to you, but it can and it will. A good percentage of consultants are workaholics and they put in a tremendous amount of energy into their work. They are paid accordingly. And making big money starts to feed on itself, such that you get used to those big checks and you actually become a slave to them. The thought of not working starts to scare the hell out of you. So what happens is that as soon as one contract is over, you rush off to another.

This could prove to be a big mistake. You have been told that you are going to work hard, much harder than you did as a full-time employee. Well, if you keep up the pace to long, you are nothing more than a heart attack or nervous breakdown waiting for a place to happen. And once it happens you have no choice but to take time off and recover.

When you feel you are starting to burn out, take some time off. No matter what the deadline is, your physical and mental health are more important. Try to remember the reasons why you went into consulting in the first place. One of them was so you could be your own boss and work when you wanted. Well, when your mind or body starts to say that you have worked yourself to a frazzle, be your own boss and order yourself to take a short vacation.

> *TIP: Try to schedule your vacation(s) and work them into your contract when you take on the project. This especially necessary when you take on a long-term project.*

It would seem that the natural time to take a vacation is when you are between contracts. Unfortunately, most consultants find themselves so preoccupied with the fact that they are out of work and will have to do marketing upon return, they don't really enjoy their vacation. Take a lesson from Joan Fields of Miami:

> When I first started out, I was scared to death of being out of work. When a contract was over, I rushed out to find another. I don't think I took a vacation for three years. When I finally did take one, I didn't really enjoy it, as I was worried I wouldn't find another contract. Well, I always did. Now I just don't worry about it. When a contract is up, I take a week or two off. I become refreshed and I don't find the marketing task as hard as it was when I used to just dash from one contract to another."

> *TIP: Whether you schedule your vacations or just take them when there is a break in the action, the important thing is that you get away from it all. Or, buy some stock in medical companies and start making payments on a cemetery plot. You can recover from the stress of consulting in Hawaii or in the intensive care unit. Take your pick!*

Giving It Up

You may even decide to get away from it all permanently. You have to be honest with yourself. If you are unhappy as a consultant, you should get the hell out. There is no disgrace here. Why do something you hate? Why be in a situation you feel uncomfortable in?

Many people go into consulting with the hopes of building an empire of their own and becoming a big business mogul. They are actually "management types" who don't really want to "do" the work... they want to direct it. Guess what happens when they realize they are not going to be able to build the General Motors of consulting? They become very unhappy campers working at a job they can't stand.

And they do it because they have become a slave to the money. It is tough to give up a $80,000 a year income and go to work for $60,000 if you are a slave to the almighty dollar.

If you are not happy, go find a full-time position. There is a good chance one of your old clients would be glad to have you. The fact that you were an independent consultant will stand you in good stead when you re-enter the job market. The fact that you could sell yourself and deliver the product will make you an attractive candidate to some company.

> **COMMENT**: *Didn't your parents tell you (and don't you tell your kids) that money is not the most important thing in life? Maybe you should convince yourself.*

You don't need a weatherman to know which way the wind blows.

Bob Dylan

Subterranean Homesick Blues (1965)

13

THE BROKERS: INDUSTRY PIMPS

A Few Words About That Chapter Title

No, I am not being insulting. This is the standard term that has been applied to agents. However, most consultants that you will speak to will tell you that the term is very applicable for *most* brokers. (I use the term agent and broker interchangeably - although in legal terms there is a difference). They are called pimps simply because they sell our services and make money off of our efforts. There is not much difference in the service they provide than that of a literary agent, or show business agent. But the "pimp" term seems reserved for our industry, not the others. If you ever use brokers in your career you will see why... you can count on it (unless you get real lucky with a good agent the first time and never use anyone else).

If I raise a firestorm of criticism, so be it, but my research shows that the majority of agents are bad. The majority of consultants that I have had dealings with over the past fifteen years have had far more negative comments about brokers than positive. The overwhelming number of consultants I spoke with in researching this book honestly believe that agents have been a negative factor in the business.

What I find interesting is that this is just the opposite of most business groups. Whenever you read critiques of one business sector or another (doctors, lawyers, bricklayers, etc.) the research almost always suggests that the "bad apples" are in the minority and that most of the participants in the industry being looked at are fine, honest, diligent etc. companies or people. (Notice that the "bad apples" usually get most of the press, doing a severe disservice to the majority of others!). In the high-tech consulting industry, it seems that the majority of agents are viewed with negative (sometimes furious) feelings and that most consultants feel that only a small (in some areas, very small) minority are honest, diligent, fair, etc. It is curious. If you ask ten people how they feel about lawyers, doctors, literary agents, they say "most are fine, a few are terrible". Talk to consultants about brokers and you get the reverse. Read on and you will find out why.

They are not *all* bad. I want to go on record with that. I have had the privilege of working with some really fine broker companies, some large, some small. And every consultant I have spoken with has the name of at least one agent they prefer to deal with over all others. While the computer consultant broker industry appears to have overwhelming numbers of less than ethical and less than honest members, there are some agents who do the business fairly, with concern, and with pride. I will highlight one of these later on.

During the first editing of this material, the readers all asked, why is the chapter on brokers at the *back* of the book, not the front. I purposely wanted you to know about *our* industry before you learned about *theirs*. We are not in the same business, for the most part. We are in the technology business, they are in the merchandising business. It is probably *more* important to know all you have read up to now if you use a broker, then if you don't. Many consultants have the mistaken idea that all they need is a good agent and they can get all the work they want. Not true. You need to know all you *now* know in order to be successful whether you use an agent or not.

> **COMMENT**: *The agent can package and merchandise you. But you have to sell you.*

Also, had I put this part up front, I was afraid you would read only one chapter and decide to use a broker and assume a "mind-set" that you could not do it on your one. Nothing could be further from the truth. Most consultants work through brokers. It is a fact. The reason for this is because most have never learned how to market themselves. They never had access to the material in this book. Almost every (like 99%) consultant you speak with who works through a broker will tell you that they would rather go direct to the client. But they don't. Why? Because they didn't know how (until, perhaps, now).

> *COMMENT:* If it is not evident by now, let me spell it out. I don't like most agents. I don't like their role most agents play in the industry. I don't care for their concept of ethics. I don't care for their greed. I don't care for their lack of consideration.
>
> I don't care if this book has not helped you learn anything about sales and marketing of your services. I don't care if you never follow any of the advice in its pages. It is not important to the author if you think much of this work is gibberish. But if you come away with one and only one remembrance, this book will have succeeded: You don't **NEED** an agent!

However, there are times when you may want to use one. There are some companies that you just won't be able to "crack". There are some opportunities that may be presented by agents that are so attractive from a technological standpoint that you just have to take it. And there are times when you will want to take a contract in a different geographical area, such that only an agent will be able to help you, short of you traveling to the city, and spending several weeks learning the "lay of the land".

You should view agents as industry resources... not as a means of entry or continued existence in the industry. Like any resource, you have to learn how to use it effectively. A word processor is a resource. Knowing how to use it is not going to get you a Pulitzer prize. The same is true with an agent. Relying on agents exclusively is one of the quickest ways to failure in the business. They can only do so much for you. They are only a resource. Again, *you* have to sell *you*.

What's An Agency

A lot of people are confused about just who is a broker and who isn't. First, let me tell you what a broker is not. There are many companies who hire hundreds, even thousands of computer literate people and provide consulting services to business and industry. The key word is *hire*. With these firms, the people are the product. They hire for the long term, seek long term opportunities with their clients, and usually make a great effort to keep their people employed even when there is no project for them. These are not brokers. First of all, they are looking for employees. Secondly, they pay their people as employees. Even though they may pay on an hourly rate basis, the rate is determined pro rata on what the person would earn as a full-time employee. They do not pay consulting rates. For example, if you are worth $40,000 a year on the open market, the company would divide this by 1920 hours in a year and pay you about $20.00 an hour; less if you want their benefit package. If you work for one of these firms (and some are excellent) don't mistake yourself for a consultant, even though that may be your job title. You are an employee who will go from project to project, but with the security (and pay) of a full-time employee. And these firms will treat you like an employee, usually with dignity and respect. They will make an investment in you through training, and they hope you will stay with them as a career.

> **COMMENT:** *Most of what is in this book is very applicable to people who work in these companies... and I have no problem with these firms so long as they really make an attempt to "keep people on the beach" and not just lay them off after an assignment.*

This chapter is about the type of company that acts as an agent for you, the consultant. They find a client, they send your resume to it, they set up an interview, they bill the client, they take a commission from each pay period, and send you a check. At the end of the project, you are history. You will do business as either an independent (a 1099 sole prop or corporate) basis, or as a W-2 employee. But this employee status is different than the above, because brokers make no illusion about keeping you on after the project is complete: you are gone.

An agent's job the same as a pimp's job. They match consultants up with clients that need work done, and take a commission for their efforts. Unlike the consulting firm above, the agent does not care about your welfare, your needs, desires, loves, or problems. You are only as important as the revenue (commission) you generate.

There is a organization called the National Association of Computer Consultant Businesses. This purports to be the umbrella under which all the brokers can gather to lobby for repeal of 1706 (more on this later) as well as to provide insurance and legal services. They have what they call a "Statement Of Business Principles", the important points are outlined below (as printed (with permission) on page 5 in the Jan. 93 issue of *Technical Consultant Magazine*)

> **COMMENT:** *I offered the NACCB a thousand or so words (two or three pages) for material on their organization. The article they sent is in the Appendix.*

- NACCB members DO NOT defame clients, consultants or competitors.

- NACCB members DO actively avoid misrepresenting a consultant's skills or experience..

- NACCB members DO NOT misrepresent a consultant's pay rate, contract terms, assignment duration or other subjects pertinent to the business relationship.

- NACCB members DO NOT have unreasonable non-competition clauses or unfairly prevent a consultant from pursuing other opportunities.

- NACCB members DO refrain from soliciting employees of their own active clients

- NACCB members DO NOT induce consultants to breach or improperly interfere with a contractual relationship with a client or competitor(s).

- NACCB members DO have a clear policy for payment of consulting, marketing and recruiting personnel.

> *COMMENT*: You have heard the slogan, "Look for the union label"? NACCB is a good idea, but it ain't the union label. Just because a broker belongs to NACCB is not an assurance of quality. It has been the author's experience that NACCB members have been more prone to be anti-consultant in their conduct and contracts than non-members. Notice they don't call it a Code of Ethics.

Why Are There So Many?

On the scale of difficulty of entry, the broker business ranks pretty low. It doesn't take much in the way of brains or money to start-up an agency. And it is not a difficult business to run; surely more difficult than being a long-ranger consultant, but not as involved as, say a law practice or a medical office. You don't need to be a rocket scientist to get started and be successful in the consultant broker business. A sales background is the basic requirement.

Becoming an agent is a logical progression for a consultant. If you can find and obtain work for yourself on a consistent basis, you can do it for others. And if you have worked with (through) brokers, it is not hard to figure out their operations and duplicate them.

> *COMMENT*: I sometimes think it is the goal of every consultant in the San Francisco Bay Area to become an agent. Ten years ago there were about five. Now there are well over a hundred and five.

It also does not take a Nobel Prize winner to figure out that the profits in the business can be staggering. Make ten dollars an hour off of twenty people and you have the potential of grossing around $400,000 per year. At a 50% margin (which is a low estimate) you are looking at $200,000 before taxes. Twenty people is a small agency. Most of the mid-sized firms have around 100 consultants at any given time, and the large houses have up to 500.

No one is saying that the work is easy. But it sure beats flippin' burgers. And getting started is not an easy task, in a market that already has many agent firms. One San Francisco agent told me that:

> it as quite hard to get any business started, but when you start a business that has lots of competition and is

hard to differentiate our service from theirs; the potential for success is not assured. Things were so slow in the early going that I used to have these two dreams. The first had me in front of a desk and microphone and I was saying "I want to thank the Chamber of Commerce for their award for....". The other dream had me also in front of a table and microphone where I was saying "You want fries with that...".

There are three other factors that contribute to the proliferation of brokers. First, it is not labor intensive; you can do it part time to get started. Second, there is obvious demand for the service. There are clients looking for consultants (your product). And finally, there is supply; there are employees and ex-employees (a.k.a. redundant workers) who want to go into consulting.

Why They Are Loved

The overriding reason why consultants like to use agents is because most contractors (think they) cannot market themselves, or they don't want to do what it takes to get a client on their own. There is no denying that using a broker is an easier and faster way to get a client *if* you don't have any experience in marketing, don't really know the consulting business, don't know your locality, *and* haven't read this (or similar) book.

If you have banged your head against the wall for three weeks trying to find a contract, and a broker calls and has an assignment that is tailor-made for your skills, it is difficult to say no (at least until you find out the details).

Some agents truly understand the psyche and ego of consultants (some having come from the consultant ranks). These brokers know that consulting can be a lonely work-life with little psychological reinforcement. (Remember, there are damn few "attaboys" in the business; it's the money, stupid). Agents who lavish praise and attention on their consultants are often beloved, even if they are taking 50% of the gross. It doesn't matter. To some (though not many by this author's count), the work and praise are just as important as money. There are some brokers who become surrogate parents to their consultants, just the same way that some literary agents become friends, lovers, and counsel to their authors. It is not unknown to find a coach/player relationship among consultants and their agents.

> *COMMENT: There has been psychological research indicating that whores are really and truly in love with their pimps.*

Many consultants give credit to brokers in helping to get them in the business. These contractors report that with only technical skills on their resume, they could never have found their first client on their own. Many were, indeed, recruited by brokers who had consultants at the client company.

There are some clients that you can only get to through a broker. For example, the State of California has a short list of brokers that all contract programming consultants must go through if they want to perform services for the state. When a state agency has a requirement, it must call one of these brokers to get a contractor. So, if one wants to consult to the state, they have to use one of these agents, who have already bid the rate for various skill levels.

> *COMMENT: This supposedly saves the state money but many departments have trouble getting contractors beyond minimal skill requirements. So they get around this by issuing what is called "personal service" contracts.*

Clients say they like using agents when they have to staff several, indeed sometimes many, contract positions, all with different skill requirements. They can make one or two calls to their broker vendors and get hundreds of resumes by fax in a few hours.

> *COMMENT: This of course often leads to the client receiving the same resume from several brokers. To combat this occurrence, the Sacramento Municipal Utility District has a policy that if they get the same resume from more than one broker, they won't consider the consultant at all. Sure, why not punish the victim?*

Some clients have a comfort level in dealing with large broker firms. They like the attention and lunches that the marketing reps of the big brokers provide.

> *COMMENT*: When I did a contract at IBM, the project leader knew his power with the brokers and played it for all the lunches, sporting event tickets, and golf outings he could. I believe he is now selling a very interesting line of casualty insurance right outside of Peoria.

From the client perspective, finding the "right" consultant is a critical move in the game. Customers believe that they have a better chance of finding that hard-to-find person if they put the requirement out to several large brokers. The corollary to this is the client also feels it can get this "guru" cheaper by dealing with an agency. They feel the agency will do whatever it takes to 'convince" the consultant to take the assignment at whatever the client is willing to pay.

> *COMMENT*: Some client companies are downright squeamish about money. They prefer to use brokers so they can "test" the market to see what price good talent is going for and let the broker do the hard bargaining with the consultant.

Finally, clients assume that large brokers can provide project continuity. This is industry lingo for replacing bodies as they quit or burn out during long multi-year contracts. Clients like the concept that if one CASE consultant gets hit by a bus, the broker can crowbar in another without much trouble.

Why They Are Hated (Do You Have All Day?)

A long (and very interesting) book could be written on why agents are despised in *every* industry; theater, literature, insurance, sports, etc. No one seems to appreciate these individuals. Why is this? My conclusion, based upon interviews and surveys, is that (in the consulting industry) there are far more agents who practice unethically, then those who adhere to a code of ethical behavior. And even many who adhere to ethical practice, tend to hold consultants in very low regard, such that we are only mindless techno-nerds lacking the ability to survive without an agent.

The biggest myth that agents spread about us to clients is that we cannot be successful in marketing ourselves. They constantly tell consultants and prospective consultants how "hard it is out there" and that unless they sign on with an agent, they are doomed to never finding a client. In the past ten years this line has been repeated so often that many consultants actually believe it. So do clients. Since you have read this far in the book, you must realize by now that this is pure garbage. It is propaganda. It is a self-serving lie. In fifteen years in the business I have met many contractors who *didn't* market their skills. But I never met one who *couldn't* after being shown how.

> **COMMENT:** *I'm sorry, but you can't be smart enough to know the complex nature of your particular niche, be it analysis, programming, communications, etc., and not be able to master the relatively simple principles of marketing and sales.*

The second great myth the agents perpetuate is the replacement principle mentioned earlier. This is nothing but a scare tactic that broker marketing reps use with clients to scare them from doing business with us. A broker with their collection of resumes will have no easier time finding a replacement consultant than would a client that had their own collection of resumes. All a client need do is "put the word" out either by small classified ads, a call to the local computer consultants association (such as ICCA), or by making a few calls to some consultants asking for referrals for a specific qualification.

> **COMMENT:** *Several years ago when I did a contract at Pacific Gas and Electric, one of the consultants broke a leg skiing and would be out for six months. PG&E did an experiment. They called two brokers with the requirement and also asked their three consultants to assist. The word went out on the consultant grapevine. In two days PG&E had three solid candidates to choose from. The brokers were able to come up with several resumes, but none of the consultants were available immediately. This may not be scientific methodology, but it convinced me of the myth of replacement.*

Clients and consultants hate agents for the money they make. The argument is that brokers not only drive rates up, but also take "all the money". Evidence suggests (although it is not conclusive) that clients who use brokers pay more for consultants, then they would if they dealt directly with the contractors.

Contractors want a certain rate. Brokers need to pay close to that in order to attract consultants. Most brokers add 25% to 45% on to the rate the consultant gets. For example if a consultant wants $40 an hour and the house has a 25% market up, they charge the client $50 (.25 x $40 = $10, $40+$10=$50). If the house can talk the consult into taking $35 an hour, and still charge the client $50, the house getting a 42% mark up. ($50 - $35=$15, 15/35=.42). Another way of looking at this is percentage of billing. On the $40-$10 split, the agent is taking 20% of the total ($10 is 20% of $50). On the $35-$15 split the house gets 30% of the billing ($15 is 30% of $50). No matter how you figure it, the price a client pays goes up noticeably.

Brokers argue to their clients that if the customer didn't pay it to the agent, they would pay it to the consultant. If the house can get $50 an hour, why shouldn't a consultant dealing direct with the client also charge $50, the agents ask? The first answer is that the consultant will take less in order to compete with the agent. *But the real truth is that if there were no agents is it is unlikely the rate would be $50 in the first place.*

An analogy that can be made is in real estate. Studies have shown that comparable houses (usually tract homes) sold by-owner are cheaper than those sold with agents; usually by half the agent commission. Thus a client that pays a consultant $45 on a project that they would have paid an agent $50, saves 10%. If they pays the consultant $40 as opposed to the agent $50 fee, they save 20%.

The payment practices of most agents have received much scorn from consultants as well as clients. The bottom line is that many agents try to delay payment to the contractor for as long as possible. They try to talk the consultant into not demanding payment until the client pays the agent. It doesn't matter that the whole business world runs on payment due on invoice or net 30. Agents want to live by another set of rules.

There are many cases of agents receiving money from a client and either floating it, or worse, using it to pay *another* contractor who is threatening legal action because the client he is working at is *really* a slow pay. So you could be working for a client that pays its bills to the agent quickly, but the agent is using the money for someone else or something else. Nice, huh?

> *COMMENT: Look up the term Ponzi-Scheme in your Funk&Wagnels Encyclopedia.*

Sometimes you don't get paid at all. The agent just steals the last two or three payments and goes out of business. One unhappy consultant told me this story and it was confirmed by a broker:

> The agent owed me about $3,500 when the contract was over. Two weeks later I learned his corporation had gone Chapter 11. I also learned that there were over 50 other consultants that he owed money to. Yet the books looked good. He had cooked them to perfection. There was nothing we could do. We "knew" he skimmed the money. It was even more disheartening when a month later he went back into business under a new corporate name, in a neighboring city, about a hundred miles away. Even tough "we" put the word out on him, he was able to pull the same stunt there.

> *COMMENT: I must have heard over a hundred sad stories from consultants about payment problems they had with agents. I don't know how many of them were true, but I had no reason to suspect these contractors of lying. Several agents also told me how easy it is for an unscrupulous broker to "screw over" s consultant. Who can afford to sue for a few thousand dollars.*

Another complaint is the freeze-out. This is the non-compete clause found in most consultant/agent contracts. Many agents attempt to retain an exclusive on the consultant's services by prohibiting him or her from working at the client for a certain length of time. If the time period is reasonable, this is no big deal. But some agents have clauses that prohibit the consultant from working at the client, or any company that could be considered a client, for a period of one year, in a geographical radius of 100 miles from the agents office. I've known agents that make consultants sign an agreement that they won't work for any client that the agent even introduces them to (via an interview) for a period of six months.

> **COMMENT:** *The worst was an agent that wanted me to agree that they would have right of refusal (not <u>first</u> refusal, but refusal) on the client for life... I could never work at that client through another broker or on my own without the express written permission of the broker (and the commissioner of baseball!).*

Another abusive practice of many brokers (especially some members of the NACCB on the West Coast) is what I call the "indentured servant" clause. This give the agent the right to cancel the contract at any time, for any reason, with no notice. However, the consultant cannot cancel his or her services for any reason without being considered in breach.

The editors thought I was making this up. But I have it in writing. Item 2, Term of Agreement for Chamberlain Associates, Inc. in San Mateo, CA,(an NACCB member) states *"Contractor may not voluntarily terminate its services under this Agreement before the end date unless, as stated in writing by the TPU, the project has been completed or the services are no longer required".* My attorney told me that if I signed this, I should just deed over my house to them and save everyone a lot of time and trouble should I break my leg or have an emergency.

To go one step further, the NACCB standard contract, at this writing, also provides for *liquidated damages.* Some agencies strike this but Midcom of Mountain View, CA has contract wording that states (I have it in writing) that if the contractor has to bail out *"Contractor shall be liable for liquidated damages in the amount of $80 per day for each non-holiday weekday between the date of termination and the end date to compensate the BROKER for its lost commission not to exceed ten (10) eight hour days at Contractor's billing rate."* If they bill you at $50 an hour, you owe Midcom $4,000 ($50 x 8 hrs. x 10 days) if you suffer a broken leg 2 months before the contract end date.

When unethical business are mentioned, the one that occurs most often is called the "take out". Here is what happens, and judging from my research I suspect it happens more often then one would think.

The broker gets a requirement that he knows has been put out to several houses. Because they might have dealt with you before, or you are well known, they think you would be favored to win. But, they know you are high priced and they can get a better "return" by using someone else. Or they want to use one of their "favorites" so they don't lose them to another broker.

The agency calls and finds that you have not been contacted by anyone else for the assignment. They seek to represent you at any rate you wish. You say "great". However, what you don't know is that they can get a better commission by using the other person. So they represent you at a price that guarantees you won't even be considered. Or, worse, they don't even submit your resume. Or, they submit, and if the client wants to interview you they say you are now unavailable. They actively pitch their favored candidate. A consultant friend from New Jersey had this happen to her:

> A large regional agency called me and told me about a contract at MCI. They knew I was a shoo-in because I had done work there a few years back and knew the people and systems. I gave them the go-ahead to submit me for a rate of $40 hr.

> For over three weeks the agent never returned my calls. Finally, I called a friend at MCI who told me they had no record of my resume being submitted. The person who won the contract was from "my" agency. I also learned that MCI was paying $50 an hour to the house. I contacted the winning consultant, told her my story, and she told me that her rate was $36 hr. Obviously, the broker would make far more with her, then with me.

> When I confronted the agent with all of this they swore up and down that I had received bad information and that the client had rejected me over the other consultant. Since everything was told to me in confidence, there was nothing I could do.

> But every chance I get, I tell this story to clients and consultants alike. Maybe it does some good. It makes *me* feel better.

A variation on the above is when an agency finds out you are being represented by a competing broker. It can happen that the agency's marketing rep will say some rather disparaging things about you to the client, in the hope of discouraging them from considering you. They have your resume so they know something about you. They make up the rest. Fortunately, most clients don't believe agency sales reps any more than they believe hardware or software sales reps!

Some agents are not just content to take a vast portion of the billing, they expect the consultant to act as a sales rep at the client's office. There are contracts the impose a penalty if the consultant learns about a possible client need and does not report it to the agent. The penalties get even higher if the consultant tells another agent or consultant about the opening. I have found these clauses to be more prevalent on the West Coast, especially Southern California.

A practice that happened all the time several years ago has been pretty much eliminated by most brokers, but some still are guilty of "papering". This is the practice of sending out a "book" of resumes (with or without names) to clients without the permission of the consultant. The reasoning being that if the broker sends out your resume and then you later (not knowing of the broker's submission) send it direct, the broker can claim an "imputed" representation of your services if the client wants you. The legal implication was that if you send your paper to an agent, you are giving implicit permission for them to circulate it. With the increase in the number of brokers, a great deal of duplicate submissions were occurring such that the clients were being dragged into the "who do you want to represent you" dispute. Due to client pressure, (not consultant pressure) an unwritten rule has been established that a resume does not go out without the contractors permission.

> **COMMENT:** A consultant in Santa Clara, Ca. had his resume repeatedly circulated without permission by a small broker house. He decided to get even. He forwarded a new resume to the house and put "Copyright 1990 by John Jones, all rights reserved" on the bottom of each page in small lettering. Sure enough he found that the resume got into the hands of a prospective client. He called his lawyer and filed an infringement of copyright suit. It was slam dunk, cut and dried. He settled for a tidy sum. I understand the broker went out of business.

Each of the above items constitute a pretty awful picture of brokers. And surely most brokers are not guilty of *all* of these abuses. They could not stay in business. When I asked consultants what sin the majority of agents were guilty of, well over 90% of those surveyed talked about the neglect, curtness, coldness, and downright rudeness they received from brokers they had worked with.

I'll go on record and say that the majority of brokers treat us like bad meat. Their attitude is that there is an endless supply of horseflesh out there. So, why knock yourself being nice and returning calls. We consultants understand that it is strictly a business relationship between them and the agent. But it should be a *pleasant* relationship. Most often it isn't.

The loudest complaint I've heard is how the brokers put on the hard sell to get the consultant to lower their rate. There is no doubt that some consultants are not realistic about what they are worth. But that is their choice. The agents don't have to deal with these people.

But, many brokers feel that it is their duty to "crunch" the consultant's rate down as low as they can get it. This is not so much to make a "sale" but to make as large a commission as possible. Many of the brokers have their reps on commission and they train these "bull dogs" into the fine art of high pressure tactics in order to squeeze out an extra dollar or two from the contractor. It is not a pretty picture to see these "used car" manipulators go to work on a young consultant or one they know is very hungry.

As for the personal side of the business, this affects some people more than others. Many consultants would rather do business with people they like and trust, and perhaps pay a bit more, than get top dollar and have to work with asses. Their feeling is that if a house can't return their calls, keep them informed on the client's selection process, and treat them with respect and dignity, than to hell with them. Others don't seem to care one way or the other.

One of the reasons why so many broker reps are so negligent in the simple protocols of business, like returning calls, treating people with respect is due to age and pressure. So many houses hire young people out of school who have never been trained in "traditional" business behavior. They are trained in high pressure "make that sale and get that commission" marketing organizations. They start making some good money and believe that the more abusive they are the more they will make. When the broker manager says "Don't worry Susan, I know you can grind the guy down five bucks an hour", what do you expect Susan's attitude will be?

1706

Section 1706 of the 1986 Tax Reform Act is the most important piece of federal legislation effecting the consulting industry. In a nutshell, this act virtually outlaws three party consulting arrangements where the consultant acts as an independent. The three parties are the client, the broker, and you. The law says , in effect that anyone who is a subcontractor (i.e. you) to a prime contractor (i.e.. the broker) must have *employee* status, not *independent* status.

It is a long story how this law came into effect with lots of different elements of the computer industry all pointing the blame at their "competition". The loudest outcry is from the brokers who say that the big consulting houses like Price Waterhouse and EDS lobbied Congress to pass legislation so that brokers could not undercut the "big houses" during the bid process. Since brokers used 1099 people, they did not have to have the costly infrastructure to take money out for taxes, offer benefits, etc. This gave the brokers an unfair advantage over any bidders who "helped the economy by employing people". The charges and counter charges have been going on for years.

The real support for 1706 was probably the IRS and the tax agencies of the states. The IRS has claimed for years that independent contractors (in all businesses) cheat on their taxes by not declaring their total income; and it is difficult for the IRS to track this income down. This was a way for the IRS to eliminate the problem. If everybody is an employee of a corporation (i.e. nobody is self-employed) taxes are withheld and there is a clear cut audit trail.

The software consulting industry was probably singled as a "test" case. We were not organized and with several large firms (the big guys) backing the legislation, it was easily passed.

The law applies only to self employed 1099 people.... sole props. It says nothing about corporations. Thus, there has been a tendency for many consultants to simply incorporate their business, make themselves an employee of the corporation, and contract with the broker. On the other hand, many consultants decided to simply take W-2 employee status with the broker and suffer withholding and loss of several tax write-offs.

> *COMMENT: The main tax difference between working W-2 and being independent is that an independent uses a Schedule C for their deductions and the W-2 must claim employee business expenses. Doing a Schedule C is easy. But it takes a good tax person to help you claim all the possible employee deductions and document them correctly.*

Section 1706 should *not* dissuade you from being a consultant. The law is only concerned with three party arrangements and has no effect when you contract directly with the client. In addition, it is widely held that the law is unconstitutional in that it discriminates against a class of people - technical specialists. As a result, many agents simply ignore the law and have continued to contract with sole prop consultants. Others, out of fear, will only work with you on a W-2 basis. And some, only deal with consultants who have incorporated. Either way, there is no risk to you. If the broker signs you as a 1099 and is audited such that the IRS says you were really an employee, the agent, (not you) is liable for the back taxes and penalties.

> *COMMENT: As you can guess there has been a "whole lotta shakin' goin' on" over 1706 the past several years. The NACCB and the ICCA who are often on the opposite side of the fence on many issues, are actively lobbying the Clinton administration for a change. The early line is that the Congress will do away with 1706 and substitute a flat 10% withholding for all contractors (in all industries) who work on jobs that gross them over $10,000. (Otherwise you would have to withhold 10% of the baby-sitter's pay, the kid who mows your lawn, etc.)*

Finding And Choosing An Agent: The Ads Lie

Obviously, the best agent is the one that is referred to you by someone you trust, so ask around. If you are referred to an agent by some well meaning person, be sure to check the broker out by asking other consultants.

> **TIP**: *It is considered very bad manners in the business to give out the names of consultants to agents unless you have the permission of the consultant to do so. Brokers will always ask. Tell them your policy is not to disclose names. They will understand (at least the good ones will) and not hound you.*

Your first direct experience with an agent will probably be over the phone because of a newspaper ad. Please, please, please, don't trust the ads.

Many states have laws that say an employment agency can't advertise jobs that don't exist. However, brokers are not employment agents (and are not licensed as such unless they do placements). Resumes are the brokers stock-in-trade. Brokers never really know what requirements they will receive from a client and they like to have a fresh stock of resumes for many different skill-sets (this is the new industry buzz-word). Therefore brokers are always advertising for skills that they don't have actual projects for. They need fresh meat to throw at the clients when feeding time comes around!

So, if you see an ad, it does not necessarily mean that a project actually exists. The agents want to qualify you and your resume for potential assignment. There is noting wrong with this so long as you understand it. This is why, when you call the agent, unless you have a skill where there is an actual requirement, (which is not likely as they would already have several potential contractors from 'yesterdays' stack of resumes), they are not going to fawn all over you.

> **COMMENT**: *So why do the brokers continue to run long ads listing every skill-set (that word again) under the sun? They take contracts with the newspaper for so many lines of classified space (usually thousands) at a discounted rate. If they don't use the contracted space by the end of the year, they are back-billed for the difference between the regular rate (known as the open rate) and the contract rate.*

When you call the agency you are likely to find yourself talking to a young kid on his or her first job. They have no idea about what you really do for a living. They are just salespeople who often don't even know "what" they are selling. Many of the senior reps at the agency often employ "bird-dogs" who's job it is to make the calls, handle the walk-ins, and make the initial call from a list of qualified contractors. Don't be surprised if you get a message that Sue Smith called from XYZ Agency and that you should call back a Mr. John Jones.

> *TIP*: Don't deal with the bird-dog. It is a waste of time. Trust me on this. Better yet, don't deal with brokers who use them.

Many consultants report that the size of the broker has a direct bearing on how they are treated and the deals they make. I've never head a consultant say that they would rather do business with a "good" large house over a "good" small one.

> *COMMENT*: The large houses always say that they have the resources to pay your invoices... yet almost every house has a "no pay until we eat" policy. They also say they have more project leads. Very few clients give exclusive requirements... they call every broker in town when they want to fill an assignment. The small brokers get the same leads as the big guys. Why do you think there are so many small brokers? Because they can survive.

Usually before they will meet with you they will want you to fill out a skill sheet. This lists every conceivable computer, software, industry, application, methodology, etc. in creation. You are to check off those you have worked on and usually circle an experience level... like from 1 to 10.

> *TIP*: Check off everything you have ever worked on as well as anything you want to work on. Even if you can't do it, check it off. You can learn it. This sheet goes into the computer and is used for selection purposes. If you don't check it, you won't be called for it.

When you meet with the agent, try to get a lunch out of it. Many agents work out of their home and will be pleased to take you to lunch. Getting them out of their offices sometimes gives you a better idea what they are *really* like. Anyway, they are on expense account. You usually don't have to put on a dog and pony show for agents. They meet 50 to 100 people a month and they know all the tricks. Just be yourself and be honest. But don't talk money (see below). When they ask your rate, tell them you are flexible, or give them a range between $10 and $100 an hour!

Sometimes you will be in the wrong place at the right time. You will have a skill where the agent has a client with a dire need, but who doesn't want to spend any money. You will get a big lunch, lots of compliments about your background, and will be introduced to everyone at the office as if you had just thrown a no-hitter at the World Series. You are being set up to accept a less than adequate rate for your services. Agents do it because we fall for it.

> *TIP*: *If you want lavish attention paid to you, buy a dog, not a broker.*

One last thing on personally dealing with agents. Don't let them talk you into doing a technical phone interview with their clients or even with one of their in-house people. This tactic is used to screen you out, not in. Simply tell them you don't do phone interviews except to out-of-town clients on a direct basis.

> *TIP*: *Over the years I got tired of answering the question of "why" I will or won't do something. I was told by Ross Perot when I worked at EDS to simply tell people what your "policy" is. People don't argue with "policy", and "policy" is never rational... it is just "policy". When they continue to ask why, something is "your policy", simply say it is "your policy". For example, Question: "Why is it your policy not to do phone interviews?" Answer: "It is a policy that has served me well". With agents (and sometimes clients) it is often best, as someone said, to "never apologize, never explain".*

Dealing For Dollars: A Few Rules

Negotiation of a rate with a broker is not difficult if you know what you are doing. If you follow a few common-sense rules you will do o.k. Just remember that whatever money you leave on the table is picked up by the broker. It is not like you are giving the client a discount as you would if you were dealing direct. Always remember that the agent pretty well knows what he is going to charge (i.e. what he can get from) the client.

The first rule of rate negotiation with brokers is not to be the first to mention money. No matter what you say, *you loose*. You will be either too high and force the broker into some hard ball position, or (more likely) you will be too low, thus accepting a bad deal.

Always let the agent tell you what he is willing to pay. They will ask you point blank what your rate is. Your job is to be stupid. Tell them you have no idea what it would take to "win" the contract, and that you usually leave it up to the agent to suggest a fair amount.

The second rule is never to accept the first offer. The agent is going to do what is in his best interest *not yours*. You will probably be low-balled. Even if you are not, you can always do better.

The third rule is to re-read the second rule.

The fourth rule is never, never, never, sign "something" concerning *anything* before you interview. Some brokers use this ploy to lock you into a low rate for a particular client.

> *TIP:* I won't sign anything with a broker except a final contract. Some try to get non-disclosures signed before they will reveal the client. Don't do this. If you can't come to terms with the agent you would be prohibited from going with another agent for that client should one call. Let them take the risk.

The final rule is to find out what they are going to bill the client. Ask. They will tell you that it is confidential, or not policy or whatever. Ask what they have to hide, since you will probably find out once you are on the contract.

> *TIP:* If a broker won't tell me the rate or a close approximate, I walk. If we can't trust each other, we can't do business. I've walked from many, many agents.

It is permissible to go on a client visit/interview before you have established a rate with the broker. Sometimes this is to your advantage, because you will have more ammunition that you and the broker can use to pry a higher price out of the client. Many agents have to deal with clients who have unreasonably low expectations of what a good consultant will cost. By sending you out there with the hope you will be impressive as hell, the client will be willing to face "rate reality".

Many consultants adopt a policy of not giving up more than 20% of the billing. Others will give away more if they really want the assignment or if they are very hungry. You have to decide your own comfort level. You have to decide if it doesn't matter what the broker charges so long as you get your rate; or if it is important that you keep a certain portion of the billing.

> **COMMENT**: *Consultants are split right down the middle on this one. Half don't give a damn what the agent gets so long as the consultant gets his. The others, like myself, do not believe it proper for a broker to take more than 20% of the billing, no matter what he pays me. I believe (but could not prove in court) that a broker has a fiduciary relationship with the consultant. This means the broker has to put my interests before his. Lots of people think I live on Planet Zardo.*

On W-2 status, agents take your rate, add 14% to it and then add their profit to arrive at a billing rate to the client. The 14% covers their FICA, FUTA, and other payments. Thus if you get $40 an hour, the agent will bill around $60.60 if he takes a $15 profit. To get an accurate picture of the percentage of the billing you get subtract the 14% from the total amount and divide that into your billing rate. (14% x $40 = $5.60, $60 - $5.60 = $54.40, $40 / 54.4 = 73% , leaving the broker with about 27% of the billing.)

Finally, if you had verbally agreed to a rate before you interviewed and upon meeting the client find that they want a much higher skill level, decline the assignment if the broker can't get you more money. There is no worse feeling in this business than to know you are working for less than you are worth on a particular project. Every once in a while business conditions warrant it, but not often, and not long term.

> **COMMENT**: *In bad business cycles I have had to work for less than the rate I felt was due. So, don't sit home as a hold-out if your local economy is in the dumps. But in normal times you should refuse to design the space shuttle if they are only going to pay you a junior engineer rate. If you can't get a good rate, get a job with benefits.*

Selling The Broker's Product: (You)

The rule still holds. No phone interviews unless it can't possibility be avoided due to distance. Brokers like to use phone interviews because they can submit more clients that way. Usually when you do a phone interview it is not with a manager who can sign you, but with a lower level technical person who's job is to see if you know what you know.

> **COMMENT**: *A friend of mine who is world class in a particular database did a phone interview with someone who had no idea what the database product was or how it worked. It was apples talking to oranges. He never made that mistake again.*

Making the sale when you are working through a broker is pretty much the same as selling direct; except easier. You have already been pre-sold by the agent. If you follow the sales cycle presented earlier you will close most of your interviews.

And you do have to close. You won't do it with a contract, but you will want to get a client commitment if you can. If you can't, don't expect the agent to do it for you. Probably the strongest close when going on an agent sponsored client call is to let the prospect know that you are registered with many different agents and that the client should make up their mind quickly because you are waiting to hear about another project through another agent.

If you can't close the deal, you have probably lost the project. Many consultants falsely believe that the agent is going to close for them on the phone later. It is hard to close a deal that has gone cold. Also, agents are not necessarily the best salespeople either, since may of them were consultants who didn't really know how to sell (that's why they are working as salespeople now...you figure it out!).

One additional selling point in your favor when you go through a broker is that you can pitch the strengths of the broker's organization. If the client has done a lot of business with the broker they will have a positive feeling that you can do the job; based upon the quality of consultants the broker has provided in the past. One consultant from New York told me:

When I go through a broker I do what I always do at a clients office, I just don't go into as much detail and I try to get to the close as soon as possible. Since I've already been pre-sold, I take the attitude that it is a certainty that the client will want me. I tell the client that since they have been happy with the other contractors from this agency, they will be just as happy with me. I'm real hard nosed about it. I'd say "Mr. Jones, you know the kind of consultant I am by who is representing me. When do I start and where will I sit?"

It is a good idea to find out the billing rate. Simply ask. If you do it in an offhand casual way, most often you will get an answer. You have to play off of the personality type you are dealing with. If you have a rather sympathetic client, tell them you want to know so you are not being taken advantage of by the agent. If you have a hard nosed business type, say something like "I'm curious, what do you folks pay for someone like me..... $50 an hour?" By putting a price in you are likely to get a "more than that" or "less than that" answer. All that's left is to find how much. It is easy. Think about it.

By the same token, don't tell the client what rate you will get. Simply tell them that it is still under discussion and change the subject.

> **COMMENT:** The broker may have given the client a different "consultant pay" rate (usually higher) so as not to tip the client off to a possible exorbitant profit. Agents don't always deal straight with client's either.

Finally, it is best that you go to the client meeting alone. Many brokers will want to accompany you, especially the first time they work with you. There is not much you can do about it unless you can set up the meeting when only you are free. If the broker has a strong rapport with the client this may work to your advantage but most often agents go on these calls simply to get out of the office for a few hours. More often than not they open their mouth and screw things up; so say many consultants.

Avoid The Contract From Hell

Contracts are very important and you should read the one presented to you very carefully. Better yet, take it to your lawyer for review. And it goes without further comment that you should never do any work through a broker without a written contract.

You will have to negotiate several points with the broker because they will present you with a "standard" contract. It is "standard" for *them* because everything in it will be in *their* favor. You have to look out for your own interest because the "standard" contract *won't*.

> **COMMENT:** An ideal contract should be "interest neutral" where both sides have the same rules, for example in termination notice. But most of the contracts you will see will be "interest negative" to you. Every item is a positive for them and a negative for you.

The most important part of the contract concerns money. The document will spell out how much you will be paid, usually on an hourly straight time rate. On a 1099 contract make sure it stipulates that you get paid for *every* hour you work, not just up to some maximum.

Just as important as how much, is *when* they will pay you. Many brokers pop a clause in that says you wont' get a check *until* or *if* the broker gets paid. Of course this means you are taking the risk along with the broker. But that is not why you signed on with a broker. Don't let them do this to you. Insist on net 30. Make them strike any language with an "until or if" clause. They will fight you like a tiger on this. They will tell you that they "always pay" net 30 but still want this clause in. Again, if you allow this to stand, you are asking for trouble. Every consultant will tell you the same thing. Please believe me! Don't allow any contingencies with respect to your rate or timeliness of payment. Don't sign anything that is "interest negative".

> **COMMENT:** If they don't pay you because the client didn't pay them and you signed the contract allowing this, you have no recourse. However, if they don't pay you net 30 you at least can take them to court (if you can afford to).

If you are working as a W-2 you will not have to worry about when you will be paid as by law they have to pay you every two weeks.

However, they may insist that you are not allowed to get overtime (at the straight time rate), even though in most states you are entitled to it.

Contract termination is another issue where brokers take advantage of us. Most brokers will put a contract before you saying that they can cancel you anytime with no notice, but you can only get out by giving thirty days notice. Earlier I talked about one broker who had a contract that said you couldn't terminate the contract at all! What goes for them should go for you. If they insist on two weeks notice from you, they should have the same terms. Many times they will try to intimidate you by saying that you must be less than honest if you are considering breaking the contract. Don't comment. Just tell them you object to the unequal treatment and that you insist on parity. They will amend it. Don't sign anything that is "interest negative".

Some brokers will try to include liquidated damages in their contract, should you decide to terminate early. This is a somewhat new development in broker contracts, and I have seen it mostly in NACCB contracts. Often the contract allows the broker to collect a specified sum of money, usually equal to their billing rate for two weeks. Some contracts allow the broker to sue you for the total value of billing remaining on the contract! Some agents will exempt damages if you have to leave due to an emergency, but they want to keep your last monthly payment if you leave for any other reason. Don't sign a contract with liquidated damages. It is a scare tactic. I've only known one agent who would not delete this clause.

> **COMMENT**: *I could understand this clause if the broker was going to suffer payment of some penalty to the client. But I have never heard of such a thing. Don't sign anything that is "interest negative".*

The term of the contract should be for a fixed period and should not have an automatic extension feature. Some brokers try to slip this in to keep you at the same rate for projects that tend to run months (or years) over schedule. Some consultants try to keep their contract term very short with the hope of re-negotiating the rate. This is a mistake. Sign for the expected length of the project. If you are in a "position" to re-negotiate later on then do it, otherwise keep your rate and sign an extension. The option should be yours. Don't sign anything that is "interest negative".

Every broker will have some non-compete language in the contract. Nobody will argue that brokers are entitled to some protection from an unscrupulous consultant. But, some contracts are more obnoxious than others. A fair contract would read that you won't do business for 90 days after the contract, in that client's *one* division, at the client's *one* location. Agents will often try to lock you out of a client, its customers, all its subsidiaries, and in a worldwide area. But, they will back down on this if you propose the 90 day clause outlined above. Don't sign anything that is "interest-negative".

Along with the non-compete will be paragraph after paragraph of language concerning confidentiality of both the clients business and the brokers. Most consultants have no problem with this. However some agents go to an extreme and do not allow the consultant to reveal their rate or where they are working to anyone but their spouse. This is ridiculous. I've always had this language removed because it think it demeans me. But if you have no problem, then forget it.

You are signing a contract to perform consulting services, not sales and marketing services. Many brokers surreptitiously try to make you their salesperson by including language making you report any openings you might hear about to the agent's rep. Some brokers have written in damages if an opening pops up and you don't report it. This is another new development in contracts. Again, it is put in because we are stupid and don't contest it. If you don't mind being the on-site rep for your agent, by all means go ahead. But you should get some kind of commission if you help the agent fill another consulting spot.

> *TIP*: Don't complicate your life. Stay out of the sales and marketing game, even if you are promised a big commission. The client hired you to do a specific job... not to go bird-dogging around the company looking for open slots. Don't ask for trouble. Have the agent strike the clause. They will.

Finally, most brokers believe that if the client wants to hire you full time and that you agree, they are entitled to a commission. This often equals one third of your proposed yearly salary. Half the consultants surveyed had no problem with this, the other half do not like the idea. If you have no problem with the concept, at least put a time limit in, say any hiring done during the contract or for 90 days after allows the agent to collect from the client.

> *TIP*: *Did I say it often enough?   If not, here is my heartfelt advice to all consultants engaged in contract negotiation:* **Don't sign anything "interest-negative"**.

Broker Relations

You have obligations to act in an ethical manner, if you expect the broker to act the same. Brokers always tell horror stories about how they have been screwed by consultants; and many of these stories are valid. It is an open question as to whether the rather one-sided contracts that we are presented with by brokers are a result of unethical behavior on our part or greed on the broker's part. Your answer will depend on whether you are a consultant or broker; and I have spoken to them both.

There several "rules" that you should follow in dealing with your agent.

Don't do an "end-around" the broker. This is their number one complaint. Don't try to terminate your contract with the client and then try to sneak back in a week or two later at a higher rate. Many clients like this because even though you get more money, they are paying less. Often times you will split the broker's commission with them. Not only is this unethical, but when the word gets around in broker circles, you won't work through any broker in your area again. They will black-ball you.

> *COMMENT*: *In the early eighties I did a contract through a large house. The regional office manager was known far and wide as a top notch, straight shooter, and he had the respect of clients and consultants. They had interest -neutral contracts, paid good rates, and paid their contractors two weeks from date of invoice like clockwork. One young man decided to do an end-around by making a separate deal with the client (a utility company). He terminated his contract and went direct to the utility. When the broker heard about it, he went ballistic. Because the agent had such respect, indeed power in Sacramento, the young man didn't work again in this town, and was actually forced to move to San Francisco in order to work. Was this fair? You be the judge. Be careful out there.*

Along the same line, if you sign a non-compete clause, honor it. If the situation comes up where you have another broker call you for an assignment at a client where you are frozen out, call the agency and see if you can get it lifted. Most brokers will cooperate. If they won't, don't bother suing, you will lose. Just ask them to take your name and skill-set off their computer and never to call you again.

Don't pimp for any other agent at your client's site. This goes for whether you are direct or through an agent. I said earlier it is best not to be a sales rep for your broker. It is definitely a sign of bad faith to scout for another agent. You will be offered all sort of incentives to pimp for other brokers (as well as for full-time headhunters). Maintain your independence and keep out of the agent business.

Don't blab to your broker about the operations, management, or any gossip you might hear at the client's office. If the client finds out, you are in deep doo-doo. Lots of brokers will want to know the "latest and greatest" from the client's shop. They use the information as a sales angle. The big problem is that the sales rep will say something like "I heard it from Al Canton that....". That's just what you need, right?

> *TIP: I alluded to this earlier. At the client's office, keep your mouth shut, your ears open, believe half of what you see and none of what you hear. Use any information you might obtain to your own advantage.*

If you are not paid within a reasonable period past your invoice date, don't work. Sometimes the only way you can squeeze a check out of the agent is to withhold your services. But don't do this one day past the 30 days from date of invoice. Talk with them first. Most are reasonable and will try to get some money to you quickly. Some agents are so small that they really can't pay you until they get paid by the client. Hey, you took the risk, so you better learn to live with it. If you don't get paid, sue.

> *TIP*: I put the following on every invoice, either to a client or a broker. It leaves nothing open to question.
>
> *A-Systems Payment Policy:*
>
> *We work very hard to earn your business and trust. Nothing is too difficult or short notice for us. Whatever it takes ... we will get it done. We ask for nothing up front. We have a long and successful client track record. All we ask is that your understand our situation.*
>
> *A-Systems is a small business. As such, we depend on our customers and agents for prompt payment so that we can continue to provide the best professional programming and consulting services possible. Please understand that we will absolutely withhold continued services on any account in arrears over 60 days.*
>
> *You or your clients have received our services with no advance fee. We feel it is only fitting and proper that we be remitted on our invoices in a prompt and timely matter.*
>
> *If you are appreciative of our service and expertise, please remit the total due amount at your earliest convenience. It's right and it's fair. We hope you understand.*

Finally, when I asked contractors the best way to insure good broker relations, almost all of them replied in one word: lunch! That's right, lunch. Take your agent to lunch once every three months. Discuss whatever issues you have with them. Treat them like a client. If they offer to pay, let them (they are making big bucks off of you), otherwise you pick up the tab. Also, do lunch (o.k. it's a yuppie California term... I'm sorry) at a nice place. The other guys are taking their brokers to Burger King. Who is going to be the first guy called by the agent when a new requirement comes in?

The "Almost" Ideal Broker: Abator Information Inc.

In the research for this book, I looked at the policies and contracts of many brokers, some large and some small. There are many that I would be pleased to work with. However I came across one that I could endorse as a model that other agents could follow. This is Abator Information Services, Inc. of Pittsburgh, PA.

Abator is not perfect. I have a problem with the liquidated damage clause in their contract. But by and large, these folks are what you should be looking for in an agent.

> *I am reprinting their marketing material as they sent it to me:*

Abator - General Information for Consultants
1-800-544-1210

Abator's objective is to provide quality systems resources and support to our clients.

A brief outline, in case you don't like to read long-winded promotional material:

- Abator pays a minimum of 80% of the billing rate to the consultant performing the work.

- Payments are made every two weeks, regardless of when Abator collects funds from the client.

- Abator contracts only on a 1099 basis with independent consultants. This means that consultants are responsible for appropriate taxes and quarterly filings, and that expenses are included in the negotiated rate.

- If you desire W-2 status, Abator may be able to refer you to an affiliated vendor however, we can not dictate other vendor's payment percentages or schedules. Please request additional information if this is of interest to you.

- No resumes are submitted to potential client projects without your prior approval, including your agreement as to an acceptable payment rate.

- No resumes are submitted to clients until references are verified.

- Abator can't tell you about projects if we don't have phone numbers and a completed skills inventory!

Abator was founded in 1983, almost by chance. Our president's previous employer closed their Pittsburgh operation, with virtually no notice. After ten years project staffing and marketing in contract services, she wasn't prepared for an alternate career. Collecting unemployment was not particularly attractive so a business plan was created, funds borrowed and the new company began soliciting contracts and consultants. Abator is 90.3% owned and operated by women.

Since then, Abator has developed what we feel to be rather unique practices in our industry:

Everybody has a skills system and Abator's is probably not unique. How we use it may be! The application was developed to eliminate typographical errors in technical resumes (you know, where the typist can't spell IBM!), and evolved into a new, complex networked system which tracks a huge amount of data on skills and contact information.

When a new project is defined to Abator, the skills are automatically searched and qualified candidates are contacted with details about the project's description, duration, location and compensation. Based on this information you decide whether or not to pursue the opportunity. Abator does not submit technical presentations to its clients without the prior approval of the individual involved! So, even though it can be a real hassle, completing a skills inventory insures that you will be contacted about a wider variety of potential assignments.

The new system also serves as a standalone marketing tool. Using a laptop, the Guest password allows clients to perform searches and look at resumes based upon whatever criteria they wish to specify. Name, contact and compensation fields are blanked so that Abator has an opportunity to discuss details with you before a formal presentation actually occurs. In this way, your background can be reviewed by clients for potential assignments without compromising your confidentiality.

Compensation & Tax Status
Lots of vendors advertise big compensation. Abator's practices are clear cut. We pay minimum of 80% of the billing rate to the consultant performing the work. We will tell you the expected billing and payout rates before a formal presentation is made. Payout rates are all inclusive in most instances, with no additional compensation for expenses and you are responsible for your own tax deposits. This means that compensation may fluctuate based on the assignment, but it is for you to decide if the financial arrangements are suitable.

Payments to consultants occur every other week, regardless of when the client pays Abator. Since 1983, Abator has never missed (nor been late with) its payments to consultants.

1099 Rationale

Section 530 of the 1978 Tax Reform Act granted safe harbor from tax withholding to independent technical consultants. Section 1706 of the 1986 Tax Reform Act was surreptitiously passed to eliminate 530's safe harbor. Abator views 1706 as discrimination against a class of people preventing technical specialists from participating in the American Dream of self-employment, while allowing this freedom to others. Beyond philosophy, prior to 1986 Abator offered both W- 2 and 1099 status. Experience had demonstrated that 1099 was preferred and Abator had no W-2 consultants in December 1986. We completed the SS-8 test (20 questions) and were exempted from conversion of 1099 staff to W-2 status. Abator believes this decision was predicated upon not treating consultants performing similar tasks differently for tax purposes. Consequently, Abator is offering only 1099 status, to protect the independents already affiliated with us. If you're interested in W-2, we can recommend you to vendors through which Abator occasionally subcontracts. We can not, however, guarantee the level of compensation offered by these vendors.

Despite the independent status of Abator consultants, we are interested in establishing long term relationships. We have been fortunate in this regard, continuing to re-assign many of our original consultants to several consecutive assignments. On the other hand, we recognize that independents can not afford to put all the eggs in one basket. We make a practice of
encouraging consultants to pursue all the opportunities available to them, and we work with them to prevent duplicate submissions by multiple vendors to the same client site.

References

Abator asks for, and verifies, at least three references on each consultant. In all cases, Abator insists upon verifying references before submission of a resume to any Abator client.

Presentations/Technical Summaries

A professional summary, otherwise known as a resume, is compiled by the skills inventory system into a standard format. The skills are entered from your completed forms, and the projects are taken directly off your resume and sorted in reverse chronological order. We may make minor editorial changes, but we make it a point not to misrepresent skills or experience. This resume with a formal quotation form specifying your availability and billing rate are combined to create a presentation to the client.

Current Operations

Abator is involved with on-line, database oriented applications development and systems support, essentially performing tasks encompassing feasibility, design, construction, testing, installation and documentation as well as database design and administration, systems programming technical support and project leadership. Abator tends to represent senior level consultants, providing clients with exceptional expertise and consultants with high visibility projects.

Our goal is not to be either huge or extremely wealthy. Our commitment is to quality and longevity, not glitz. Should you visit our offices in Pittsburgh or St. Louis, you'll find moderately sized, comfortable space with low overhead. Sales, staffing and administrative functions are supported by about a half dozen people. We all work together to achieve common objectives for consultants and clients. This structure ensures a high level of personal contact and interaction with consultants and clients.

Initially, Abator's marketing strategy was to pursue major corporations not dependent on one particular industry. For example, Westinghouse is involved in electrical distribution, transportation, elevator, defense, soda bottling and distribution, watch (wrist watches!), and real estate development businesses. Subsequently, our secondary approach was to major corporations in slightly more remote locations. The premise was that these clients would be willing to pay a higher rate to attract talent and there would be less competition for their projects. Currently, we market both those segments and general industry everywhere.

Abator has provided services in such diverse locations as Alabama, Alaska, California, Connecticut, Florida, Illinois, Indiana, Iowa, Kansas, Kentucky, Louisiana, Missouri, Montana, Nassau (the Bahamas), New Jersey, North Carolina, North Dakota, Ohio, Oklahoma, Oregon, Pennsylvania, Puerto Rico, and South Carolina. Our marketing staff continues to develop rapport with potential clients in all fifty states and, to a limited extent overseas.

Standard Abator Contractual Agreements include:

- Two week cancellation clause.

- A non-disclosure agreement protecting the materials used and developed for clients. The results of the work performed for the client belong to the client.

- Abator does not sell its services based on a placement option, however we are realistic ... should you and an Abator client determine that it is in your best interests to negotiate permanent employment, Abator will not oppose such activity after twelve months on assignment. Prior to twelve months, a fee to the client would be assessed.

- The non-compete clause used by Abator is limited to 90 days, although Abator may elect to release consultants from this clause. It is also limited to those Abator clients with whom a consultant becomes familiar during the contract period, either through work performed or interviews scheduled.

And that's what Abator is all about. If we've missed a topic of interest to you, don't hesitate to call any one of us ... that's what we're here for!

Lorraine Douthett-Clements
Joanne E. Peterson

--- --- --- ---

The following is a sample of their contract. This will give you a good idea of what a "good" broker contract looks like. It will also give you a "starting point" when you begin contract talks with a broker.

Sample Time and Materials Service Agreement
For Independent Sub-Contractors

This agreement made the 00th of Month 1900, between ABATOR Information Services, Incorporated, referred to as ABATOR, whose address is 1601 Penn Avenue, Suite 602, Pittsburgh, Pennsylvania 15221; and (NAME), referred to as CONTRACTOR, of CITY, STATE, to fulfill an ABATOR project with XXXXXXXXXXXXXX, referred to as CLIENT.

Term: This contract will become effective on (DATE) and will expire on or about (DATE).

Rate: ABATOR agrees to compensate CONTRACTOR the sum of $00.00 dollars per CLIENT approved billable hour.

Termination: This agreement may be terminated by either party, without cause by giving (FIFTEEN/THIRTY) days written notice to the other. Such termination shall not prejudice any remedy which either party may have against the other either at law, in equity or under this agreement.

Termination Penalty: Should CONTRACTOR voluntarily leave contract early, with insufficient notice (excluding illness or other extenuating circumstances acceptable to ABATOR), a penalty of forty (40) hours may be collected by ABATOR from contract payments otherwise owed to CONTRACTOR.

Scope/Direction: CONTRACTOR shall perform DP services for CLIENT pursuant to the contract between ABATOR and CLIENT. These services shall include, but are not limited to: conceptual/functional analysis, design and specifications, programming, testing, implementation, documentation and user training. The entire direction, scope, control and interpretation of any systems work to be performed by CONTRACTOR shall be made exclusively by CLIENT.

CONTRACTOR shall perform the services at any designated site of CLIENT. The job site is to be determined exclusively between ABATOR and its CLIENT. It is understood that the primary site shall be (CUSTOMER)'s facility in (CITY, STATE). CLIENT shall provide the facilities and services necessary to the successful completion of this effort.

CONTRACTOR shall devote as much of his/her productive time, ability and attention to CLIENT as required by CLIENT during the term of this agreement. CONTRACTOR shall not directly or indirectly render any services of a business, commercial or professional nature to any other person(s), firm(s) or organization(s), whether for compensation or otherwise, without the prior written approval of CLIENT and/or ABATOR.

Environment: Subject to CLIENT changes, the environment is understood to be ---------. The project involves a (senior) position with responsibilities for -------- duties in conjunction with (support of) or (development and/or enhancement of) ------------.

Confidentiality/Non-Compete: CONTRACTOR covenants and agrees as follows:

- 1.1 CONTRACTOR shall not directly or indirectly, within existing or future marketing areas begun during this agreement, enter into or engage generally in competition with CLIENT (CUSTOMER NAME) in the business of developing computer programs or systems, either as an individual, partner, joint venture or as an employee, agent, officer, director, shareholder of a firm or corporation, or otherwise for a period of one year following the date of the termination of this agreement.

- 1.2 CONTRACTOR shall not for a period of ninety days immediately following the termination of this agreement either directly or indirectly call on, solicit or take away any of ABATOR's clients on whom CONTRACTOR calls or with whom CONTRACTOR became acquainted during the term of this agreement with ABATOR, either for him/herself or for any person(s), firm(s) or corporation(s), without the express written approval of ABATOR.

- 1.3 CONTRACTOR shall not for a period of one year immediately following the termination of this agreement either directly or indirectly:

- 1.3.1 Make known to any person, firm or corporation the names and addresses of any ABATOR clients, employees or agents or any other information pertaining to ABATOR.

- 1.3.2 All records of the accounts of ABATOR and any other records and books relating in any manner whatsoever to the business of ABATOR shall be the exclusive property of ABATOR regardless of who actually purchased or prepared the book of record. All such books and records shall be immediately returned to ABATOR by CONTRACTOR upon termination of this agreement.

- 1.3.3 CONTRACTOR hereby assigns to CLIENT any right, title and interest on any invention or idea, patentable or not, hereinafter made or conceived jointly with CONTRACTOR, while working on CLIENT'S project, which relates in any manner to the actual or anticipated business or research and development efforts of CLIENT, as suggested by or results from any task assigned to CONTRACTOR or work performed by CONTRACTOR for or on behalf of CLIENT.

CONTRACTOR Responsibilities:

- 1.4 CONTRACTOR shall at all times be deemed an independent sub- contractor and s/he shall do nothing to create a principal/agent or employer/employee relationship with respect to her/himself and ABATOR and or its CLIENT. CONTRACTOR shall have no authority to bind or obligate ABATOR or its CLIENT in any way whatsoever, or to accept service of process in their behalf.

- 1.4.1   All taxes applicable to any amounts paid by ABATOR to CONTRACTOR under this agreement shall be his/her liability and neither ABATOR or its CLIENT shall withhold nor pay any amounts for Federal, State or Municipal income tax, Social Security, Unemployment or Workmen's Compensation. In accordance with current law, ABATOR shall annually file with the Internal Revenue Service a form 1099-MISC., U. S. Information return for recipients of miscellaneous income, reflecting the gross annual payments by ABATOR to him/her, net of any reimbursed expenses incurred by him/her on behalf of ABATOR, pursuant to this agreement. CONTRACTOR hereby acknowledges his/her personal income tax liability for the self-employment tax imposed by Section 1401 of the Internal Code, and the payment, when applicable, of estimated quarterly Internal Revenue Service forms 1040-ES, declaration of estimated tax by individuals. Upon request by ABATOR, CONTRACTOR agrees that s/he will provide documentation evidencing compliance with all applicable Federal, State and Municipal income tax and/or self-employment tax laws in regard to amounts received under this agreement.

- 1.4.2   CONTRACTOR shall at his/her own expense procure and maintain comprehensive general liability and worker's compensation insurance, and provide a certificate of insurance upon ABATOR's written request.

- 1.4.3   CONTRACTOR shall indemnify and hold ABATOR and CLIENT harmless for and against any claim, suit or other action whether to person or property, whether injury or damage arising out of services or work to be performed under this agreement while CONTRACTOR is on the premises of ABATOR or CLIENT, including but not limited to injury and damages to CONTRACTOR and property.

- 1.4.6   CONTRACTOR shall complete ABATOR project status reports and time sheets at the conclusion of each week, and call his/her hours into the Pittsburgh office each Monday prior to 12 noon Eastern Time.

<u>ABATOR Responsibilities:</u>

- 2.1 ABATOR   shall be responsible for the handling of all administrative matters relating to this project - CLIENT billing, CLIENT interface (administrative), and CONTRACTOR's compensation.

- 2.1.1 Invoicing/Payment: CONTRACTOR shall submit invoices with each weekly time sheet. ABATOR shall make payment on invoices every other Friday according to its normal payroll schedule following a two week delay.

- 2.1.2 ABATOR   will make advance payments on invoices when deemed necessary between CONTRACTOR and ABATOR.

- 2.1.3 CLIENT shall advance/reimburse CONTRACTOR for any travel expenses incurred at the request of CLIENT, according to CLIENT's then published or oral expense reimbursement policy.

- 2.2 In accordance with federal tax laws governing independent contractor status, ABATOR reserves the right to hold CONTRACTOR financially liable in the event CLIENT refuses payment for services due to inadequate technical performance.

Conclusion: This agreement may not be modified except in writing, signed by authorized representatives. This agreement shall be governed by the laws of the Commonwealth of Pennsylvania, and all actions, regardless of who brings such action, must be litigated in the Commonwealth of Pennsylvania.

Consultant Confidential Information
Noncompetition Covenant and Invention Agreement
Relative to Clients of Abator Information Services, Inc.

In consideration of my contract with Abator Information Services, Incorporated or its allied, affiliate or subsidiary companies (hereinafter referred to as ABATOR), and in consideration of one dollar ($1.00) and other good and valuable consideration, the receipt of which is hereby acknowledged, the undersigned CONSULTANT agrees as follows:

CONSULTANT during the term of the contract with ABATOR will have access to and become familiar with various trade secrets, consisting of formulas, patterns, devices, secret inventions, processes and compilations of information, records and specifications which are owned by (CLIENT NAME) (a company which is a client and customer of ABATOR) and which are regularly used in the operation of the business of said client. CONSULTANT shall not disclose any of the aforesaid trade secrets, directly or indirectly, nor use them in any way, either during the term of this agreement or at ANY time thereafter, except as required during the course of CONSULTANT's contract.

All files, records, documents, drawings, equipment, specifications, and similar items relating to the business of (CLIENT NAME) whether prepared by the undersigned CONSULTANT or otherwise coming into his possession, shall remain the property of (CLIENT NAME) and shall not be removed from the premises under any circumstances whatsoever without the prior written consent of (CLIENT NAME).

CONSULTANT covenants and agrees as follows:

- On termination of his/her contract with ABATOR for any reason whatsoever, CONSULTANT shall not directly or indirectly, within the existing marketing area of, or any future marketing area begun during the term of this agreement, enter into or engage generally in direct competition with (CLIENT NAME) either as an individual on his/her own or as a partner, joint venturor, as an employee or agent for any person, or as an officer, director, shareholder or otherwise, for a period of one (1) year after date of termination of his/her contract with ABATOR.

- This covenant on the part of CONSULTANT shall be construed as an agreement independent of any other provision of this agreement and the existence of any claim or cause of action of the CONSULTANT against ABATOR or (CLIENT NAME), whether predicated on this agreement or otherwise, shall not constitute a defense to the enforcement by ABATOR or (CLIENT NAME) of this covenant.

- CONSULTANT shall not for a period of one (1) year immediately following termination of this contract with ABATOR, either directly or indirectly:

- 1) Make known to any person, firm or corporation the names and/or addresses of any customers or clients of (CLIENT NAME) or any other information pertaining to it or;

- 2) Call on, solicit or take away, or attempt to call on, solicit or take away any of the customers or clients of (CLIENT NAME) on whom the CONSULTANT called or with whom the CONSULTANT became acquainted during his contract with ABATOR, either for him/herself or for any other person, firm or corporation;

- 3) All records of the accounts of (CLIENT NAME) and any other records and books relating in any manner whatsoever to the customers or clients of (CLIENT NAME), whether prepared by CONSULTANT or otherwise coming into his possession, shall be the exclusive property of (CLIENT NAME) regardless of who actually purchased or prepared the original book of record. All such books and records shall be immediately returned by the undersigned to (CLIENT NAME) upon termination of CONSULTANT's contract with ABATOR.

I acknowledge receipt of a copy of this agreement and agree that with respect to the subject matter herein that it is my entire agreement with ABATOR and, this agreement being in addition to a sub-CONSULTANT's agreement executed between the undersigned, the even date hereof, and ABATOR.

The effective date of this agreement is the (the day of MONTH /YEAR).

Try It Once On Your Own

You have to decide whether to go on your own or use a broker. Many consultants won't use one, not because of money, contracts, or hassle, but simply out of pride. When you go to a new client that has several contractors, or whenever you come into contact with other consultants the first question that will be asked is "Are you on your own or are you with an agency.?"

The basic fact of life is that consultants who make it happen for themselves and do not use brokers are held in much higher esteem by their peers then those who do use agent services. I am not saying this is right or wrong. It is just a fact.

To me, anybody who braves the marketing wars and is able to put up with an unsteady cash flow is certainly a more "admirable" type than the consultant who just gets a call from an agent. When people talk about a self-made person as opposed to a person with inherited wealth, what connotation do *you* get?

Many consultants talked to me about self-respect and achievement. Those who had gotten their work through their own efforts (especially those who had used agents previously) felt a certain degree of self-pride. As one consultant from Atlanta put it:

> I used to use a large body-shop to supply me with work. I knew I was just considered by my peers as a member of a "stable", but I did not care. However when I figured out what they were making, and that I surely could get some of that money, I decided to go it alone the next time. It wasn't easy, but then it wasn't that hard either. When you sign that contract directly with the client, you really get a feeling of pride and accomplishment. Your first contract signing is a day you will never forget.

I have tried to present the positive and negative sides of dealing with a broker. You will have to decide for yourself whether or not you want to deal with them. The only guidance I can give is, everything presented before this chapter is predicated upon the eventual success of the consultant who does it him/herself.

If everything you have read seems too difficult or too time-consuming, then you might be better off going through an agency. On the other hand, if you feel that you can successfully market yourself, then you should give it a try and go for all the gold.

For many, making this decision often depends on how they feel about themselves. Some really don't give a damn about how they get their work, so long as it is steady and the money is reasonable. They are not really into the whole concept of being an independent business person, and as such, they are very comfortable working with agents. The others have deep-seated needs to be as independent as possible and be totally responsible for their own success or failure. They want the big reward and are not afraid to take the big risk. They do not go through agents. They want it all for themselves.

So, search through your own feelings and try to determine what you want to do. Do what suits you and not what other people (or me) are going to approve. It is your future at stake. One thing you might want to keep in mind: the brokers are not going anywhere. You can always try your own marketing campaign, and if it goes flop, you can always go to an agency. But, I think you should try it on your own *first*. A young consultant with two years of experience laments:

> When I first got into consulting I went through a broker for the first year or so. Then I decided that I wanted to really by my own boss and get my own contracts. It was a real adjustment to make in having to do my own marketing, instead of just waiting for the agent to call. I also had to get used to an uneven cash flow. I wish I had never started in the business through an agent. It would have been better had I started all on my own from day one.

Do what is best for you, but don't sell yourself short. If you want, you *can* do it on your own. However, you don't have to be locked into an "either-or" situation. Naturally I do most of my assignments on my own, but every once in a while an opportunity comes up through a broker that I can't resist. So I do it.

COMMENT: But I don't just sit around wishing and waiting for some agent to call. You can starve just as quickly that way as by doing it on your own, and not doing it right.

> *When the President does it, that means that it is not illegal.*
>
> *Richard Nixon*
>
> *Interview with David Frost (1977)*

14

BIG TIME OPERATOR

Starting Up Is Hard To Do

We all secretly desire to be president of General Motors (or perhaps nowadays Honda would be a better example). Every time you hear someone say that their business is small because that is the way they want to keep it, you are listening to a person who desperately wants to run a large operation. Whether they run an ice cream shop, a law firm, or a publishing company, this rationalization is just a cover-up. I've know a few consultants who simply want to run a one-horse shop, but the vast majority of contractors I have met desire to have from three to a thousand people working for them. They all want their own systems house.

It can be done. Lord knows, the demand for good software talent has never been greater.

The problem is the cost of quality people available to work for you. You might be able to take on some lightweights and give them heavy training but even this has built-in costs as well as risks. Most entrepreneurs face the universal lack of capital. It is difficult to attract good people if those people have to wait a month or two to get paid.

You might be able to get a line of credit at the bank, however, you won't get enough to really keep you going. Banks don't like to lend on start-ups and neither does anyone else. Taking a second on your house is not going to buy you that many quality employees (unless you have a mansion). Thus, unless you are already cash-rich, it is quite hard to undertake a new start-up, even one that involves no product and no inventory.

Form A Syndicate

One alternative is to form a syndicate with one or two other consultants and market yourselves as a team. The problem here is that everyone always wants to be the boss and nobody wants to be the employee. People who successfully go into consulting for themselves seem to find it very difficult to work with/for someone else, even as an equal partner. There is just too much ego involved.

However, there are scores of four or five person consulting firms around the country. They market themselves under one business name and try to get contracts where all of them can work on the same project. The head of one such firm in the Boston area says:

> Our concept is to give the client relief from project management. We like to come-in like ghostbusters and take over the entire project so that it is done right and on time. We then get out. Of course, we are available for maintenance. When a client brings us in, they can turn the whole ball of wax over to us and relax. We will do it all.

The usual structure of the syndicate is for all parties to contract separately with the syndicate (which is a separate entity, either corporate or someone's sole prop). In arrangements like this, all the consultants agree to be paid when the client sends the check. They have some pretty big parties around the first of the month!

COMMENT: Many contractor/sub-contractor syndicates are formed to get work under the MBE-WBE (called mibbie wibbie) programs. These are initials for Minority Business Entrepreneur and Women Business Entrepreneur. Many states and the federal government have stipulations that a certain portion of government sub-contracted work must go to mibbie-wibbies.

This format works pretty well so long as all the parties can get on the same contract. Guess what happens when the next assignment comes along and there is no room at the inn for one or two of the principals? It can get ugly.

Form An Agency

You can start your own agency. By now you should know all you ever want to know about broker-agents. Obviously, it is no big trick to forming an agency; the fact that there are so many of them testifies to this fact.

If you only deal with consultants who are incorporated, you probably won't have a 1099 vs. employee problem and if you can arrange with them that they won't get paid until you do, you've got it made. However, you know full well that you are not going to find too many intelligent consultants (at least not the ones who have read this book) who will go for such an arrangement.

Also, some clients will require your people to be employees, and many of your people may opt for W-2 status. This brings us back to money. If you can take the cash-flow hit of paying your employees before the client pays you, again you've got it made.

A variation of the theme is to bring very light-weight recent graduates and put them to work on a project at a client where you are assigned. This way, you can keep an eye on their work, and since they are not experienced, you won't have to pay them very much. But keep in mind that as soon as these people feel they have the right set of skills, they are going to leave you and go on their own. They will probably do exactly what you did. So keep your contacts open with the local junior college or technical school. They can be an endless source of good trainees.

One other point. Unless yours is a city without too much consulting work, you will find that the "smart money" got into this business years ago and are well established both in the client community and with the consultant community. The competition will be fierce.

> *TIP: What you will read next is, alone, worth the price of the book. Here is a concept I have always wanted to try, but don't have the skills or experience to do. **Please steal this idea!** Open up the Five Dollar Agency. Deal only with 1099 or incorporated consultants and clients that don't require employee status. Mark up your "take" at only $5; no matter what the dollar amount per hour the client is paying. Finally, spell out the fact to the consultants that you won't pay until the client pays. Not only will you be able to under price the established agencies who are taking 20% - 30% of the billing, but you will be able to attract better consultants because you will be able to pay them more. Take the case of the agency that pays a consultant (1099) $35 and bills $50. You can pay $40 and bill $45. Once you have ten or fifteen people out there, you will be doing pretty well. And the consultants will love working for you... we hate the idea of giving up 30% of the billing (15/50) but we can live with 11% (5/45). Someone is going to become the Price Club, Costco, or Schwab of consulting, will franchise the operation, and clean up. I hope it is you.*

Big $$ and Bigger Ulcers

Before you run out and buy your first limo, there are a few things you should consider. In the first palace, you are going to have to spend more time managing people and projects than doing the actual work. Many consultants start out thinking they can do both. No way.

When you get bigger you are going to find that you spend much more time doing marketing. After all, your main function as a manager is to find enough projects to keep your people busy. If you don't have enough work for your people, whether they are partners or subcontractors, or employees, they are going to pull up stakes and leave. The only reason they are with you is because they hate to market their skills or because they want to learn from you.

You also have to take a hard look at the profitability of the enterprise. Say you have two people working for you and you are making ten dollars an hour off of each. And let us assume that you can get forty dollars an hour for your services. However, you are tied up half the time doing marketing, making decisions, working on the books, etc., such that you can only bill out twenty hours a week of your own time. So you make $800 for your time and $800 off of the employees. You gross the same $1600 you would make if you worked alone and were able to bill more hours.

You have to decide if all the headaches and possible ulcers are worth the net take. Once you get past a certain level of growth, the money flows in, but it takes a lot to get to that level. This is why there are so many lone-ranger consultants out there. Sure, they would all love to run a large organization, but the price one has to pay in founding and managing a company through its growth stages is just not worth the return for a lot of contractors.

I have known many consultants that if offered a chance to step right in and run an already-existing agency, they would leap at the chance; and probably do pretty well. But these same people just don't have what it takes to do a start-up. It is just human nature. We all want it easy.

> **COMMENT:** *Several years ago I watched a friend co-found an agency. He eventually did all right, but it took several years of struggle. He called the experience "lots of bottle washing, little cooking"! He was one of the technical types who thought he wanted to run a company. But he really missed the creative challenge of writing software. He missed doing the work, and didn't really like finding the work. He sold the company and went back to being a lone-ranger; a much happier person I might add.*

The Fix Is In

Whether you are a one-gun operation or you have several associates, you can make a terrific amount of money by doing fixed-bidding. There is no magic to this, but it does involve some risk. Most consultants bill themselves out using the time-and-materials method. It is a very simple and up-front method. However, there are only so many hours in the day, so there is a limit on what you can make. This why the more experienced (and richer) consultants are moving toward fixed-bidding.

The key here is that you form a small consortium of people that will last the life of the project. For example, say you hear of a twenty-week project. You rush out and tell the client you would like to make a fixed bid for the whole project. You should be able to sell the concept as many companies are seeking fixed bids from their vendors so that they can more easily predict their technology costs. If the client goes for it, you get on the horn and roundup some people, put together a proposal, and hope for the best.

> *COMMENT:* Many agencies are starting to move away from body brokering to putting together fixed-bid total project management proposals. This is in line with the current out-sourcing craze many companies are experiencing.

You will have to spend considerable time with the client in order to see if their estimate of the time factor is accurate. On many projects, the client has no idea of how long it will take and will expect their vendors to include that in the bid. It is important that you ask the right questions of the right people before you make the proposal.

The reason fixed-bidding is profitable is that you can hide many of the costs in the total price. If you are using more than one person, your client will have a hard time figuring out what each is making or what individual costs are; nor will they care.

The way many consultants make a killing in fixed-bidding is through the incentive payment for finishing quickly. There is also money to be made in penalty payments made by the client when their people screw up and hold you back. Of course there is the risk that *you* will screw up and have to pay a penalty or discount the final price.

Bottom-line, the client is getting a guarantee that the project will be done by a certain date for a certain cost. You take the risk and the client is compensating you for it. They know they may be paying *more* than a time-and-materials contract might cost; but they don't know *how much* more and they don't want to find out! Upon close analysis, the risk is not that great. If you have had a lot of experience in the business, you should have a pretty good idea as to how long it will take to get something done.

Here is a simple method that many consultants use to determine a fixed-bid. If you know that you and two associates can design and write, say a new order entry system, in twelve weeks, then all you do is double the figure to twenty-four weeks. Then you figure out what your hourly time is worth and plug in the numbers. If the number looks too low, simply raise it. Fixed-bidding is not a precise methodology. While there are several established formulas for determining what the bid for a project should be, more often than not, these complex formulas will approximate the amount an experienced consultant will come up with by using the "good hunch" method outlined above.

The way you clean up on a fixed bid is by working your buns off and getting the job done in half the time for the full price plus an incentive award.

From a financial standpoint, if you work your butt off on a time-and-materials contract, you are working against your own interest. (This is why consultants are so often accused of never wanting to finish a project). If you do a twenty week project in ten weeks, the client will love you, but all you will have to show for it is a case of exhaustion and less money.

When you do the twenty week project in fifteen weeks, you might still have the exhaustion, but you will also have the equivalent of twenty weeks pay.

How can you *lose*? What happens if you or one of your people get sick? What happens if you find the project is much harder than you estimated and you have to bring on some extra (expensive) people? You could lose a lot of money on the deal.

> *TIP: Before you go into a fixed-bid deal, make sure you know what you are doing. It could be your best deal ever.. or it could be your last!*

"Hot Software Here! Get Yer Hot Software"

There is another method that can make you a lot of money if you go about it the right way and if you are lucky. This is the software vending business. All you have to do is either write or buy the rights to a good package of software and then become the salesman and installer of the package.

There is a lot of software sitting around out there because the people who have the right to it, do not have the time or money to market it.

Take the case of Bill Jordan, a California consultant who took a contract with a client that had an accounting package especially designed for a UNIX based computer. The company developed the package and owned all rights to it. He talked with management and offered to buy some rights. The company offered Bill the Northern California rights for $5,000 plus $2,000 royalty on each sale. The package retailed for an even $20,000.

Bill paid the $5,000 and took the software package around to the salesmen of various UNIX machines. The salesmen were so impressed, they made mention of the product when they made a sales call. Our hero then would accompany the hardware salesman and do a demonstration to the prospect. Bill made five sales in the first year alone. He hired a contractor to help him do the installation, which took about a month and paid the contractor $5,000. So, he took in $100,000 for the five sales. Subtract from that the $5,000 one-time fee, $10,000 in royalty payments, and $25,000 in contractor fees, and he came out with $60,000 gross profit.

> *TIP: There is a lot of software just waiting around for the right person to market it. Keep your eyes and ears open. If you develop a specialized package for a client, think about the possibility of getting permission to market it. How do you think Bill Gates got started. He wrote something (a BASIC implementation for microcomputers) and sold it.*

15

KEEPING WHAT YOU MAKE

"The Rich Are Different"

It was said earlier but it bears saying again. The reason the rich are rich is not because they *make* more (although that helps), but because they *keep* more). In other words, they spend less.

Let us assume you are either in or near the 50% bracket when it comes to all taxes. Do you really know what that means? It means that of the $50 an hour you received for your last project, you get to keep $25. It means that of the $1,500 you received for finishing a contract early, you get to bank $700.

If you are employed and earn time-and-a-half for overtime, since it is all earned on the margin, it is not such a hot deal after all because after taxes it may only amount of your straight-time rate.

Being in the 50% bracket means that the 5% interest in your savings account pays you about than 2.5%(while inflation runs at about 3%) .

Above all, being in the 50% bracket means that a penny saved, not spent, is really two pennies earned.

You plan to eat out tonight for $50 with tip. But instead you eat at home for $10. You saved $40. You have $40 more in your bank account than you otherwise would have had you gone out.

Now to earn an extra $40 for yourself you actually would have to make $80; half for you and half for the tax people.

The key here is that if you want to end up with more money at the end of the term, the first thing to consider is spending less rather than earning more. Spending less also includes paying less in taxes.

While this book is concerned with how you can earn *more* as a consultant, a few words about how to keep the tax man from taking it all is in order.

Ledgers, Journals, Books, and Records

It was mentioned earlier that you absolutely must find a good tax consultant, bookkeeper, accountant or whatever they are called in your area. Sit down with him or her and find out about some of the areas where you can find tax deductions or loopholes. I will suggest a few of them here, but your tax advisor should be the final authority.

There is no way you can measure how much or how little money you are keeping if you don't keep any records. No you don't need a $3,000 computer to do your simple ledger work. Any good stationery store will have several bound "bookkeeping methods" for you to use. One good one is the DOME Simplified Weekly Bookkeeping Record, which is available at many discount stores. All you need is a simple single-entry system to keep track of the funds you take in and the amounts you pay out as business expenses. If you wish to use your computer, don't run out and buy a complex expensive accounting package. Quicken, which is an easy to use bookkeeping/check-writing system is all you need. It cost under $100.

The important thing is to keep the record up to date. The DOME method is a weekly system. Most consultants determine their week as being from Monday to Sunday. So, every Sunday night they sit down and fill in the figures for the past week. They also enter the amounts of any checks they received. That is all there is to it. At the end of each quarter, you truck the results to your accountants and they take care of the paperwork for the tax people.

> *TIP*: *Your bookkeeper may set you up with a similar one-write system. Also, inquire about the necessity of keeping an auto mileage journal. The rules on this vary from year to year*.

Trash, Not Cash

There is one basic premise that you must understand when it comes to taxes and business: *the government does not want you to have money - they want you to have things*. Their philosophy is that loose money sitting around in the bank is really not doing anyone that much good. However, when you go out and spend it on something, you are helping to keep people employed and the economy cooking. This is why you find so many deductions for expenditures. This is why there are "investment" tax credits for capital goods. Notice that there is no reward (indeed, a penalty) for saving? The government wants you to spend, not save.

If you are an employee, there are few deductions you can take for the things you buy. If you are in business for yourself, however, you are right on par with IBM or Ford. For example, if you buy a box of disks as an employee, you might be hard pressed to substantiate a deduction. But if your consulting business buys them, the deduction is unquestioned (virtually). If you buy a modem as "an individual" you buy a modem! As a business you are buying a depreciable capital asset.

This is where a good tax advisor is invaluable. You can't have cash because all non-spent money goes to the government. But you can have "things". Take your choice; either give your money to the government or get "something" for it. Either way you come out with the same bank balance, but as a business the asset side of your balance grows. As an employee, extra cash just becomes one big tax liability.

A small business is the last real tax shelter available. Let us say that you have to pay $8,000 to the government in taxes if you had no deductions. That is $8,000 out the window and into the bit bucket. But let us say that you could "find" $4,000 worth of "trash" that you had to buy to stay in business. True, you are still out the $8,000, but at least you have $4,000 worth of stuff to show for your effort.

> **COMMENT:** Why do you think you get a nice holiday card from your lawyer or dry cleaner? They either send you a card or give that 45 or 50 cents to the government. It is far better spent by sending you a little goodwill than helping the government buy a six million dollar space shuttle toilet. How many times in your life do you think you are going to be able to use the "can" in the shuttle?

"Deductive" Logic

If you are still awake, you might realize that I lied to you in the first page of this chapter. I said you could win by spending less. What it really comes down to is that you win my spending more, because you end up spending less on taxes. You may not have more money, but you will at least have more for your money. That is a net gain when you look at yourself not as a bank account, but as a collection of assets.

For a list of good business deductions you should get one of the tax guides on the market and read through it. The DOME ledger, mentioned earlier, has a list of over 250 different deductions in the front section of the book. I will only talk about a few that are of specific use to consultants.

You have always wanted an extensive library. Well, you are allowed to maintain a professional library and take a depreciation factor on it. However, if the life of books you buy is short, you can expense the cost. In our industry as soon as a book is published, it is virtually obsolete, in light of the new technological breakthroughs, so consider writing off most of your book purchases.

You should also subscribe to every magazine and journal you can find. You might as well also join every organization and write off the dues. You never know when membership in the Friends of the Little League might get you a good contract which will lead to a big dollar contract

> **TIP:** Talk to your tax advisor about deducting dues for health clubs. The IRS, from time to time, gets cranky about this. The same goes for foreign travel abroad luxury cruise ships. Check it out before you write it off or you could be sending holiday cards from Levenworth.

How about your personal computer. While these might be dubious deductions to someone who is employed as a full-time mainframe programmer, or as a senior analyst (who uses it mostly so the kids can play Carmen Santiago), for you it is a legitimate deduction. After all, you are in the technology business, so who would need a computer more than you?

> *TIP: One point of interest. The government is constantly changing the so called "useful life" of a microcomputer, so be sure to check with your accountant before deciding how much depreciation to take.*

There is the age-old question of taking a deduction for having an office in your home. You can easily qualify for this one, but it is one of the real sore spots with the tax people. When you take this deduction you turn on the audit-bit and are just asking for an investigation. Again, the guidelines change all the time, so check it out.

> *COMMENT: Most of the intimidating propaganda coming out of the IRS about office in the home is not really geared to those of us who are self-employed but to salary earners who maintain they must do some of their employers work from home. I have never heard of a consultant who has a legitimate business being denied reasonable home-office deductions.*

You can take a deduction for the expense of driving to your client's offices. For most consultants, the flat rate per mile works out better than the actual expenses of running the car. Be sure to keep an auto journal. You can pick one up at any stationery store. Also, if you have a chauffeur, his or her salary and uniform are expenses if you use the car for business! (Just a little humor).

> *COMMENT: When I go to the airport (for a business trip) I never drive my car and pay the steep parking fee. I hire a limo service that not only takes me, but picks me up a week later. I don't worry about my car being vandalized at the airport, I get door to door service, and they serve champagne! It costs about the same as parking, and it is tax deductible.*

Don't forget to attend all of those conventions and seminars. The travel and cost of registration are deductible expenses.

Take a colleague or a manager to lunch every day. Why eat alone? It costs more that way.

I could go on. Get yourself a good tax book and compile your own list. Remember, it is either pay the government or buy a "thing". There is no choice here! Happy spending.

Finally there are the "government supported" tax shelters - the SEP/IRA and so called qualified retirement plans. These plans have lots of rules and regulations which seem to change with the tides. I use a SEP/IRA because it is simple. Basically you can put up to 15% of your earnings (up to $30,000) into the plan. The amount you put in is deducted from the "top", thus if you make $100,000, you can contribute $15,000 and your tax basis (before itemized deductions) is $85,000.

However it is not as terrific as it might sound. You are simply burying money in a box at current rates. You re not allowed to use the money until you are 59 years old and you cannot borrow on it. You can get it for an emergency.

COMMENT: *Again, it is a case of either getting a "thing" or paying the government. If you don't have a SEP/IRA, you will just be taxed on a higher income amount. If you give the money to the government it is gone for good. Instead, it only gone for twenty or thirty years. When you get it back, you might have enough to buy a pack of gum!*

Appendix
1

The NACCB Advantage

By

Phyliss Murphy

> *In response to my request, the NACCB sent the following article which was printed in the October/November issue to Technical Consultant Magazine. This is reprinted with permission of the NACCB.*

The National Association of Computer Consultant Businesses (NACCB) was established in January 1987 to provide a forum for exchange of ideas between member companies, with the ultimate goals of enhancing and helping to further develop the computer consulting business. The efforts of the NACCB are designed to improve the ability of the consulting business for the consultant and for its clientele. The

NACCB is the only national association representing companies that specialize in providing highly skilled computer professionals to clients in need of temporary support with the power to impact and enhance the computer contracting industry.

The valuable services that the NACCB provides as it continues to grow and provide leadership to the industry are numerous. The NACCB acts as an effective advocate at the national, state and local levels for the interest of the consultant community at large. As a group, the NACCB voices an collective opinion for political representation. It also plays a critical role in ensuring that clients and consultants are well informed on important issue that range from taxes to ethics that affect the computer consulting industry.

Members of the NACCB have agreed to subscribe to a high level of business professional standards in Statement of Business Principles which is significant[sic} benefit to consultants. They encourage and enforce ethical business practices between agencies, consultants, and clients.

The NACCB also acts as an effective advocate for the consultant's right to provide services as an independent contractor. The mobility that consultants enjoy is a critical means of technology transfer. This sharing of talent and knowledge with others keeps the computer industry in the United States first.

At both national and state levels, the computer industry has been the target of tax law discrimination. In order to combat this unfair action, we suggest consultants and clients deal exclusively with NACCB members, all of whom have contributed significant amounts of time and money to protect the interests of computer consultants.

Why should consultants deal with NACCB Members exclusively?

All consultants face answering this question over and over again. What does a client or consultant have to gain from using a NACCB member:

1. Member firms have agreed to be governed by a strict Statement of Business Principles. Consultants benefit from this as member firms will not knowingly misrepresent a consultant's skills or experience. Prior permission of representation as well as complete reference checking is a strongly recommended practice.

2. Member firms encourage consultants to remain until the project's completion and will refrain from soliciting consultants of active clients.

3. If a client receives the same resume from two NACCB member firms the client need not get involved in the dispute. The two firms will swiftly act to negotiate and resolve the conflict with the aid of the NACCB (if necessary). The client and consultant can processed (sic) without interruption during the interview process when NACCB member firms are used exclusively. Consultant will not lose a job or waste time because of an agency dispute. Violation of ethical standards can result in penalty fines and/or expulsion from the NACCB.

4. The NACCB contract most frequently used by members was drafted by legal counsel familiar with applicable tax and labor laws affecting the computer consulting industry.

5. NACCB firms are knowledgeable of up-to-date legislation affecting the use of computer consultants. Earlier in the organization (sic) history, the NACCB was involved heavily in supporting legislation to replace Section 1706 of the Tax Reform Act with a fair and understandable solution for the computer industry. The organization continues its dedications (sic) and commitment to supporting just and equitable regulations effecting this industry.

6. NACCB is very proud of its joint efforts in running successful career fairs and continues to recruit and place highly qualified consultants with state-of-the-are skills. We encourage our agencies to interact with each other to create a sense of allegiance and camaraderie in consultant referrals which only serves to provide a video (sic) opportunity of jobs for the consultant and level of professionalism in the industry.

Appendix
2

T.C.

> The following piece was provided by _The Technical_
> _Consultant_ which is the de facto official magazine for high-
> tech consultants. Colin Brown, the Editor-In-Chief is
> sometimes not quite with the program, as you will see from
> the article below. You will enjoy reading T.C. because you
> can never be sure what weird stuff Colin will find to write
> about!

"T.C." Magazine or "The Technical Consultant" is the iconoclastic
brainchild of jut-jawed New Zealander and publisher Colin Ingham and
thoughtful, owl-eyed Britisher and editor Colin Brown. The "TC" on the
masthead really stands for two Colins, they say, and reflects their
diametrically opposed viewpoints of a crumbling world.

The magazine has a glossy cover and in the latest issue features a
young lady on the cover, perched on a rock in a snowy landscape. "A
friend of our publisher," says Brown euphemistically.

"Our magazine doesn't intend to be a formal industry publication. We don't have the money for that. Ingham saw the need for a product that tells consultants where the jobs are. Other publications simply don't do that, " says Brown.

"Yes," says Ingham, "Our main aim is to provide a central rendezvous for our marketplace. The place to find out what's happening in the job arena.. Tips, trends and taxes are all our fodder."

"We decorate the meat and potatoes of business with desserts of lively, thought-provoking stories that aren't necessarily just the stuff of computing," says Brown. "Sometimes we delve into the worlds of high tech espionage, our recent stories about the Inslaw scandal and the Justice Department demonstrate that. We've covered AIDS as a biological weapon, a Nazi conspiracy at the highest levels of government. But sometimes we just have fun, and run humorous soap operas. We try and cover everything we become fascinated by - whether it be the intricacies of 'C', the wonderful, wacky world of 'Windows' or ... babes in bondage."

"We haven't covered that last one, though," muses Ingham.

"Perhaps our next issue," says Brown. "In the past we have covered extraordinarily interesting stories - and have had our advertisers whine because they seem a little out of place in the tight-assed, anal-retentive world of the consultant. But, in testing, we've found that advertisers have gotten the greatest response from these stories."

"And," continues Brown, "We ran a couple of issues replete with the sort of techno-geek language beloved or our competitors and our advertising responses dropped like lead weights on Jupiter. I mean, I fell asleep editing them!"

"We have a great demographic of quality consultants," says Ingham. "Our advertisers get quality resumes in response to their ads and those who have stayed with us have blossomed - the others have perished. We've now expanded out of California into the Pacific Northwest and have a booming interest there now. In fact we're now looking for partners to franchise into other cities."

"That means a local team who will write their own regional pages to insert into the base magazine," says Brown.

"And get someone else to do some work..." says Ingham.

The two Colins thoughtfully slurp their margaritas under the shade of a horse-sized cactus. The sun glints off their chunky gold Rolexes and splinters shadows onto the bleached stucco wall of their retreat. The stock of a Beretta is just visible peeping out of Brown's maroon jacket. His eyes dart cautiously behind his mirrored sunglasses. A tall angular blonde appears from the pool and climbs onto Ingham's lap.

"The image we're trying to convey," says Ingham, "is of the consultant as the last great adventurer. Let's do away with the Arthur Andersen archetype. We're the best and brightest in the business..." he smiles - "and the most dangerous."

For a free copy call TC at (310) 519-4453 or write them at 1916 Rockefeller Lane, Suite 2, Redondo Beach, CA 90278.

(Just kidding about the Beretta, the retreat, and especially the blonde)

Appendix 3

ICCA

I am happy to have some space for the ICCA. This organization is the voice for the independent consultant. People ask, why am I not a member. When I first started out in this business I was (I was one of the very early members of the organization along with Steve Epner and Sherwin Pakin. I don't belong now because there is no local chapter in my city, and the benefits of the national organization are not as much value to me, after 15 years in the business, as they will be to you if you are just starting out. The following is taken with written permission from ICCA literature.

The Independent Computer Consultants Association is a professional association for independent computer consultants. It is a not-for-profit corporation and is not connected with any commercial enterprise. ICCA was founded by consultants in 1976 in St. Louis. In addition to the national organization, local chapters have been formed in a number of major U.S. cities.

ICCA offers many benefits to its members, the most important of which is that it presents the opportunity to network. Through ICCA you will be involved with an organization that is working for the development and protection of the independent consultant profession. Through fellow consultants you will learn about market conditions and opportunities.

Many of the local chapters operate referral services, which is used by those seeking consultants. The service allows ICCA to match clients' specific needs with member qualifications. Chapters also offer monthly meetings, featuring experts in the computer and/or consulting fields, and a monthly newsletter.

The National organization publishes a bimonthly newsletter, puts on semi-annual national conventions, offers group health insurance and disability plans and keeps watch over government action that may affect the way we do business.

ICCA's annual spring conference is the major event of the year. Programs feature sessions that support professional, technical, business and personal success. Major industry leaders are featured speakers. Representatives of vendor sponsored consultant relations programs participate. Attendees learn from the experience of their colleagues. Contacts made with peers from across the country can lead to business expansion beyond the local area. Conferences are fun too.

ICCA sponsors an active forum on CompuServe where thousands of consultants and others interested in computer-related issues share information and network. Have a business or technical question you can't resolve? Ask on the forum and it will be answered.

Although ICCA is a national association with far flung members, they can meet on-line any time. Special sections of the CONSULT Forum reserved for members allow ICCA to conduct association business and communicate interactively.

ICCA's vendor/consultant liaison group is sponsored by computer industry leaders who recognize the importance of the independent consultant in supporting their products and services. When vendors and consultants work together, everybody benefits, especially the end-user.

Professional liability insurance is offered to members at low rates. You can protect yourself and satisfy your client's concerns in this area.

ICCA offers members who qualify medically a comprehensive, competitively priced health insurance plan including major medical and hospital coverage. Other options include long term disability coverage, maternity coverage, dental plans, and low rate life insurance.

ICCA's legal counsel has created a standard contract form appropriate for computer consulting contracts. This standard form contract is provided to every member and maintained in the CONSULT Forum library for members to download.

Our associates specializing in computer law consider it a well constructed document. Members may adapt it in whole or in part when negotiating specific contracts with their clients, thus cutting down on possible legal fees. This contract provides a beginning document which can be adapted for use in all states with minor changes that may be required by varying state laws.

ICCA also provides members with group discounts for rental cars, credit card programs and other products and services when available.

ICCA provides a promotional brochure you can give to your clients along with your own promotional material. The brochure helps to remind the client that you are a professional who subscribes to a code of ethics, that you are truly independent, and that you belong to an industry that is truly professional.

ICCA is constantly alert to government regulations and tax-related laws affecting our industry. Members in key states and Washington, D.C., monitor legislative activity, reporting to the membership regularly on issues that potentially impact small businesses offering technical services.

At the state and local level ICCA has lobbied against tax laws that threaten our industry's independence. In California members influenced favorable decisions defining contractor versus employee status.

Experienced computer professionals must race to keep ahead. Every expert brings a unique set of experiences, skills and talents to the table. ICCA is taking a lead in establishing independent computer consulting as a recognized profession.

ICCA is one of twelve major computer-related associations represented on the board of directors of ICCP. ICCP has established a recognized program for identifying and measuring the technical skills of computer professionals.

The art of consulting may be more difficult to measure. ICCA is working to build a body of knowledge that clearly identifies the standards and practices which will describe the essence of the consultant/client relationship and ultimately define the professional computer consultant.

The Independent, ICCA's substantive bimonthly newsletter features information on the business of consulting. You will find regular updates on legislative issues; news about allied organizations; technical advice; essays on client/consultant relations; articles on how to succeed in business; marketing tips; and opinions form colleagues on issues of importance to our membership and profession.

A database of members with descriptions of their businesses is maintained in ICCA's national office. It is possible for ICCA to respond at both the national and chapter level to those who inquire about the services independent consultants offer.

The dues are currently:

$160 for a one person firm or individual associate

$200 for a 2-9 person firm

$250 for a firm of 10 or more

Chapter dues vary from $75 to $180. You do not have to join the local chapter, however you cannot join the local chapter without being a member of national.

ICCA, 933 Gardenview Office Parkway, St. Louis, Missouri 63141

1-800-438-4222 - voice

1-314-567-5133 - fax

Appendix
4

CCN Publications

> A few days before we went to print I spoke with a woman named Wendy Vandame. She runs a company called CCN Publications. While I can't endorse her company or its products, I was very impressed with her knowledge of the consulting industry. I think it would be worthwhile to get in touch with them. The following is re-printed with permission.

For east coast residents seeking contract and subcontract or consulting assignments, as well as news concerning the availability of assignments, a long-standing source is CCN Publications.

Based in Boonton NJ, CCN publishes two regular newsletters, *Consultants' & Contractors' Newsletter*, and *JOB EXPRESS*. Both focus on NY, NJ and PA, but include additional information as available.

Consultants' & Contractors' Newsletter, published once a month, contains news and features ranging from changes in the tax law, IRS-related matters, to regular columns such as "Contract Watch" and the "Ongoing Exploits of Fly-By-Night, Inc." A very popular section is NY-NJ Market Update, which reports on merger and acquisition activity, new companies, and reports on who's changed firms or set up their own.

JOB EXPRESS is different in that it contains virtually no editorial, consisting of a survey of gross billing rates for different kinds of work, followed by roughly 20 pages of classified style listings of data processing work (consulting, contracting and full-time are all included). It also contains a "Positions Sought" section for people looking for work. *JOB EXPRESS* is published twice a month.

The two Newsletters are sold by joint subscription for $69.50 a year which includes both publications. There is also a 6 month trial subscription for $43.50

CCN Publications also publishes softcover books of interest to the same sorts of people. These include *CCN's Guide to Consulting and Contracting*, an entry level guide available for $21.50, *Tales From Beyond The CPU*, an advanced guide for $32.95, *The Freelancers Guide to Taxation* $15.95, and more.

You can reach CCN at (800) 836-0667 or in NJ, (201) 299-1535.

Index

COLOPHON

The word colophon *is Greek for* finishing touch. *It used to be part of all books, but has fallen out of fashion in the past several years. The colophon tells the reader the details on the production facts such as typeface, paper, etc. I thought you might be interested in the text counts.*

The main body of this book and the appendices contain 592,769 characters, 106,629 words, 10,134 lines, and 2,245 paragraphs.

The entire text was composed on an Apple Macintosh SE using Microsoft Word 5.1. in 10pt Times and 14pt Helvetica.

The cover was designed by Colleen Nihen of Right Angle Productions, (916) 783-2068.

The camera-ready copy was output via an Apple LaserWriter printer.

The paper is 60 lb. offset book stock (recycled) and the trim size is 5.5 x 8.5.

The book was printed by Griffin Printing, C. Penny Arnett, (916) 448-3511.

The text ink is environmentally friendly soy-based (but don't eat it!).

DISCLAIMER

This book is designed to provide information in regard to the subject matter covered. It is sold with the understanding that the publisher and author are not engaged in rendering legal, accounting or other professional services. If legal or other expert assistance is required, the services of a competent professional should be sought.

It is not the purpose of this book to reprint all the information that is otherwise available to the author and/or publisher, but to complement, amplify and supplement other texts. The reader is urged to obtain other available material, and learn as much about consulting as possible.

Consulting is not a get-rich scheme. Anyone who decides to go into the business must expect to invest time, effort and money.

Every effort has been made to make this book as complete and as accurate as possible. However, there may be mistakes both typographical and in content. Therefore, this text should be used only as a general guide and not as the ultimate source of writing/publishing information. Furthermore, this book contains information on consulting only up to the printing date.

The purpose of this book is to educate and entertain. The author and Adams - Blake Publishing shall have neither liability nor responsibility to any person or entity with respect to any loss or damage caused, or alleged to be caused, directly or indirectly by the information contained in this book.

If you do not wish to be bound by the above, you may return this book to Adams - Blake Publishing for a full refund.

Ordering Information
Please Print

Name _____

Address _____

City _____

State_____ Zip_____

Phone_____

Please send me _____ copies of **ComputerMoney.**

Price is $29.95 plus $2.00 for shipping. California residents please add sales tax. Express delivery available for an additional fee to credit card customers.

Method of payment:
❑   Check

❑   VISA
❑   Mastercard

Card Number_____

Expiration Date _____

Name on Card _____

Signature _____

Adams-Blake Publishing
8041 Sierra Street
Fair Oaks, CA 95628
Tel/Fax (916) 962-9296

Note: For convenience, our company has installed a combined phone/fax system which uses the same number. If you hear an answering message at the start of your fax, just ignore it. The machine will switch and receive your fax.

Unconditional 1 year guarantee: If ComputerMoney doesn't help you launch your own business or increase your current consulting earnings or for any other reason, return ComputerMoney anytime for up to one year from date of purchase for a full refund.